Running a Small Library

WITHDRAWN
Tribal Library
Saginaw Chippewa Indian Tribe
7070 E. Broadway
Mt. Pleasant MI 48858

ALA Neal-Schuman purchases fund advocacy, awareness,
and accreditation programs for library professionals worldwide.

Running a Small Library

A How-To-Do-It Manual for Librarians®

Second Edition

Edited by John A. Moorman

An imprint of the American Library Association

Chicago   2015

© 2015 by the American Library Association

Extensive effort has gone into ensuring the reliability of the information in this book; however, the publisher makes no warranty, express or implied, with respect to the material contained herein.

ISBN: 978-0-8389-1273-7 (paper)

Library of Congress Cataloging-in-Publication Data
Running a small library / edited by John A. Moorman. — Second edition.
     pages cm
  Includes bibliographical references and index.
   ISBN 978-0-8389-1273-7 (print : alk. paper) 1. Small libraries—Administration—Handbooks, manuals, etc. I. Moorman, John A., editor.
  Z675.S57R86 2015
  025.1—dc23
                              2014049139

Cover images © Shutterstock, Inc. Composition by Mayfly Design in the Minion Pro and Interstate typefaces.

♾ This paper meets the requirements of ANSI/NISO Z39.48–1992 (Permanence of Paper).

Printed in the United States of America
19 18 17 16 15   5 4 3 2 1

Contents

Contents

Preface

The goal of this edition is the same as that for the first edition. It is to provide assistance to those operating or working in small libraries, no matter the individuals served or the units with which they are affiliated. Service in small libraries remains a challenge. In an age of increasing technology, it is imperative that knowledge be continually upgraded, that all possible areas of cooperation be explored, and that funding be located to provide essential library services. *Running a Small Library: A How-To-Do-It Manual for Librarians*, Second Edition, continues to provide practical guidance for the day-to-day and the out-of-the-ordinary services, activities, and issues facing the small library community in a rapidly changing world.

This is my second go-around as the book's editor and an author of some chapters. A great deal has changed since the first edition in 2006, particularly the advances in technology that have reached even the smallest of libraries. Access to new databases has been made available through institutional funding or through state library consortia that bring basic database access to even the smallest of public libraries. With new formats such as e-books and electronic publishing, meeting the expectations of small library users is an increasing challenge. This edition is designed to present both big-picture concepts as well as specific issues facing those responsible for operations, or interested in operations, in a small library. Individual chapter authors are recognized for their expertise in content areas as well as their long experience working in small libraries. Some are new to this edition and some are returning. Each chapter has received either a thorough update or is completely new for this edition. It is the intent and hope of each author that the advice, instruction, and experienced commentary will meet your needs and the needs of the community your library serves. The small library, no matter what community it serves, is the backbone of our information society and an essential component of a democratic society.

This second edition of *Running a Small Library* again covers six major areas: management, administration, public services, collection development, computers and automation, and sources for more information.

Part I, "Introducing the Small Library," contains five chapters. Each chapter is devoted to the unique characteristics of library settings in college, community college, special, public, and school libraries. Chapter authors explore their service sectors from a variety of approaches, leaving you, the reader, with a better understanding of their libraries' history and current state and the challenges facing them in the twenty-first century.

Part II, "Administration in the Small Library," in nine chapters, delves into specific areas of importance to small library operations.

- Chapter 6, "Budgeting," assists readers in creating a financial plan that works. From types of budgets to key financial considerations, this chapter provides valuable and often overlooked guidance.
- Chapter 7, "Policies and Procedures," makes the creation of institutional regulations easier. It outlines necessary topics that must be covered and provides guidance for authoring effective statements.
- Chapter 8, "Staffing," factors human elements into the management equation, describing how to create job descriptions, interview candidates, train staff, balance schedules, and supervise and evaluate workers.
- Chapter 9, "Planning," shows why and how you should prepare for long- and short-term goals.
- Chapter 10, "Buildings," covers how to plan, finance, construct, furnish, remodel, and maintain facilities.
- Chapter 11, "Governing Boards and Governmental Relations," demonstrates both how these bodies work for you and how you work with them—from establishment to maintenance to assessment.
- Chapter 12, "Friends Groups and Foundations," explains the differences between these two support bodies; walks readers through their formation; and provides guidance for setting bylaws, fund-raising, and keeping both groups active.
- Chapter 13, "Community Partnership Development," presents solid advice for libraries looking to partner. In addition to model relationships, you will find management techniques and suggestions for maximizing the benefits to your institution.
- Chapter 14, "Development," examines traditional models of fund-raising and what it takes to implement a comprehensive advancement program for the twenty-first century.

Part III, "Public Services in the Small Library," brings together three chapters that offer guidance to individuals providing service to specific user communities and discuss the increasing role that digital materials play in daily library operations.

- Chapter 15, "Adult Services," examines reference work, programming, readers' advisory, displays, and outreach and how to work with individuals of all types in the provision of these services.
- Chapter 16, "Youth and Young Adult Services," covers the history of youth and young adult services in public libraries, services offered by youth and young adult services staff, the importance of collection development, and library programming.
- Chapter 17, "Digital Services," is a new addition to the book. It covers digital collections, programs, and services and how best to provide them to users in the small library.

Part IV, "Collection Development in the Small Library," addresses the issues and topics related to your materials and collections.

- Chapter 18, "Selection," covers the goal of selection, questions to be answered before the selection process begins, considerations to take into account when making a selection, handling controversial materials, selection resources, and funding your collection.
- Chapter 19, "Ordering," covers each of the steps required to buy an item from a vendor and get it ready to be turned over to the catalogers for additional processing.
- Chapter 20, "Cataloging," outlines the two systems of cataloging and subject headings and discusses item description, assigning subject headings, authority control, assigning classification numbers, and applying a local collection scheme.
- Chapter 21, "Circulation," gives guidance on the process of loaning items to users and obtaining the return of those items.
- Chapter 22, "Weeding," gives guidance for the process of removing materials no longer of interest or use from the collection.

Part V, "Computers and Automation," consists of two chapters addressing the issues surrounding technology in the small library.

- Chapter 23, "Personal Computers and In-House Networks," provides assistance in writing and using a technology plan and discusses the types of equipment you will need to manage in your library, key technology services to offer in your library, and supporting and securing technology resources.
- Chapter 24, "Integrated Library Systems," covers the features of an integrated library system (ILS), integration with third-party products and the ILS, ILS vendors, and the future of the ILS.

The final section of the manual, "Running a Small Library Sourcebook," provides lists of state library agencies, book and periodical vendors, library furniture and supply vendors, and automation vendors as well as information on professional organizations and professional statements. This information will prove valuable as you seek further assistance on problems or concerns or increased knowledge on particular topics. The purpose of the second edition of *Running a Small Library* remains the same: to assist you in better serving your community—whether in the academic, public, special, or school setting—by providing a better understanding of the essential functions of a small library. I hope that this second edition will provide valuable assistance to all individuals involved in the operation and use of the small library.

Part I

Introducing the Small Library

College Libraries

Cy Dillon

In the early history of English-speaking North America, small academic libraries were both simple and similar, but the three and three-quarters centuries since the founding of Harvard have produced remarkable variety among libraries that serve the smaller institutions of higher education. Whether it was Harvard's library in the seventeenth century, centered on a gift of 300 books from John Harvard (Budd 1998), or the library at Hampden-Sydney in the eighteenth century, advertised proudly in the *Virginia Gazette* as having the "best Writers, both ancient and modern" (Brinkley 1994), the book collections were usually housed in one room under the care of a professor or the president. In the case of Hampden-Sydney, for instance, the first library was housed in one of the five rooms of the president's home (Brinkley 1994).

With a few exceptions, academic libraries remained small, with untrained staff, and were open relatively few hours per week until the 1890s (Valentine 2012). In the nineteenth century, this oversight was at times corrected by libraries purchased and maintained by debate societies at institutions such as the University of Alabama (Pace 2004) and the University of North Carolina, where two debate societies had a total of 8,800 books in their libraries by 1849 (Budd 1998). But by the twentieth century, the demand for library collections to support research and teaching increased to the point that libraries evolved in divergent forms to serve their institutions. This tendency toward diversity was accelerated by the development of technology to the point that today small college libraries can range in size from a multiple-story building of 100,000 square feet to a single room of less than 1,000 square feet. Buildings can be historic or quite contemporary, be devoted to only library resources, or contain everything from classrooms and counseling centers to coffee shops and computer labs. Print collections can range in size from more than a million volumes to a small reference section supported by a virtual library of e-books and electronic periodicals. Staff, of course, can range in number from dozens to one.

This variety makes writing a succinct definition difficult unless you simply say, "A small academic library is a library that serves a small college."

One source that addresses the definition of "academic" in "academic library" comes from the National Center for Education Statistics (NCES 2014):

> An academic library is the library associated with a degree-granting institution of higher education. Academic libraries are identified by the post-secondary institution of which they are a part and provide all of the following:
>
> 1. An organized collection of printed or other materials or a combination thereof;
> 2. A staff trained to provide and interpret such materials as required to meet the informational, cultural, recreational, or educational needs of clientele;
> 3. An established schedule in which services of the staff are available to clientele; and
> 4. The physical facilities necessary to support such a collection, staff, and schedule.

An example of what is generally considered to be the size of the student body for a small academic institution may be found in these guidelines written by the American Council of Learned Societies (ACLS 2014). The ACLS defines these as "small":

- Master's Colleges and Universities I and II with FTE enrollments between 1,000 and 2,500.
- All Baccalaureate Colleges—Liberal Arts and General with FTE enrollments 1,000 or above.
- All Associate's Colleges and Community Colleges with FTE enrollments between 2,500 and 10,000.

The ACLS defines the following as "very small":

- Master's Colleges and Universities I and II with FTE enrollments below 1,000.
- Baccalaureate Colleges—Liberal Arts and General with FTE enrollments below 1,000.
- All Associate's Colleges and Community Colleges with FTE enrollments below 2,500.

Thus, leaving aside community colleges, 2,500 would seem to be the enrollment ceiling for small academic institutions, so, with the exception of relatively small community colleges, a small academic library serves a degree-granting institution of 2,500 or fewer FTE students.

Library Services

Every small academic library should offer a range of services that match the needs of the institution's academic program. The creation and revision of a mission statement for the library provide opportunities to make sure that the match of services to needs is appropriate and to plan for changing services as needs change. The library's mission should be in harmony with the overall mission of the institution. In 1999, the College Libraries Section of the Association of College and Research Libraries (ACRL) published a collection of academic library mission statements titled *Mission Statements for College Libraries* (Hastreiter, Cornelius, and Henderson 1999). This book reveals that libraries' explanations of their missions differ as dramatically as their buildings, collections, staffs, and services, but it is well worth consulting when it is time to revise the mission statement of any academic library.

One of the clearest and most direct of all the mission statements available comes from Randolph-Macon College in Ashland, Virginia (see sidebar). The categories of services this library asserts that it provides are typical of those at most small colleges: build an appropriate collection, give individual research help, offer bibliographic instruction tailored to the college, provide hardware and instruction for teaching and learning technologies, maintain a college archive, and create a space that promotes a variety of styles of learning.

Beginning with the collection, a set of policies should be in place to support the acquisition of carefully selected items from a number of media. Getting faculty to select books and make recommendations on subscriptions is ideal, but this approach usually has to be supplemented by selections made by the staff. Having general guidelines about how much to budget for each subject and how many items to attempt to add in a year helps keep acquisitions going according to plan. In addition to regular reviews of a library's acquisitions policy, it is a good practice to use products designed to evaluate collections when they are affordable. Until recently, commercially available lists of recommended materials for college libraries focused on print, books and journals, but software products such as Bowker's version of *Resources for College Libraries* are beginning to include electronic media evaluation as a service. As more extensive electronic resources become available, libraries will have to be sure that their collection development policies reflect the growing importance of those assets versus print materials. Do not give up on books, though. Most users prefer digital versions of journals, but undergraduate students are still most comfortable using books in their research, particularly humanities research.

Providing good individual help to all users is one of a small academic library's most important roles. A small campus atmosphere supports taking all the necessary time to be sure students and faculty get the help they need. The traditional approach to this service has been from behind a reference desk, but more and more libraries have switched to either roving reference staff or "one stop" service desks that answer basic questions and offer users individual appointments with reference librarians for more complex issues.

Sample Mission Statement

"At McGraw-Page Library we provide information services and spaces to foster learning communities at Randolph-Macon College. We do this by:

- selecting, acquiring, and making accessible information in diverse media,
- providing research assistance,
- integrating bibliographic instruction with the college curriculum,
- supporting a variety of educational technologies,
- keeping an historical record of Randolph-Macon College, and
- enhancing individual and shared intellectual work in a welcoming environment."

(McGraw-Page Library 2014)

The single desk also functions well to direct patrons to services such as technology help desks, media librarians, and writing centers. Other methods of individual help used in small college libraries include e-mail, chat reference, and even messages via Facebook. Whatever the context, the key to good individual reference service is matching the user with the right staff member to solve his or her specific problem.

Group bibliographic instruction, often as a meeting of a specific class, is one of the core services of an academic library. When possible, this instruction should be carefully coordinated with an assignment, so collaboration with faculty is essential. Some colleges have a required assignment in all freshman seminar or introductory composition classes, creating an excellent opportunity for librarians to be sure most students are exposed to basic research skills. An ideal structure within the curriculum for making information literacy a core academic skill might include a required short assignment to orient freshmen, a session on research papers for the second composition course, an introduction to research in a major focused on a selected assignment in foundation classes, and an intense session on information literacy in capstone classes. Convincing a whole faculty to support such a program is very difficult, but it makes a good target.

Small college libraries most often include a media library with hardware and software as well as at least one staff member with technology skills to support their use by both students and faculty. Of course, some campuses keep media services separate and some colleges are too small to support a media library, but directors should be prepared to supervise everything from a DVD collection and streaming video service to the college's learning management system. In many institutions, the library director or media librarian also has to manage classroom technology, and the technology required to deliver the library's content is also something that cannot be ignored. Libraries should be prepared for technology shifts such as the recent increase in demand for access to content on mobile devices.

College administrations usually assume that libraries conserve a wide variety of publications, documents, and media items that reflect the history of the institution. In many cases, these efforts are woefully underfunded, but the library should do what it can to maintain usable copies of items such as college newspapers and magazines, programs from graduation and other important events, historical photographs, trustee meeting minutes, presidential papers, and recordings of important speakers. The digital revolution is making this process less space intensive but not necessarily easier. In addition to maintaining an archive, most libraries will benefit from having their own digital repository as well as from locating some digital assets in resources such as the Internet Archive. Having the public access catalog link to digital files stored on a variety of servers is one strategy that improves access for most users.

While it is now possible to deliver information services to a small college with a "virtual" library, many institutions have recently increased emphasis on the value of library space as an individual and group learning environment. Open, attractive space for study, working on computers, collaborating with or without technology, and doing research is an effective draw for students, and the current tendency is to move or condense print collections—particularly reference books—to create more space for students. As opposed to earlier generations who wanted privacy, current students usually want to see and be seen when they are in the library. They are also comfortable with seeing staff (though they do not necessarily want to interact), and it is important to have someone visible at the service point at all times. Twenty-first-century students also tend to expect the library to be open both late and early, and a ninety-hour or more weekly schedule has become the norm. Relatively few small college libraries maintain twenty-four-hour schedules, but some campuses have that tradition. Libraries also often house coffee shops, technology-rich classrooms, computer labs, editing studios, group study rooms, and writing centers, so it is clear that the library as a place will be important to small colleges for the foreseeable future.

Budgeting

Most small college library budgets can be managed with a bit of knowledge about fund accounting, an acquaintance with spreadsheets, attention to detail, and a simple pocket calculator. Funds usually come from four sources: the college's current budget, endowments, gifts, and grants.

Current funds will be divided into "lines" or amounts for specific expenses such as postage or electronic resources. Library staff should know their institution's policies about transferring money between lines, and they should be aware that all money allocated should be spent within the fiscal year. Good managers usually try to avoid saving a large sum in a line for a big-ticket purchase at the last minute. Current budgets are also subject to a process of requesting funds that will likely include providing reasons for the request in each line. This process is both reasonable and helpful in that it gives the library staff the opportunity to examine their priorities for spending money each year. Online resources, because their renewals fall at various times during the year, sometimes present budgeting problems. Libraries without a commercial product for managing database purchasing should keep a spreadsheet that records each resource, its date of renewal, the cost of the last subscription, and the funding source used each year.

As opposed to current funds, endowments provide funds from the earnings of investments, with the amount available for each year calculated by a formula consistent with college policies. This requires some caution in planning because the same fund will produce different amounts as the economy changes, but endowments have the advantage of allowing money to be held over in the account if it is not spent within a fiscal year. Thus, an endowment is suitable for saving funds for a large, one-time purchase. Endowments are also relatively reliable for recurring expenses such as book purchasing as long as the librarian is conservative in forecasting the funds available for the next year. Because of the relative permanence and flexibility of endowments, libraries may designate gifts to endowments as their preferred form of donation.

Gifts may be unrestricted, that is, for use at the discretion of the library staff; they may be intended for a specific use with some flexibility, as in a donation to buy books in a designated subject; or they may be for a specific purpose or purchase. In all these cases, library staff should be careful that the donated funds are either funneled into library accounts or segregated into an account of their own. Otherwise, a gift meant to underwrite a specific library acquisition may end up in the institution's general fund.

Grants are usually received from government agencies or private foundations and often require a strict application process as well as being competitive with other applicants. Grants, which can be restricted to one fiscal year or spread over several, should be the subject of special care in the accounting process, as they often require very detailed reports. Many small colleges have grants officers who can assist librarians in designing and writing grant applications.

Statistics and Assessment

Once a library delineates its mission, the staff should take steps to ensure that their effectiveness in each area of service can be evaluated regularly. Gathering statistics on library activities is an important part of the assessment process because this enables a library to compare its efforts against past years and to look at them in the light of norms and benchmarks. Along with outcomes assessment results, such as those from information literacy surveys, these comparisons should be the subject of regular reviews, and as noted in the ACRL's (2011) *Standards for Libraries in Higher Education*, libraries should "use assessment data for continuous improvement of library operations" (6).

In addition to internal assessment, statistics are often reported annually to the institution's academic administration, and a variety of surveys and reports also require statistics from the library. Two that are among the most important are the NCES's biannual academic library survey and the ACRL's annual survey of statistics and trends (see sidebar). It is a good practice to save copies of both the NCES and the ACRL surveys. The results can help when the library's institution is up for reaccreditation by its regional accrediting agency. If your library produces an annual report for the administration, consider posting it each year as part of the library webpages. This makes statistics easy to find and is a way of communicating what the library has accomplished.

Academic libraries should have detailed assessment plans that include means of measuring student learning outcomes in information literacy. These outcomes are best explained in the ACRL's (2000) *Information Literacy Competency Standards for Higher Education*. There are a number of approaches to assessing students' information literacy, but pre- and post-testing with a nationally normed instrument is arguably the method most likely to be accepted by accreditors. Even this procedure, however, requires "closing the loop" by reviewing the results, noting where the students might improve, and devising strategies to foster that improvement. Thus, gathering statistics and carrying out assessment are important tools in the effective management of small academic libraries.

Staffing

The wealth of a good small academic library, never mind the building or the collection, lies in the skill and energy of its staff. Because numbers are limited, the staff in general, and the director in particular, must be versatile and focused on the service mission of the library. There is usually no place to hide a staff member whose abilities are below par. Most small college libraries have a director or dean, one or more professional librarians, various paraprofessionals, and student workers.

The director of a small academic library should fill a variety of roles requiring both versatility and persistence. Perhaps the most important role is leading the staff, working toward constant improvement in fulfilling the library's mission. Because the working environment in most libraries is relatively small, the director has the opportunity for daily observation of and communication with all the staff. In spite of this frequent contact, having regular planning and review meetings with the director and key colleagues is a good strategy in libraries with more than a few workers. It is most often the director's vision that drives positive change, even with a very talented staff, but the director should also help cultivate good ideas from other sources.

More roles for the director include guiding collection development and technological innovation, managing the physical facility, acquiring funding and managing the budget, hiring appropriate professionals and paraprofessionals, and participating in and taking advantage of consortia and other cooperative organizations. Directors must also maintain good relationships with a wide variety of constituencies, including the college administration, the faculty, the students, the trustees, the community, donors, alumni, and vendors. If that list is not imposing enough, add scholarly research and writing and the job seems to be too complex for anyone. Nevertheless, serving as the director of a small college library can be one of the most interesting and fulfilling positions on any campus.

Since most small college libraries employ more than one professional librarian, a person in this position can usually focus more closely on specific aspects of the library such as technical services, circulation and public services, or technology and media. Still, these librarians are usually expected to supervise paraprofessional and student staff and maintain relationships with most of the groups that concern the director. They may also be called upon to be engaged in the faculty governance process, and some institutions

Library Survey Reports

Among the most important statistical reports are the library section of the NCES's Integrated Postsecondary Education Data System, a federal report usually completed in the college's office of institutional research, and ACRL's annual Academic Library Trends and Statistics Survey. Some care is required to complete these instruments because the definitions for key terms can vary, and the directions that accompany each survey call for close reading. Results from the ACRL survey are published by the association in a variety of formats, described in detail on its website (www.ala.org/acrl/publications/trends). These results are an invaluable source for benchmarking and for identifying and understanding trends in academic libraries. Every academic library director should take advantage of them, especially since so much of the data is available free to survey participants.

Changing Standards in Information Literacy

The *Information Literacy Competency Standards for Higher Education* are currently undergoing revision. For information on the new proposed *Framework for Information Literacy for Higher Education*, go to http://acrl.ala.org/ilstandards.

For Further Information

To learn more about the recruiting and hiring process, see the ACRL's "A Guideline for the Screening and Appointment of Academic Librarians Using a Search Committee" at www.ala.org/acrl/standards/screenapguide.

assign librarians as liaisons to departments or divisions. The importance of these professional positions, which often come with faculty status, means that hiring librarians is a process much like hiring a tenure-track professor.

Small college librarians should expect—and be expected—to participate in professional organizations and engage in research related to their work. This is especially important if they will be involved in the tenure and promotion process, but it has benefits for nonfaculty librarians as well. Directors must see themselves as mentors for their colleagues, encouraging their professional activities and trying to help them find funds for conferences and workshops. The rate of change in resources and processes is such that librarians never reach a point that they can permanently know what they need to know to perform their job. With the director's support, the close working relationships, and the variety of responsibilities required of all professionals, small libraries are a good place to begin a career as an academic librarian.

Paraprofessionals should also be hired with care. Their accuracy and reliability are essential to providing good library services, and the importance of the ability of public services paraprofessionals to interact well with library users cannot be overemphasized. The best collection can be rendered inconsequential by uncooperative or disagreeable staff at points of service. As opposed to professional librarians, in most cases, paraprofessionals can be recruited locally or regionally and vetted by a committee from within the library.

The director and professional librarians should be sure that the paraprofessional staff have ample opportunities to communicate both in terms of being informed of plans and projects and in terms of offering their own ideas about processes and policies. Often the most productive ideas come from the point at which the detail work is done. This communication should include frequent contact, clear explanation of expectations, regular evaluations, and occasional meetings of the whole staff.

Like librarians, paraprofessionals are well advised to participate in organizations such as state library associations and to take advantage of professional development opportunities. More ambitious staff will consider getting a library science degree, and the recent creation of quite a few quality online master's programs makes improving your status more attractive than in the past.

Small college librarians rely on student workers to complete many essential tasks and provide core services to users. This means that professional and paraprofessional staff have to be good trainers and supervisors, developing instructional programs for a variety of student positions. As with other classes of library workers, clear communication between the students and their supervisors is essential. The hiring, evaluation, and dismissal policies for students must be clear and consistently applied. If these requirements are met, students can be given much responsibility with very good results, providing the library with more workers than it could hire otherwise and allowing young people willing to work to help pay for their education.

Challenges

Most of the challenges that academic libraries face now are the result of the unprecedented rapidity of change in the character of their institutions, the demographics of the users they serve, the budget realities for their colleges, and the technology they use but do not really control. The procedures and strategies that developed during the many years that libraries served as repositories for print resources are no longer adequate in an environment rich in new problems and priorities. Clearly libraries are "at a critical time in the realm of library technologies, with many organizations working to break out of established conceptual, functional, and technological bounds" (Breeding 2013b, 18). But successful use of technology alone is not enough to ensure that a library will fulfill its mission. Librarians must examine all their practices and modify them as necessary to meet the demands of their users and the needs of their institutions.

As small colleges offer a wider variety of programs of study in multiple formats such as distance learning, branch campuses, shared facilities, and international programs, libraries are finding more efficient means of delivering the information students and faculty need. Obviously, digital information resources along with technology like discovery services, link resolvers, and automated interlibrary loan are all crucial in information delivery. Nevertheless, libraries also have to maintain inviting learning spaces, book collections, and a set of services that support the academic work of students and faculty. With more and more nontraditional students entering this wide variety of academic programs, libraries also face serving multiple generations with very diverse expectations about how they should be served. Thus, the same public services librarian who keeps up the library webpages, Facebook presence, and Twitter account may have to be able to teach a traditional bibliographic instruction session and answer traditional reference questions, and the technical services librarian might have to master batch downloading MARC records from multiple vendors and help standardize the metadata for the digital repository the same year he or she catalogs a set of centuries-old Latin books for special collections. Needless to say, all these activities have to be undertaken in an environment of flat, if not sinking, financial support for the library. Many small colleges are struggling with discount rates that make it very difficult to increase budgets; at the same time student demand for amenities is at an all-time high.

One of the most difficult current challenges is competing for the user's attention. The Internet experience of students and faculty exposes them to resources that set "an almost unreachable bar for user experience and breadth of content" (Breeding 2013a, 18), but librarians have to convince users of the value of the resources and services their own technology offers. As more content becomes available on the web, e-books become easier to use, open access flourishes, and new forms of digital scholarly work become accepted, successful academic libraries "will need to: deconstruct legacy print collections; move from item-by-item book selection to purchase-on-demand

and subscriptions; manage the transition to open access journals; focus on curating unique items; and develop new mechanisms for funding national infrastructure" (Lewis 2013, 159). Clearly, collaboration, particularly shared systems and resources, is a strategy that no library will want to avoid in a situation that is at once demanding and potentially very rewarding.

Conclusion

The small academic library offers a dynamic working environment with an opportunity to fulfill a service mission while developing as a professional. Librarians are called upon to be versatile, innovative, collegial, and resourceful in a time of tumultuous change in most aspects of their work. A small campus offers the opportunity to work directly with students and faculty while making meaningful contributions to the evolution of the institution as you pursue a satisfying career.

Further Reading

In addition to journals focused on college libraries, such as *College and Research Libraries*, *The Journal of Academic Librarianship*, *Journal of Library Administration*, or *College and Undergraduate Libraries*, academic librarians should read the *Chronicle of Higher Education* regularly. It is important to keep in touch with developments in the college and university sphere because trends and issues for these institutions are bound to influence their libraries. The *Chronicle*'s annual *Almanac of Higher Education* is a particularly useful source of statistics on the American academic scene.

In many cases, RSS feeds and electronic discussion lists are excellent means of keeping up with specific journals or entire fields of study, and their immediacy makes them hard to ignore. These resources are particularly good for following a specific area of research or keeping current with an organization. It is best to be selective about signing up, however, since having too much to select from can be a hindrance to productivity.

Academic librarians should be aware of the many publications of the ACRL, described at www.ala.org/acrl/publications. This page links to sources that range from journals to dozens of monographs on all aspects of academic librarianship. Some of these resources are open access, and some are for sale, but the quality is always good and the coverage broad. ACRL publications are especially good sources for widely accepted sets of standards for library practice (www.ala.org/acrl/standards).

References

ACLS (American Council of Learned Societies). 2014. "ACLS Humanities E-Book 2014." Fact Sheet. Statewide California Electronic Library Consortium. http://scelc.org/sites/default/files/offers/fact-sheets-2014.pdf.

ACRL (Association of College and Research Libraries). 2000. *Information Literacy Competency Standards for Higher Education.* American Library Association. www.ala.org/acrl/sites/ala.org.acrl/files/content/standards/standards.pdf.

———. 2011. *Standards for Libraries in Higher Education.* American Library Association. www.ala.org/acrl/sites/ala.org.acrl/files/content/standards/slhe.pdf.

Breeding, Marshall. 2013a. "Library Technology Forecast for 2014 and Beyond." *Computers in Libraries* 33 (10): 18–21. *Business Insights: Essentials,* EBSCOhost. Accessed May 6, 2014.

———. 2013b. "Library Technology: The Next Generation." *Computers in Libraries* 33 (8): 16–18. *Computers and Applied Sciences Complete,* EBSCOhost. Accessed May 6, 2014.

Brinkley, John Luster. 1994. *On This Hill: A Narrative History of Hampden-Sydney College, 1774–1994.* Hampden-Sydney, [VA]: [Hampden-Sydney College].

Budd, John. 1998. *The Academic Library: Its Context, Its Purpose, and Its Operation.* Englewood, CO: Libraries Unlimited.

Hastreiter, Jamie A., Marsha Cornelius, and David W. Henderson, comps. 1999. *Mission Statements for College Libraries.* 2nd ed. Chicago, IL: College Libraries Section, Association of College and Research Libraries.

Lewis, David W. 2013. "From Stacks to the Web: The Transformation of Academic Library Collecting." *College and Research Libraries* 74 (2): 159–76. *Library, Information Science and Technology Abstracts,* EBSCOhost. Accessed May 6, 2014.

McGraw-Page Library. 2014. "Mission Statement." Randolph-Macon College. Last updated September 26. http://library.rmc.edu/mission/mission.html.

NCES (National Center for Educational Statistics). 2014. "Library Statistics Program: Academic Libraries." US Department of Education, Institute of Education Sciences. Accessed December 29. https://nces.ed.gov/surveys/libraries/academic.asp.

Pace, Robert F. 2004. *Halls of Honor: College Men in the Old South.* Baton Rouge, LA: Louisiana State University Press.

Valentine, Patrick. 2012. "The Origin of College Libraries in North Carolina: A Social History, 1890–1920." *Information and Culture,* no. 1: 79. *Literature Resource Center,* EBSCOhost. Accessed May 6, 2014.

Community College Libraries

Rodney Lippard

The community college library, much like its parent institution, is a fairly new creation in comparison to other libraries and educational institutions. Having begun just after the turn of the twentieth century, community colleges were originally designed to train tradesmen to join the postindustrial workforce. It was not until after the world wars when community colleges really started to grow, as servicemen and -women were coming home to a different world from the one they had left and were in need of training in particular skills. Community colleges have continued to adapt and change, as have the libraries that serve them.

According to the American Association of Community Colleges (AACC 2014b), there are currently 1,132 community colleges in America; this number has grown drastically since the "oldest existing public two-year college," Joliet Junior College, was founded in Illinois in 1901 (AACC 2014a). However, according to the US Department of Education, in 2001, there were 1,655 combined public and private community colleges (OCTAE 2005); this discrepancy in recording points to the complexity that is community colleges. What defines a community college? From their beginnings when community colleges were extensions of high school engaged in training workers in the new industrial age, to preparing students with the first two years of college at a location closer to home, to working with returning World War II soldiers and back-to-workforce development, community colleges are responsive to their communities' needs and, therefore, always changing and growing and often difficult to define. In the past decade, more community colleges have found themselves offering bachelor's degrees (Gonzalez 2012); whether this becomes a national trend remains to be seen. Crumpton and Bird (2013), in *Handbook for Community College Libraries*, give a succinct history of community colleges from those early beginnings in Illinois to the issues facing community colleges today.

To understand the history and the complex relationship of the library in relation to the community college, you can again turn to Crumpton and Bird (2013). The authors point to the work of D. Joleen Bock, whose seminal article in "one of the first volumes of *Community and Junior College*

Libraries," titled "From Libraries to Learning Resource Centers," "reflects one of the most important innovations" and "indicates the movement toward an expanded view of the library both as a place where more than books can be obtained and as a service central to learning" (Crumpton and Bird 2013, 3). As the parent institution of the community college library continues to evolve, so does the library itself, coming a long way from its beginnings, when "it was thought that textbooks were sufficient for supporting learning" (Crumpton and Bird 2013, 3). The library or learning resource center of the community college today may find many services located under its roof or under the directorship of the library director. Some may include media services, housed within the library, that support technology both within the classroom and for individual use. While classroom technology is becoming more the responsibility of the information technology department, media services help to support areas where extra technology is needed or, for example, when an individual faculty member or student wants to add media to a presentation or website. Some libraries find themselves adding testing to the services that are provided, both academic testing for classes as well as placement testing for entering students. With the advancements in online education and many colleges and universities offering classes using this method, many of these testing centers and libraries are also providing proctoring for these classes. An additional service area being added to libraries or learning resource centers in community colleges is that of tutoring. These tutoring services can take many forms, such as a writing center or a center that offers tutoring in all subject areas of the college. The writing center could, for example, help students with researching and writing papers, which may also fall under the purview of the library through reference desk services, thereby making a logical connection between the two.

Taking cues from trends in both public and academic libraries, the space that the community college library inhabits has evolved to encompass the learning and studying needs of its patrons. While some students need quiet spaces to study, others are looking to study in group spaces, and the library has responded to these diverse needs by creating quiet areas as well as expanding the number of group study rooms. Many faculty members, responding to requests from employers, are creating exercises that require students to work in teams; libraries at community colleges are providing study rooms that are wired and feature collaborative technology to assist with these exercises. The community college library's electronic space is changing as well. Websites are becoming more dynamic and offering features such as discovery services, chat reference, and research guides.

> From a library to a learning commons to a learning resource center with multiple services, the community college library is ever changing.

Community

The community college library serves a large and diverse community with its mixture of programs in both curriculum and continuing education. However, the community that this library serves is larger than just the academic community; it includes the local community as well, especially as most community colleges have open enrollment and may find those who are public patrons one day becoming students the next. In addition, library staff must be aware of the library community as well as the global community to which the library belongs; knowledge of these communities will help staff stay on top of current trends in services to patrons, gain knowledge about cultural issues, both globally and locally, and assist in providing excellent customer service, internally and externally. While knowledge of these areas is important to running any library, not just a community college library, covering all of these areas is far beyond the scope of this chapter, so the focus here is on the academic community.

The academic community consists of the faculty, staff, and students of the college, and while these categories are similar to what you might find at four-year academic institutions, there are considerable differences. The staffs at both institutions are the most alike and would be those individuals who, for the most part, are not responsible for teaching semester-long classes; of course, many community colleges have staff teaching college orientation types of classes. The faculty members at the community college teach a variety of subject areas, from the traditional curriculum areas in the arts, humanities, and social and natural sciences to continuing education subjects such as cosmetology, auto mechanics, basic law enforcement, nursing and allied health, or any number of other subjects covered under this category. While the majority of faculty members at four-year institutions usually have a master's degree, at the minimum, faculty at the community college can carry a variety of educational credentials, from associate's to doctoral degrees. A practitioner in the field is often preferred for continuing education classes, to bring a workforce-experienced voice to the classroom; working with faculty members who have not frequently used the library when at work can be particularly challenging to the community college librarian.

Students at the community college are where you will find the most diversity in such areas as age range, racial and/or ethnic identity, socioeconomic levels, and educational preparedness. Many community colleges offer a type of early college program or dual enrollment with local high schools for students to earn associate's degrees alongside high school diplomas. Students in these classes can be as young as fourteen years old, while those at the upper end of the age range may be retired community members who are interested in learning a new skill. Some students may be returning to school at the community college to earn the equivalent of a high school diploma due to any number of factors that interfered with their educational process early on. While many students had already discovered that an affordable alternative is to complete the first two years of a four-year degree at a community college, the economic crisis in the first decade of the twenty-first century saw these numbers increase dramatically. Another outcome of the economic crisis was that community colleges started seeing many students who needed workforce development and training due to massive layoffs and unemployment. These students bring with them different educational

> Any library, to be successful, must know the community it serves and be responsive to that community's needs.

abilities, and the library needs to be aware of this. Students can range from those who may be in the college transfer program and are very comfortable with visiting and using a library to those who may be in the high school diploma equivalency program or looking for workforce training who may not be familiar with the library or the services provided. The library must be prepared to address any needs or skill levels presented by the students.

Collection

Once you have an understanding of the community that is being served, then you can begin defining the collection needed to serve this community. Supporting the learning experience is the primary objective of collecting at the community college library; therefore, most community college libraries will include a breadth of subject areas but usually not in-depth coverage of any particular area. In curriculum areas, the collection will focus mostly on the last two years of high school and the first two years of college; however, for continuing education classes, you cannot rely on this same policy and must focus on the particular needs in each area. Working with the faculty in all areas is the best method for finding the resources needed to support the students' educational needs. However, this is not always easily accomplished, so you should complement this method by accessing bibliographic tools for collection development.

No matter what method you use to identify and collect resources to add to the collection, the nature of the collection will continue to change. While electronic resources are becoming more integrated into the collection of the community college library, print resources are still an integral and important part of the library's collection. Currently, the best format for the circulating collection is print; this is not the only format that is circulated, but many students are more comfortable with print. Today, the largest percentage of collection resources is in electronic format, including databases, journal packages, electronic books, and streaming media. As libraries need to reclaim space, moving the collection to a digital environment helps with this by reducing the amount of space needed for the physical collection. An additional benefit of digital resources is that they are accessible to distant and online education students, an important factor now that most community colleges are offering online or hybrid courses. Additional collections and resources to consider are media, archival, and technology. The media collection, like the print collection, is moving into the digital realm with streaming media that integrates seamlessly with the course management system used by the college. Archival collections may be found at some community college libraries, but the majority of items in such collections relate to the history of the college, as archival material in other subject areas is not core to the mission of this type of library. The technology collection may be another growing area in the community college library because it is

> Supporting the learning experience is the primary objective of collection efforts in a community college library.

needed to supplement classroom technology and students need technology to access, not only library resources but also classroom assignments, and not all students can afford the required technology.

As mentioned in the previous section, the community served by the community college library varies in economic and technological competencies, so access to the resources is an important factor in deciding on format. A comprehensive collection development plan is imperative in addressing the issues you face in collecting for the community college library.

Collaboration

Collaboration can take many forms, from the simplest directional or reference transaction to the more complex formal collaboration with community partners. Collaboration happens at the academic level with students, faculty, and staff. Librarians collaborate with students through the reference interview, by providing resources that assist with homework, and in helping with writing papers and creating citations. Staff collaboration most often happens when creating programming for the library or planning for library-hosted student events such as registration or advising. Faculty collaboration is probably the most familiar form. Working with faculty is very important in building the collection; to understand what resources are needed to support the curriculum, librarians must have an understanding of what is being taught, which means communicating with faculty. Instruction sessions are another method by which community college libraries collaborate with faculty; consulting with faculty, librarians can customize instruction to best benefit students. Research guides are another student aid that are best created with assistance from faculty, as these guides can be created from a subject macro level to a class or project micro level. One of the most recent collaborative efforts is community college librarians embedding in classes, particularly online classes. Many libraries create liaison programs, whereby librarians are assigned to programs or departments to facilitate these collaborative efforts.

Collaboration also happens outside of the academic community through working with other libraries or other entities. Community college libraries are teaming up with other libraries, particularly public libraries, to hold community-wide reading events during which a single book is selected for the whole community to read and programs are held around the themes of the book. The community college library can host programs in its buildings or facilitate book talks and even coordinate faculty presentations on the themes. Some public and school libraries are collaborating with community college libraries to share spaces and services, especially in more trying economic times. Parks and recreation departments and extension services are other entities with which the community college library can partner as it integrates itself into the local community. Whether the collaboration is

> Collaboration, both internal and external, helps the community college to remain relevant by meeting the ever-changing needs of its patrons.

internal to the college or external within the larger community, community college libraries must be engaged in order to remain relevant and to meet the needs of their patrons.

Conclusion

Whether it is the community, the collection, or collaboration, communication is what brings it all together for the community college library. Understanding the community requires assessment of the community's needs; sometimes this is done through conversations with students and faculty in the hallways or perhaps through a more formal assessment structure such as focus groups or surveys.

Community colleges resist clear-cut definitions because they change to meet the needs of the local communities that they serve. Likewise, the community college library or learning resource center has multiple definitions and may include many different service areas. However, if the community college library is attentive to its community, collects resources to provide for that community, and collaborates with its community for services, then it will be successful and remain an integral part of the learning community.

References

AACC (American Association of Community Colleges). 2014a. "Community Colleges Past to Present." Accessed December 29, 2014. www.aacc.nche.edu/AboutCC/history/Pages/pasttopresent.aspx.

———. 2014b. "Fast Facts from Our Fact Sheet: Number and Type of Colleges." Accessed December 29, 2014. www.aacc.nche.edu/AboutCC/Pages/fastfactsfactsheet.aspx.

Crumpton, Michael A., and Nora J. Bird. 2013. *Handbook for Community College Librarians*. Santa Barbara, CA: Libraries Unlimited.

Gonzalez, Jennifer. 2012. "Go to Community College, Earn a Bachelor's Degree: Florida Likes That Combination." *Education Digest: Essential Readings Condensed for Quick Review* 77 (5): 19–22. ERIC. Accessed July 13, 2014.

OCTAE (Office of Career, Technical and Adult Education). 2005. "Community College Facts at a Glance." US Department of Education. Last modified October 25. www2.ed.gov/about/offices/list/ovae/pi/cclo/ccfacts.html.

Special Libraries

Richard E. Wallace
Revised by Elizabeth Terry Long

A special library is one that is set up to serve the information needs of a defined set of users by facilitating access to and dissemination of needed information. Its collection of resources is maintained and organized in a manner that enhances (and can be determined by) the ways in which users access the resources to acquire the information they need.

Many organizations use names other than *library* for their information unit, names that include variations on information, knowledge, and analysis, for example, information center, knowledge center, market research and analysis. For the purposes of this chapter, they are all called *special libraries.*

A special library can be a physical collection of resources, a person with the means (e.g., computer or telephone) to access internal or external resources, or something in between. These libraries are found in all types of for-profit and nonprofit organizations, colleges, and universities. They may serve the entire organization or just one of its subunits or some combination of both. The user group(s) served depends on who is willing to provide managerial and financial support.

Each library's collections and resources are determined by the interest of the users it serves and the types of resources necessary to provide the needed information. Thus, the collection and resources will change as the parent organization's interests change. The size of the staff varies from one person (solo librarian) to twenty or more.

A special library usually has one or more of these characteristics:

- Staff are subject oriented (by education or training).
- The library exists so long as it is considered an asset to an organization's mission.
- The resource collection is subject specific—*specific to the parent organization's needs.*
- The library has a usually small and well-defined user group.
- The library depends on outside resources—*staff will travel to the resource site.*
- The resource collection is virtual.

- The resource collection is very current.
- Staff usually know all their users by name.
- Many users may not be in the same physical location as the library.
- The collection is organized and defined by the users and their needs.
- Staff are highly user oriented.
- Staff members usually have more than one of the normal library-related job functions—*the larger the staff, the more individual jobs become specialized.*
- The size of physical facilities is no indication of resource or staff size.

Using this description means that a large number of libraries can be classified as special libraries. However, due to similarities among libraries, special libraries can be divided into a number of classes, including medical, law, church/synagogue, departmental libraries within public and academic libraries, advertising, newspaper, and chemistry. The *American Library Directory, 2013–2014* noted that there were 7,616 special libraries in the United States (McDonough and Williams 2013). These numbers do not include government and armed forces libraries or those special libraries housed within public and academic libraries.

When to Establish a Special Library

For a library to exist within an organization or one of its subunits, there has to be recognition of the need for economical, efficient, and effective ways to access and retrieve information. In addition, there must be a willingness and desire to make a direct commitment of some of the organization's or subunit's financial and physical resources to achieve this goal.

An information audit should be arranged when someone in authority in an organization without a librarian and/or library realizes employees are spending an exorbitant amount of time looking for information to do their jobs. Although this is usually done by an outside consultant, there have been instances where a librarian has been hired to conduct the audit. The purpose of the audit is to help determine (1) what internal and external resources are currently available within the organization; (2) what types of resources might be required; (3) how information is used and knowledge shared among the potential users; (4) how and where the users currently acquire such information; and (5) the knowledge and skills the library staff will need to ensure information is effectively and efficiently acquired, organized, and distributed.

Formal and informal user surveys need to be conducted throughout a special library's existence. The data gathered help the library manager prove the value of his or her unit's contribution to the organization's bottom line.

Kno... ...titive Intelligence

Librarians have had a long and rich experience in the management of information. These skills of librarianship can be applied to knowledge management and competitive intelligence. Librarians can work with information technology professionals to develop appropriate knowledge management systems.

As a result of assuming responsibility for the management of digitization projects, knowledge management, and the proliferation of electronic information managed by the library, many libraries have changed their name to information center. Job titles for those employed in information centers also have changed to reflect the responsibility of each employee, for example, content strategist, information services librarian, library services analyst.

MICHIGAN eLIBRARY mel.org

RETURN THIS ITEM TO: FRASER PUBLIC LIBRARY

KEEP THIS BOOKMARK INSIDE THE ITEM WHEN RETURNING TO YOUR LIBRARY

RENEWALS MUST BE DONE AT LEAST 1 WEEK BEFORE DUE DATE. CONTACT FRASER PUBLIC LIBRARY TO RENEW.

- 7 Day loans may not be renewed.
- 3 Week loans may be renewed once.

DATE DUE: 8/3/21

Fines are $0.25 a day.

The ... ...ational Unit

...must the librarian educate the supervisor about what the library does; he or she must also show why the library is a real asset to the organization or subunit. The library is a service unit and is therefore always subject to closure if it cannot prove that it is contributing to the bottom line. This aspect

Recommended Written Policies/Procedures in a Special Library

Statements
- Mission/vision
- Strategic plan
- Marketing plan
- Goals and objectives

Policies
- User services
- Collection development (including deacquisition)
- Copyright
- Cataloging/indexing
- Records management

Procedures
- User services (including circulation)
- Acquisitions
- Cataloging/indexing
- Records management
- Procedures for jobs not covered in the previous four items

Other
- Budget
- Job descriptions
- Organization chart with responsibilities
- Purposes and responsibilities of library committee

of a librarian's job is called *marketing*. The selling of the library as a valuable asset goes on continuously and must be done at *all* levels of the organization.

As part of a marketing strategy, vision and mission statements need to be drafted. This requires knowledge and understanding of the parent organization and should take into account its vision and mission statements.

Staffing

Although special library staffs vary in size, most are staffed by one professional librarian, with sometimes one or two clerks or paraprofessionals to help. This lone professional has become known as a solo librarian, and there is a division within the Special Libraries Association (SLA) devoted to this type of library service.

A solo librarian is responsible for all aspects of library operations. This position requires the use of time management and the acceptance of some isolation because there are no colleagues close at hand with whom to collaborate. The solo librarian must be flexible and willing to adjust to the continuously changing demands for service. Deadlines create pressures and long hours because the users require information that often impacts, directly or indirectly, the organization's bottom line.

Not only must the solo librarian provide service to his or her users; he or she must also find time for training and continuous education; performing the technical functions (cataloging, circulation, shelving) required to keep the library operating; and performing the functions of a manager (preparing budgets, writing monthly reports, marketing, supervising and preparing performance evaluations, if lucky enough to have help). Some librarians, including solos, even manage other departments, such as mail/receiving, corporate records, reproduction/duplication, or information technology. Several librarians in for-profit organizations have moved up the organizational chart to supervise the library and other departments.

There are special librarians who do not have a physical library to maintain. These librarians use telephones, computers, and the resources of other libraries to obtain the information their users need. They may be employees of the organization, consultants, or contract employees. They may not even be in the same physical location as their users.

Special libraries were the first type of library to utilize the services of contract employees. While the librarian and other staff members are independent contractors hired by an employment agency, the library's physical space and its resources belong to the organization being served. Difficulties with this situation include the contract librarian and other staff not being stakeholders in the mission of the parent organization and a possible disconnect between the contract terms and the expectations of both parties.

Although many special librarians have professional degrees, in some instances, persons with subject expertise and/or training are selected to set up a new library or manage an existing one. This happens because someone in authority knows the library is essential but has no idea how a library functions. In this instance, it is helpful if the employee is supervised and/or mentored by a professional librarian.

One of the things an experienced librarian can do is take advantage of the special librarians' proclivity to network among themselves. This networking takes place across special libraries regardless of subject or type. The willingness of special librarians to help one another is one of the strengths of special librarianship. A good place to start is to join the SLA. Membership in SLA allows you to belong to local chapters of the association. See the sidebar for a partial list of specialized library and professional information associations.

Another way to get help is to join some of the library-related electronic discussion lists. You do not have to be an active participant to learn about new ideas, but participation is a good way to obtain input when you would like help with a question or problem. Library-related electronic newsletters also provide a way to stay current.

> **Professional Associations**
> - American Association of Law Libraries: **www.aallnet.org**
> - Association of Independent Information Professionals: **http://aiip.org**
> - Medical Library Association: **www.mlanet.org**
> - Music Library Association: **www.musiclibraryassoc.org**
> - Special Libraries Association: **www.sla.org**
> - Strategic and Competitive Intelligence Professionals: **www.scip.org**

Budgeting

In order to exist, a special library needs financial resources to pay staff and to acquire the information needed by users. Budgets and funding mechanisms vary widely. The budgeting system and financial record keeping used by a special library are determined by the parent organization.

Staff and information resources cost money. An organization having a good library understands this and is willing to take the expenses from the income or profits every year because the library helps the organization's employees do their jobs better. If the library staff is perceived as not helping the organization achieve its goals (including making a profit), then the library may be discontinued.

The budgets for most for-profit and nongovernmental special libraries are not publicly available because it is thought that such data could help competitors determine undisclosed financial information about the parent organizations. The actual budget for special libraries varies widely; examples include no formal budget, a lump sum spent at the librarian's discretion, and a detailed budget similar to those used in public and academic libraries.

The size of special libraries' budgets is as varied as the budget systems used. Library budgets can be (1) a percentage of the parent organization's or unit's sales or profits; (2) a percentage of the R&D or marketing budget; or (3) a system of charge-backs in which each unit using the library pays a percentage of the library's budget. The percentage may be based on the percent of the library staff time used or on some form of head count.

There are also differences in what line items are included in a special library's budget. For example, some or all of these items may be included:

- Accounting
- Association memberships

- Computers and peripherals
- Furniture and shelving
- Maintenance
- Postage/shipping
- Property taxes
- Space allocation
- Staff benefits
- Travel
- Utilities

Final authority for purchases (up to some fixed amount) usually rests with the library manager, although in some cases this authority rests with a committee or the library manager's supervisor.

The methods used for ordering and receiving and paying for materials vary also. Methods of ordering and receiving can include one or some combination of these:

- Library uses the parent organization's purchasing department.
- Library generates own purchase orders.
- Library orders online or by telephone without formal purchase orders.

Payment methods include check, petty cash fund (usually limited to payments of less than $100), company-issued credit cards, or expense account (librarian uses own money and is reimbursed).

User Services

The types of services that special librarians offer their users are diverse and many. These services may be determined by formal and informal information audits or surveys. The analysis of the information needs of the users is ongoing and helps the librarian determine the types of services required and how they will be offered.

Because the user group is finite and static, a special librarian can get to know the ways individual users work and the types of information required. This gives the librarian an opportunity to provide very customized and personal service, which may be difficult to do in a public or academic library. This knowledge helps the librarian to evaluate current and future services to be offered.

Special librarians do as much of the information work (e.g., identify, obtain, analyze) as users request. By letting a librarian do the legwork, the user can utilize his or her time on other job-related activities. The librarian can do the work more efficiently and effectively because he or she knows how to obtain what is needed, and the cost per hour for finding the information will be less.

In addition to the normal user services offered by public and academic libraries, special libraries offer the following:

- Reference referral
- Literature/patent searches of databases
- Current awareness alerts
- Analyses of information found
- Competitive intelligence
- Journal routing
- Answering the request rather than just teaching the user to look for answers
- Connecting the user with an outside expert
- Translation of foreign language materials
- Document delivery of even the most obscure material
- Willingness to travel to a resource when necessary

Many special libraries offer their users direct access to online hosts such as ProQuest, EBSCO*host*, Bloomberg BNA, LexisNexis, or Westlaw to do their own database searching. Some librarians still do the actual searches or hire information brokers (expert online database search consultants) for several reasons:

- Librarian is more proficient in database searching.
- Librarian may have subject expertise (e.g., patent searches).
- User feels uncomfortable searching because "the clock is ticking" while connected to the database.
- Librarian's time is cheaper than the user's time.

When a user has an information request that is beyond the library staff's knowledge or the resources available, special librarians look for help beyond the library. Special librarians tend to have an intimate knowledge of the organization's employees' expertise and interests. Thus, they are often able to refer a user to someone within the organization. Librarians belonging to professional associations make valuable contacts that they can call or e-mail when necessary to fulfill a request. Many libraries subscribe to OCLC, an online database of information sources, to borrow materials from other libraries. If necessary, outside experts or consultants are hired to help. In all scenarios, a librarian acts to protect the identity of the patron when a request is of a sensitive matter; the name of the patron is not divulged to anyone.

The existence of a special library within an organization depends on the value of the services offered to users. To maintain this value-added service, special librarians will go all-out to find the information users need.

Librarians seek "the answer" because they are more efficient and effective at locating "the answer" and because in most cases their hourly salary rate is lower than that of the users.

Copyright Considerations

Copyright is an important issue for special librarians, especially those in for-profit organizations, since most of the materials acquired are subject to copyright law. Staying up-to-date with the law can help prevent the parent organization from being sued for infringement. In many cases, the librarian is the most knowledgeable person in the organization when it comes to copyright law and its ramifications. Librarians should be familiar with the following copyright-related topics:

- Copyright Clearance Center
- Fair use
- Licensing
- Obtaining permission of copyright owner(s)
- Preservation/archiving
- Reproduction rights (paper, electronic, audio/visual)
- Resource sharing (including interlibrary loan)

Acquisitions

Special libraries that have physical collections of paper and/or electronic resources need to acquire new materials in order to remain relevant to their users' needs. Like a number of other processes and procedures used by special libraries, the ones for acquisition of resources will follow those of the parent organization. These methods may be totally different from those used in public or academic libraries.

Special libraries should have a formal and/or written collection development policy. The librarians will acquire material in whatever formats will provide the users with the information they require. The only limitation might be cost or copyright considerations (see sidebar).

Sometimes a special library acts as the total organization's purchasing agent for books, journal and newspaper subscriptions, videos, and so on. The item ordered may be outside the scope of the library's collection, and there may be a charge-back or the library may absorb the cost into its budget. Acting as the central purchasing agent allows the special librarian to create bibliographic records in case other employees want to use the item.

In addition to the items regularly acquired by public or academic libraries, special libraries may acquire some of these items:

- Association publications
- Patents
- Sheet maps
- Standards
- Trade journals
- Translations of journal articles and/or patents

Also, an item will be acquired even if it will be used only once.

Special libraries use not only the traditional material selection tools but also jobbers and publishers' announcements and catalogs, bibliographies, and word of mouth. If an item is on a subject directly pertinent to users, it will usually be acquired before reviews are published.

Expediency is the concern when ordering materials. The special librarian will order from whichever source provides the item(s) wanted in the most cost-effective manner. Sources include traditional and nontraditional publishers, bookstores, jobbers, second-hand dealers, or whoever can supply the item. If an item is from an unusual source or difficult to find, the librarian will employ a jobber. The special librarian is able to use some of these unusual purchasing sources because he or she is allowed to pay for the item(s) with a credit card and/or without a formal purchase order.

Special libraries may not be able to acquire all the resources they need because of cost and lack of physical space. In such cases, they are dependent upon public and academic libraries and other special libraries for resources such as journal articles and electronic databases as well as books, government reports, and so forth. Journal article photocopies are one of the most commonly ordered items.

Special libraries maintain runs of journal titles directly relevant to their users and depend upon other libraries, publishers, and vendors for articles from journals that they do not have. Many small special libraries use the services of vendors or the fee-based services of academic libraries. These usually charge a service fee plus the copyright charge, but the charges are usually nominal and are less than if the libraries subscribed to the journals themselves.

Only the largest special libraries can afford to contract for access to the electronic journal databases of Elsevier, Wiley, Thomson Reuters' Web of Science, HeinOnline, or Gale. The subject of contracting for database usage is beyond the scope of this chapter. The readings at the end of the chapter include several books on contracting.

The need for currency of resource materials and a lack of physical space require special libraries to continuously review their collections. Weeding, or deacquisitioning, must be a regular activity. Methods of disposal of the discarded materials depend on the parent organization's policies. The methods used include (1) giving materials to employees; (2) donating to public or academic libraries; (3) selling to secondhand dealers; (4) donating to an organization that will send them to developing countries; or (5) placing them in the trash or recycle bin.

Organization of Materials for Access

The types of resources housed by special libraries vary from the traditional to the unusual. Common types of materials found include the following:

- Advertisements
- Engineering drawings/models
- Internal reports/documents
- Maps
- Musical scores
- Operator's manuals for machinery
- Patents
- Slides/pictures

The storage, organization of, and access to the libraries' resources are done with the users in mind and vary from traditional book classification schemes to systems designed just for a specific library's collection(s). While computers are the most common tool for accessing the content of nonelectronic resources, a very few libraries may still use paper-based indexes (including the card catalog). Special libraries tend to provide more comprehensive subject analysis and access methods for their collections than do public or academic libraries.

Also affecting the organization and access methods used is that many of the items housed are generated by the library's parent organization. The

---

Contents of a Collection Development/Acquisitions Procedures Manual

While St. Clair and Williamson (1992) provide two lists of items to consider when developing a policy, this list specifies what should be included in a manual:

- Organization and library mission statements
- Acquisitions policy
- Handling user recommendations/requests
- Subjects and formats acquired
- Deaccessioning
- Purchasing versus borrowing
- Charge-backs versus library payments
- Purchase approval procedures
- Purchase order procedures
- Payment methods (charge card, checks, cash)
- Vendor selection criteria
- List of vendors currently used
- Replacement (new, used)
- Gifts (including exchanges)
- Journal article photocopies (including who purchases and/ or pays)
- Supplies

librarian is expected to organize and provide the access that will allow users to easily access and utilize these materials in their daily job-related activities. Since access is usually by electronic means, familiarity with digitization and scanning of older materials is needed.

Most special libraries have some form of library automation software to help organize and maintain the collection. Although this topic is beyond the scope of this chapter, it is important to note that some special libraries participate in the automation systems offered by consortia or larger library systems or Web-based systems to reduce the cost of acquiring and maintaining the software and equipment needed for a library automation program.

Special libraries even provide access to materials housed elsewhere within the parent organization. Documents and other resources needed by a department to function are housed in the department with subject and content analysis done by library staff so all employees may know of their existence. Methods for organizing and accessing its resources are an essential item for any special library.

Conclusion

One of the biggest challenges facing small special libraries is going to be the ubiquity of electronic resources. More and more resources are going to be available in only electronic format. E-books will become more common, journals will be available in only electronic format, and more scientific information is going to be made available electronically.

The special librarian will have to provide the right mix of online and paper resources so as to be as comprehensive as possible. This will take ingenuity and resourcefulness because of budgetary restraints and the rising costs of electronic and paper resources. The special librarian's role will continue to involve selection, control, and gatekeeping.

Finding the needed information will continue to play an important role in user services. Special librarians need to embrace the technology supporting electronic resources and exploit those technologies which will best serve their users. In addition, because the Internet has become ubiquitous in the delivery of information, librarians will need to train users to search resources effectively and efficiently and teach them to evaluate what they find.

As electronic resources become ever more prevalent, the special library as a physical space will probably decline, with the exception of libraries dealing with certain subjects (e.g., science) that rely on information contained in older paper resources. The digitization of older resources means users will have less need for special libraries but not special librarians. These information gurus will still be needed to help find answers among the trillions of bits of data. Users will find that even though they can find information, good enough will not be acceptable.

To determine what services and resources to provide for their users, special librarians must be knowledgeable about the needs and requirements of their users. They must listen and understand the problems and issues users face in doing their work. The special librarian will do this through informal and formal market research methods (surveys, focus groups, and getting out of the office/library for one-on-one meetings). The special librarian will continuously analyze and review the procedures and activities used to meet user information requests. Lack of money, staff, space, and time will require eliminating, or revising, inefficient and ineffective procedures and activities so new services and/or resources can be added.

Journals

- *AALL Spectrum* (American Association of Law Libraries)
- *Information Outlook* (Special Libraries Association)
- *KM Today* (Information Today)
- *MLS: Marketing Library Services* (Information Today)

Further Reading

American Library Association. "ALA Library Fact Sheets." Last updated August 2014. www.ala.org/tools/libfactsheets.

———. "Setting Up a Special Library: A Resource Guide." ALA Library Fact Sheet Number 16c. Last updated August 2014. www.ala.org/tools/libfactsheets/alalibraryfactsheet16c.

Bassett, Dawn, Jenny Fry, and Brooke Ballantyne-Scott. *Facelifts for Special Libraries: A Practical Guide for Revitalizing Diverse Physical and Digital Spaces.* Oxford, UK: Chandos, 2010.

Broadbent, Marianne. "The Emerging Phenomenon of Knowledge Management." *The Australian Library Journal* 46, no. 1 (1997): 6–24.

Correia, Cynthia C. "How Competitive Is Your Law Firm? Competitive Intelligence for the Legal Industry." LLRX.com (Law and technology resources for legal professionals). Published January 2, 2003. www.llrx.com/features/ci.htm.

Financial Times and Special Library Association. "The Evolving Value of Information Management: And the Five Essential Attributes of the Modern Information Professional." Accessed December 30, 2014. www.sla.org/wp-content/uploads/2014/03/FT-SLA-Report.pdf.

Matarazzo, James M., Toby Pearlstein, and Sylvia R. M. James. *Special Libraries: A Survival Guide.* Santa Barbara, CA: Libraries Unlimited, 2013.

Matthews, Joseph R. *The Bottom Line: Determining and Communicating the Value of the Special Library.* Westport, CT: Libraries Unlimited, 2002.

McKendrick, Joseph. *Funding and Priorities: Special and Corporate Libraries, Government Agency Libraries; The Library Resource Guide Benchmark Study on 2011 Library Spending Plans.* Chatham, NJ: Unisphere Research, 2011.

Pacifici, Sabrina I. "Competitive Intelligence: A Selective Resource Guide—Completely Updated, August 2014." LLRX.com (Law and technology resources for legal professionals). Published August 8 2014. www.llrx.com/features/ciguide.htm.

Rinaldy, Caroline. *Trends in Rare Book and Documents Special Collections Management.* New York: Primary Research Group, 2008.

Semertzaki, Eva. *Special Libraries as Knowledge Management Centres.* Oxford, UK: Chandos, 2011.

Siess, Judith A. *The New OPL Sourcebook: A Guide for Solo and Small Libraries.* Medford, NJ: Information Today, 2006.

References

McDonough, Beverley, and Jennifer Williams, eds. 2013. *American Library Directory 2013–2014.* Medford, NJ: Information Today.

St. Clair, Guy, and Joan Williamson. 1992. *Managing the New One-Person Library.* London: Bowker-Saur.

Public Libraries

John A. Moorman

The Federal-State Cooperative System, charged with the annual collection of public library data, defines a public library as follows:

> A public library is an entity that is established under state enabling laws or regulations to serve a community, district, or region, and that provides at least the following: (1) an organized collection of printed or other library materials, or a combination thereof; (2) paid staff; (3) an established schedule in which services of the staff are available to the public; (4) the facilities necessary to support such a collection, staff, and schedule; and (5) is supported in whole or in part with public funds. (IMLS 2014a, 56)

While this is a good, all-purpose definition, some public libraries operate with volunteer staff, and a few public libraries (the exception by far) operate totally off of endowment funds and receive no public support. But for the purposes of this chapter, and the book overall, the previous definition serves as a good basis for indicating what is meant when the term *public library* is employed.

Types of Public Libraries

There are three main types of public libraries. The most familiar type is the stand-alone public library, or a public library that is a separate entity and not part of a larger system or regional entity. These libraries go by a variety of names: city library, county library, municipal library, township library, and district library. The differentiation here is that the public library is a unit that serves a defined local, single-jurisdiction legal entity. Its governance, which comes in many forms depending on the state laws defining its establishment and operation, is discussed in the following section of this chapter.

The second type of public library is a regional library. This library consists of public library locations serving more than one unit of local government,

IN THIS CHAPTER

✓ Types of Public Libraries

✓ Governance

✓ Staffing

✓ Funding and Budgeting

✓ Services

✓ Conclusion

✓ Further Reading

✓ References

What makes a public library different from other types of libraries? These are the main areas of difference:

- A public library serves all age groups, all economic groups, and all racial and gender groups.
- A public library is primarily funded by local government.

There are 9,082 public libraries in the United States (IMLS 2014b, 6).

such as a city or county. The degree of independence of the local public library location will vary according to the setup of the regional system. Some public library locations within a regional system have considerable autonomy and depend on the regional library for specialized services, such as materials purchasing and cataloging. Other public library locations are just that, locations, and the regional library has total control over their services and programs.

The third type of library, much smaller in number, is the combined public library, meaning that the public library location exists in combination with another entity. One such combination is the combined school/public library where the public library is connected with a K–12 school, most often a high school. These combinations are mostly found in small communities where it is not feasible to have a separate public library facility. A growing combination is one where the public library and a community college library are combined in one facility. A good example of this is the branch of the Virginia Beach (VA) Public Library that shares a facility with the Tidewater Community College Library. A third option is the combined public/university facility. A good example of this is the main library of the San José (CA) Public Library that shares a facility with the King Library of San José State University.

Governance

Public library governance is also a mixed picture. A board of trustees governs most public libraries. This board may be appointed by the local governing entity or elected from the area in which it serves. Most district libraries are self-governing entities with the ability to set tax rates as well as having a governing body elected by the people within their boundaries. The powers of the board of trustees vary according to the state, city, or other code under which they were established and operate. Most boards have control over library operations outside of the budget process, where they must go to another governmental entity for final funding approval.

In the regional library setting, the board may be composed of members from individual political units within the library's area of operation. These may be elected, appointed by local library groups, or appointed by units of government, such as cities or counties, within the area served by the regional library. As with other types of public libraries, control over operations varies, although most have control over all operations outside of the budget process, where they must also go to other governmental entities for final funding approval.

In the combined library setting, there is generally a public library board for the operations of the public library part of the combined library. The other governmental entity for the library will be the entity for the partner organization. In these cases, there is usually a formal signed contract between the unit of government for the public library and the unit of government for the other entity, outlining in detail who is responsible for each aspect of library operation and where the financial responsibility lies for library operations and services. This contract is essential for the continuance of this type of library.

The final type of public library governance occurs when the library has no board of trustees but is considered a direct part of local government. In these cases, the library administrator reports to an elected or appointed official of city or county government and the library is considered the same as other departments of that unit of government.

All of the previous methods of public library governance have their advantages and disadvantages. What makes them work are the people who participate in whatever governance structure is present and the trust and respect that the library has on the local level.

Staffing

Staffing in the small public library varies considerably. The smaller the library, the less likely there will be someone on the staff with a master's degree in library and information science. The smallest public libraries may have only one employee, and this individual may be employed for fewer than forty hours per week. Some states have specific requirements for educational attainment for directors of public libraries. There may be various levels of public libraries depending on population served, with lower levels requiring of their director only a high school education and some library experience. Other states take a different approach, for example, Virginia, where all libraries serving a population of over 15,000 must have an ALA MLS-degreed librarian as director to receive their full state aid allocation.

Funding and Budgeting

As indicated earlier, local units of government primarily fund public libraries. While most states provide some level of state support in the form of state aid grants or grants through the state library for a variety of purposes, generally 80 to 90 percent of the library's operating budget comes from local government sources. Other sources of funding include library revenue from fines, fees, gifts, and grants. Most public libraries receive little or no direct federal funding.

Another, and not to be overlooked, source of funding is that provided by Friends of the Library groups and Library Foundations. These volunteer groups, organized to assist the library in providing services and programs not provided through regular budgeted funds, can be a valuable resource in enriching a library's offerings to the public. One challenge with these groups is in seeing that regular funding bodies do not look upon them as a means to lessen their financial responsibilities for the public library.

The annual process of obtaining funding for library services is a challenge for any public library. Part of this challenge is the relationship that most public libraries have with their local funding entity or entities. As mentioned earlier, while most libraries have a board of trustees invested with governing responsibility for library operations, this authority does not extend to the establishment of the budget. With the exception of such libraries as district libraries in Illinois, where the board of trustees has taxing and revenue-collecting authority, most libraries have to request their annual funding from either city or county boards. This can be a difficult task because the public library is competing against a wide variety of interests, including public safety, parks and recreation, and health and social services. An important part of successful budget planning is positioning the library in the community as a vital community resource. To do this, the library must be more than a passive part of the community and the library director needs to be an active participant in community life. It is also important for the board of trustee members to be well connected in the community.

Services

Most public libraries offer a standard list of services (see sidebar). This section takes a look at each one individually.

Materials Checkout and Return

This service raises two questions in the public library that are not as prevalent in other library settings.

The first question is, Who may use the library? At first glance, the answer is obvious: those who through their taxes pay for the service. However, the situation is more complex. Public libraries deal with individuals who may work in one jurisdiction but live in another, or who find one library's location to be more convenient than the library located in their unit of government, or who think that another library may be better than a neighboring one. Many public libraries are part of cooperative agreements that allow their residents to use area libraries on the same basis as their local libraries, and vice versa, but some are not. This question becomes particularly vexing when use of a public library's services by those outside the jurisdiction covered by the library exceeds a level that is politically comfortable to the funding body. Then the question arises as to whether you charge for this use and, if so, how much. The author was once director of a public library where almost half of its use came from those outside its geographic boundaries. Another question arises when the political situation may require limiting public library service to those within the taxing area of the library's governmental funding entities, a situation the author has also faced. These are not easy situations to handle. However, these questions occur with frequency in areas of concentrated population growth where library service is uneven in its distribution and level of funding.

Standard Public Library Services

- Materials checkout and return
- Collection development
- Adult services
- Children's services
- Teen services
- Outreach services

The second question deals with material return. As public libraries serve all citizens within their service areas, the ability to conveniently return materials is one that is of more concern than it is in special, school, or academic settings. How do you handle the desire for off-site return? This involves questions of where to place these return vehicles, what types of return should be permitted, what staffing is needed to provide transportation of these items back to the library, and how often do these return locations need to be checked?

Collection Development

In many small public libraries, collection development becomes the responsibility of the library director. In some libraries, this individual does both selecting and ordering as well as processing of incoming materials. What is ordered depends on the financial resources available and the demands that the community places on the library. In recent years, the explosion of information in electronic format has placed a significant burden on the small public library, as these resources are expensive both in licensing cost and in the technology needed to support them. Yet public libraries are expected to have access to these resources. Many state library agencies have statewide database programs that supply selected databases to all public libraries within their states. These programs are a godsend to the smaller public library.

The public library, as with other types of libraries discussed in this book, places a strong emphasis on obtaining what the user desires. In addition to the purchase of materials for the collection, this involves the use of interlibrary loan to acquire access to materials that the library does not own outright. Most small public libraries are net borrowers rather than net lenders where interlibrary loan is concerned. However, many small libraries have items in their collections, particularly where local history or genealogy are concerned, that are desired by users in other communities.

Adult Services

This service area includes what is commonly called reference service, readers' advisory service, access to the Internet, and a variety of other services, including public copy services. Unlike other types of libraries where this service is limited to clientele such as company employees, faculty, or staff, public library adult services includes individuals of all ages and economic, social, and racial backgrounds. The information needs of this wide and varied group pose a challenge to everyday library service. Any hour serving at a reference desk can bring a vast array of questions, for example: Who is my local council representative? How can I use the computer to apply for a job? What are five sources for my term paper? What are the main factors in the economy of San Salvador? Another challenge in the provision of reference service in the small public library is the increasing presence of technology. All public libraries are expected to provide access to the Internet along with word-processing and spreadsheet programs, at a minimum. This access requires personal computers, printers, telecommunications, and the hardware and software to make this possible. Now more than ever before, public librarians are expected to be knowledgeable in the technology of information access as well as in the methods of information access and be able to demonstrate that knowledge to users on a daily basis.

Children's Services

This area of service is one of the first that comes to mind when public libraries are discussed. It is also one that can be used to good effect with the public when discussing financial needs. Even for those individuals who do not use the public library, the inherent goodness of providing access to information and assisting in acquiring and enhancing reading and comprehension skills gives most citizens a warm and fuzzy feeling for the public library.

A major focus of this area is on programming. From a variety of story hour formats, including lap-sit, preschool, and elementary programs, library staff provide children with a personal connection to the world of literature. These programs are highly interactive and use the full complement of audiovisual stimuli. A major emphasis is on the development of language skills and socialization in the young child. In providing story-hour opportunities that include educational components, the public library is working with the school system to enhance the ability of the young child to comprehend and enjoy the printed word. Many libraries have active partnerships with their local school districts, and some public libraries receive assistance from their school districts for these activities. The term *pre-emergent literacy* is used to describe public library efforts in making children ready for kindergarten.

A second area of programming that most public libraries do is the summer reading program. Here, creativity abounds, as all sorts of activities occur during this period, such as visits from staff of local nature centers, programs with jugglers or musical ensembles, the creation of story gardens, and many craft programs. The challenge facing public libraries with summer reading programs is deciding how competitive they should be and what awards they should give for successful participation or completion. Each library must find its comfort level with this challenge.

Teen Services

This is a challenging aspect of public library service. It is generally defined as serving individuals between the ages of twelve and eighteen. Individuals in this age group mature at different times and in different ways. Thus, what might fit one individual will not necessarily fit another and what appeals to males will not necessarily appeal to females.

In serving this age group, printed materials need to be attractive and in touch with current interests. Graphic novels, manga, and anime are examples of genres that are currently popular with this age group. Audiovisual materials need to be selected with an understanding of the interests of your teen library users. The website and publications of *VOYA* (*Voice of Youth Advocates*) are useful for those dealing with teen collections.

Programming is a vital part of library service to teens. Programs must be interesting, involve teenagers in their planning, and be held at a time when teens can attend. It is important to remember in planning that younger members of this age group depend on others for transportation to the library. Technology is another important part of program planning for teens. For more on the role of technology in teen programming, see chapter 16.

Outreach Services

Webster's Third New International Dictionary's definition of outreach includes "to go beyond . . . to go too far . . . to reach out." In the public library setting, outreach usually refers to library services and programs that are held outside of the building(s) that the library occupies. However, some public librarians would be partial to the second definition.

Public library outreach refers to any service or program that is conducted outside the library. These may include bookmobile or mobile services, remote site materials return, and programs such as book-by-mail, remote access to databases, and 24/7 access to library collections and services via the library's website or social media presence. By reaching beyond the library building(s), the public library provides services to day-care centers, retirement communities, assisted-living centers, and locations geographically remote from in-house library services. An important aspect of library outreach is the community organizations in which library staff participate. Examples of this type of outreach include service with United Way and membership in Chamber of Commerce and other civic organizations.

Conclusion

The coming years will be full of challenges to public libraries. The first challenge will be to the very existence of the public library. This is nothing new, for as each new technology has arisen since the 1940s, there have been those who have stated that it threatens the existence of the public library. However, with the Internet and its huge variety of information and information sources, as well as the arrival of numerous search engines to locate and present the information, this is a threat not to be taken lightly. Information is now readily accessible in many homes without the necessity of a public library visit. Music is readily downloadable from Internet sites and the e-book is becoming an easier option than the traditional book format. Both are available without library participation in the process. In recent years, many small communities and larger cities and counties have downsized or closed their public libraries or have turned to employing private contractors to provide library services to their communities.

The second challenge is the tremendous explosion in both knowledge and the formats in which it is delivered. With limited funding, it is a challenge to know which formats have staying power and when to abandon formats that have been superseded by newer and more effective means of information delivery. With this knowledge explosion comes the need for more staff training and development to keep current and be able to provide proper service to library users. This is a financial issue as well as a time issue in libraries with limited staff.

The third challenge is technology itself. Rapidly changing technology is a costly proposition. With new software, expanding databases, advances in printing technology, and information storage and transfer requirements comes the continuing necessity for equipment updates and replacement. In the small public library with limited resources, this will remain a challenge for years to come.

The fourth challenge is the increasing lack of graduate schools of library and information science. Also, the curricula of these schools may not always teach the knowledge and skills necessary for providing quality public service in the small library setting. The author is but one example of the many librarians who have recently retired, are considering retirement, or will retire in the next five to ten years. Public libraries need to look at creative ways of ensuring that there will be an adequate supply of trained, qualified librarians in the years to come. Distance education is one answer but not a total solution. A question that must be examined is the level of education that is needed for the provision of public library service in small libraries. Are there other ways than an MLS education for individuals to gain the knowledge necessary to provide quality library service to their communities? Libraries should also look at their own staff members and encourage and support those who desire graduate education so that they will be ready to take over when retirements occur.

The final challenge has two sides to it: the first is population decline; the second is rapid growth. In the case of population decline, the challenge becomes how to serve an ever-receding population while still existing as a viable entity. This is the situation faced in many rural areas in the United States. The case of rapid growth is the other side of the coin but just as problematic. Growth presents significant challenges, particularly in an era where politicians are elected on a platform of tax cuts. The expectation is that growth will enable enough increased revenues to provide expected services. So far, reality has not shown this to be the case.

While the public library faces significant challenges in the future, the situation is nothing new. For public libraries to survive and prosper, the following elements need to be in place:

- A board-approved planning document that provides a guideline for library operations and services. This document must be active, revisited annually, and used regularly in library operations.
- The planning document should include in addition to directions and goals

- a mission statement,
- a vision statement, and
- a statement of core values.
- An understanding of, and agreement on, the niche your library serves in the community. This is essential and will be different in each library setting.

With the previous elements in place, libraries stand a better chance of obtaining the necessary local support and funding required to provide effective public library service.

Further Reading

In addition to the following sources, go to ALA's website (www.ala.org) and check out its publications and web education offerings. This is a valuable resource for small public libraries and their staff.

Hernon, Peter, and Joseph R. Matthews, eds. *Reflecting on the Future of Academic and Public Libraries*. Chicago: ALA Editions, 2013.

Institute of Museum and Library Services. *The State of Small and Rural Libraries in the United States*. Research Brief #5. Washington, DC: Institute of Museum and Library Services, 2013.

Leeder, Kim, and Eric Frierson, eds. *Planning Our Future Libraries: Blueprints for 2025*. Chicago: ALA Editions, 2014.

Matthews, Joseph R. *Research-Based Planning for Public Libraries*. Santa Barbara, CA: Libraries Unlimited, 2013.

McCook, Kathleen de la Peña. *Introduction to Public Librarianship*. 2nd ed. New York: Neal-Schuman, 2011.

Pearlmutter, Jane, and Paul Nelson. *Small Public Library Management*. Chicago: ALA Editions, 2012.

Prentice, Ann E. *Public Libraries in the 21st Century*. Santa Barbara, CA: Libraries Unlimited, 2010.

Velasquez, Diane L., ed. *Library Management 101: A Practical Guide*. Chicago: ALA Editions, 2013.

References

IMLS (Institute of Museum and Library Services). 2014a. *Public Libraries in the United States Survey: Fiscal Year 2011*. www.imls.gov/assets/1/AssetManager/PLS2011.pdf.

———. 2014b. *Public Libraries in the United States Survey: Fiscal Year 2012*. www.imls.gov/assets/1/AssetManager/PLS_FY2012.pdf.

School Libraries

Linda Williams

The National Center for Educational Statistics (NCES), the primary federal entity responsible for collecting and analyzing data related to education, defines the school library or library media center as an "organized collection of printed and/or audiovisual and/or computer resources which is administrated as a unit, is located in a designated place or places and makes resources and services available to students, teachers, and administrators" (3). School libraries are distinct from public libraries because they serve as "learner-oriented laboratories which support, extend, and individualize the school's curriculum. A school library serves as the center and coordinating agency for all material used in the school" (Morris 2004, 32).

The school library has one central function—to be an integral part of the instructional process by providing curriculum-related materials and working with teachers and students to produce effective learning experiences for the students. "The school library media specialist has the opportunity to be the essential member of the instructional team in each school" (AASL 2009a, 7). The fiscal and human resources are directed to this end. There are many secondary, albeit important, functions that the school library performs as well. It stimulates the imagination of young people, it promotes critical thinking, it exposes young people to diverse points of view on important topics, it provides exposure to the cultural differences that exist in the world, and it provides some entertaining diversions as well.

School libraries are embedded in much larger organizations. On one level, although there may be a school librarian who exercises immediate control, ultimate control and supervision of the library is the concern of the school's principal. Alternatively, school libraries may be governed by a special administrator in charge of curriculum for the entire school system or an administrator specifically in charge of the school library program who may be responsible for selection or approval of materials for all of the schools' libraries. Finally, because school libraries exist as part of the entire school system, they are governed by a school board whose administrative powers are delegated to a school administration. This administration often consists of a superintendent and assistants. Although these individuals seldom get involved in direct supervision or control, they often become involved when there are complaints about materials.

History of Standards Development

School libraries in the United States have nineteenth-century origins, but there were actually very few of them until the twentieth century. Their development was accelerated in the twentieth century by many factors. In the 1920s, the impetus for school libraries grew because of the development of regional accrediting agencies that promoted the need for trained librarians. At this time, the American Library Association (ALA) endorsed the "Certain Standards" and published the quantitative standards for high school libraries produced by the National Education Association (NEA). In 1925, the NEA created standards for elementary schools. By 1939, the Middle States Association had developed "Evaluative Criteria" for school libraries, including them in their school reviews, many of which were used until the 1950s. In 1945, the ALA published *School Libraries for Today and Tomorrow*, including both quantitative and qualitative standards, which was used as a guide for future standards. By 1951, the American Association of School Librarians (AASL) realized the need for periodic revision and updates to the standards in response to changes in the educational field. As a result, *A Planning Guide for the High School Library Program* was published.

In the 1950s, another push was given when the Soviet Union launched *Sputnik*. The successful placing of a satellite in space by this rival of the United States created considerable social and political upheaval, as Americans feared they would soon be militarily inferior to their adversary. The space race thus gave a strategic significance to efforts to improve the American educational system. As a result, the 1960s were one of the greatest periods of growth and development for school libraries due to an increased flow of money and support from the private sector and public funding for education. Most notable during this time was the Knapp School Libraries Project that established model school libraries across the country. Hundreds of school libraries were expanded and renovated during this time" (*Wikipedia* 2014).

The 1960s also saw the development of strong political support, expressed primarily through the passage of the Elementary and Secondary Education Act (ESEA) in 1965. This act provided federal support to purchase materials for schools and libraries, which in turn resulted in a tremendous expansion of school library collections. This growth also resulted in new standards; in 1969, *Standards for School Library Media Programs* was published by the AASL and NEA's Department of Audiovisual Instruction (DAVI). The growth of school library collections and the variety of formats collected, including audiovisual materials, led to the creation of new standards; in 1975, *Media Programs: District and School*, published by the AASL and the Association for Educational Communications and Technology

"As we approach the second decade of the twenty-first century, school library programs continue to undergo momentous changes that have heightened the importance of technology and evidence-based learning. The focus has moved from the library as a confined place to one with fluid boundaries that is layered by diverse needs and influenced by an interactive global community. Guiding principles for school library programs must focus on building a flexible learning environment with the goal of producing successful learners skilled in multiple literacies."

(Martin 2009, 5)

(AECT; formerly NEA-DAVI), emphasized the importance of a strong media collection.

Most recently, school libraries have been defined by three major standards/guidelines documents. *Information Power: Guidelines for School Library Media Programs*, published in 1988 by the AASL and the AECT. This document defined the school library media specialist as an instructional teacher and emphasized that the program's success depended on the library media specialist. Ten years later, in 1998, the revised document, *Information Power: Building Partnerships for Learning*, also published by the AASL and the AECT, expanded the role of the library media specialist to include teacher, information specialist, instructional partner, and program administrator. This was the first time that quantitative standards were not included. The current standards, published in 2007 by the AASL, *Standards for the 21st-Century Learner*, shift the focus from what needs to be taught and take place in the library to a focus on the student or learner and what he or she needs to know and be able to do to be information literate. "It builds on a strong history of guidelines published to ensure that school library program planners go beyond the basics to provide goals, priorities, criteria, and general principles for establishing effective library media programs" (Martin 2009, 5)

Collection Management

The major emphasis of a school library collection is to provide materials that meet the needs of the curriculum. To assess these needs, the school librarian must have knowledge of the curriculum and have curriculum documents readily available. The school librarian needs to be familiar with any changes or additions to the curriculum, as those in turn will change the needs assessment and the collection development process. All districts or schools should have a selection policy, containing procedures for review, evaluation, selection, acquisition, and reconsideration. This policy should reflect the philosophy and goals of the district or school as well as support the principles of intellectual freedom as described in the "Library Bill of Rights" (www.ala.org/advocacy/intfreedom/librarybill), "The Students' Right to Read" (www.ncte.org/positions/statements/righttoreadguideline), and any position statement on intellectual freedom from the ALA or the AASL.

School librarians are responsible for implementing the selection policy and, in doing so, work cooperatively with administrators and teachers to provide resources that represent diverse points of view, stimulate growth in thinking skills, and promote the overall educational program. The rapid growth of knowledge brings with it many challenges, especially with today's shift toward digital resources. School librarians take leadership in communicating to the educational community the purpose and scope of the selection policy. The reconsideration policy, which should be included in the selection policy, identifies the procedures to follow when a library

"The school library program provides learning opportunities in multiple literacies that enable students to become efficient and effective in the pursuit of information. Further, the school library program encourages a critical stance as it encourages students to examine the authority of authors and the bias of sponsors; to assess the importance of currency of information to the topic at hand; and to determine the scope and relevance of information to meet their needs. This instruction occurs best in the context of the school curriculum where students have a need to know and are guided by a standard of excellence set by their classroom teachers in collaboration with the school librarian."

(AASL 2012)

material is challenged. Having a selection policy in place will provide evidence of reasons for the selection and purchase of a material when faced with challenges or censorship, and the reconsideration policy puts into place a standard approach to reassess the material. No materials should be removed just because there is a challenge/complaint. If materials need to be removed, then the reconsideration policy provides the means for doing so.

Schools have traditionally been vulnerable to censorship attempts, especially because they are supposed to serve in loco parentis. Among the crucial issues that define school censorship problems are

- the differing views of the function of schools and school librarians and
- the rights and powers of school boards versus the rights of students and parents.

These issues have been battled out in years of court cases, many of which have resulted in unclear or contradictory conclusions. This judicial ambivalence was highlighted in one of the most important school library cases, *Board of Education, Island Trees Union Free School District no. 26 v. Pico* (1982), which reached the United States Supreme Court. This case is now referred to as the *Island Trees* or *Pico* case, named after Stephen Pico, the student who filed the complaint. The following is a brief discussion of some of the fundamental issues raised by the legal and philosophical arguments found in the various cases. Awareness of these issues is important to any understanding of this situation for today's school library.

The Functions of Schools and School Libraries

Defining the functions of schools can have profound consequences on how you perceive the functions of school libraries. There are at least two fundamentally differing accounts. One perspective is to view the schools as a place to inculcate the values of the local community—the majority values. Such a view perceives the school as an instrument of particular values. Children, in this sense, are perceived as highly vulnerable to outside influences and need protection until they are old enough to know that these influences are problematic. Such a view is, in itself, not wholly unreasonable. It seems obvious that children do need protection from physical abuse, and some might argue that this is easily extended to intellectual harm as well. The purpose of schools is to inculcate the students with specific orthodox attitudes as well as basic knowledge. Exposure to unorthodox points of view would be undertaken only under conditions in which substantial control is exercised to ensure that the views are not mistakenly understood as acceptable or reasonable alternatives.

From this perspective, the school library represents a potential problem. Most obvious is that the school library has traditionally been a place of voluntary attendance, where the materials are voluntarily selected by the student. Some guidance may be involved, but as a rule, there is considerably less guidance and control over exposure and interpretation of materials in the library than in the classroom. If the inculcation of values is to be effected, one function of the librarian or library worker would be to monitor each student's selections. In many cases, this is a practical impossibility. The alternative is that the library exercises very careful and restrictive selection of materials and, most likely, restrictive access to materials for some, usually younger, children.

The second perspective is to view the school as a place where students are exposed to a wide variety of viewpoints. The function of the school is to familiarize students with many perspectives and to emphasize critical-thinking skills and judgment-making skills. It is not the school's place, however, to assert a particular perspective or attempt to inculcate the specific values of the local or majority community. It attempts to prepare students to discriminate among ideas so they can make future judgments on important issues about which there are many differing opinions.

The school library in this setting would likely function quite differently. The library collection would likely contain many perspectives, some unorthodox as well as orthodox, and the librarian's function would be less supervisory and controlling. Access would tend to be unrestricted.

These two perspectives have been painted here as polar opposites, although there are certainly many gradations that reflect the realities of school libraries. All schools inculcate values, and all try to get students to think, more or less. But how you perceive a school's primary purpose is likely to affect your attitude seriously when you hear that a book on suicide, one by a revolutionary, or books that contain explicit language about sex are part of the library collection. Those who subscribe to the former view are much more likely to restrict or control materials. Similarly, even in schools in which the inculcation of local or majority values is paramount, a more subtle distinction might be made regarding its school library. You can perceive, for example, that the function of the classroom is different from the function of the school library. You can argue that the classroom is the place where values are inculcated and still believe that the school library's purpose is different, a place for exposure to a wide array of ideas, even those which are unorthodox. In this sense, the concept of the library carries with it the supposition that it is a special forum—a place where many different, even controversial and subversive ideas may coexist. In this way, a distinction between classroom purposes and library purposes is possible. Obviously, if you perceive the library as a special forum for ideas, the library collection would predictably be more catholic in perspective, no matter what the defined purpose of the classroom.

The Rights of School Boards and Students (and Parents)

Censorship problems in schools also arise from the friction created by the conflicting authority of the school board and the rights of young people. Traditionally, school boards have exercised considerable legal authority and

"Beyond its curricular role, the school library program gives each individual member of the learning community a venue for exploring questions that arise out of individual curiosity and personal interest. As part of the school library program, the school librarian provides leadership in the use of information technologies and instruction for both students and staff in how to use them constructively, ethically, and safely. The school librarian offers expertise in accessing and evaluating information, using information technologies, and collections of quality physical and virtual resources. In addition, the school librarian possesses dispositions that encourage broad and deep exploration of ideas as well as responsible use of information technologies. These attributes add value to the school community."

(AASL 2012)

power in the United States. Generally, education falls primarily within the province of the states. States have delegated the authority to local school boards that have been given broad authority to run their school systems, including the selection of teachers, curricular materials, and materials for the school library media center.

There is little doubt that school boards are responsible for the school library, but it is seldom their central focus. From time to time, school boards are surprised to discover that some of the materials on the school library shelf are not to their liking or the liking of parents. Problems usually arise when parents file objections to materials their children have selected from the school library. But objections also arise from principals, teachers, students, and school board members themselves. When challenges occur, there is a tendency in many cases to restrict or withdraw the materials, especially when there are no formal policies for selection and reconsideration of these materials.

The actions of school boards to remove or restrict materials may often go unchallenged. Although the rights of young people may be limited, the courts have recognized that students do not give up First Amendment rights and due process rights just because they are in school. This highlights the delicate balance that must be struck in schools concerning the rights of school boards to run their schools as they see fit and the individual rights of citizens, including young people, to First Amendment and due process protection. The balance is dynamic.

The lack of clarity regarding the legal rights of boards, the place of the school library, and the rights of students literally ensures that more problems wait on the horizon. Such problems will be magnified as the school library collections expand to include resources on the Internet. There is certainly plenty of dissent in our society regarding what is suitable material for young people, and the school library will remain a lightning rod of political controversy in this arena.

Challenges

The contemporary school library faces many challenges, including the following:

- Ensuring that the library plays an integral role in the instructional process of the school
- Emphasizing the importance of information literacy
- Dealing with declining funds in schools
- Addressing the shortage of certified school librarians
- Dealing with increases in technology

Ensuring That the Library Plays an Integral Role in the Instructional Process

Central to the philosophy of the school library program is that the librarian and the library be perceived as central features of the school and that the librarian be seen as a collaborator in developing effective learning strategies. If school libraries are to thrive in the future, they must be recognized for their importance to the function of the school. Too often, the library is considered an expensive appendage to the educational process rather than an integral part, which is especially ironic, given the evidence of the relationship of school libraries to academic achievement. It has been shown that students who score higher on norm-referenced tests tend to come from schools with larger library staff and larger school library collections. In addition, high academic performance of students has also been correlated with school libraries in which librarians served in an instructional and collaborative role. The size of the library staff and the collection were the best predictors of academic performance, with the exception of the presence of at-risk conditions such as poverty.

These facts highlight the reality that school librarians need to communicate clearly and cooperate closely with teachers, principals, and administrators. By demonstrating the importance of the library and its ability to contribute to the school's mission, greater political and fiscal support are more likely to follow. Fortunately, there is some evidence that library media specialists are having an impact. In a survey conducted by *School Library Journal* (Lau 2002), 66 percent of the school librarians responded that their principals are very supportive of library collaborations with teachers, 46 percent of librarians teach classes, 95 percent instruct students on how to use print and online resources, and 30 percent recommend and evaluate vendors for potential classroom textbook purchases. Ninety percent report that they are satisfied with their jobs and the amount of respect they receive.

Emphasizing the Importance of Information Literacy

With the increasing use of technologies in the classroom and the school library, it is clear that students need to be well educated on how to locate and evaluate information. The underlying rationale for this education, however, has been broadened in recent years. The purpose behind developing these skills is so that students not only can be more proficient academically but also become lifelong learners.

> Learning in the 21st century has taken on new dimensions with the exponential expansion of information. Ever changing tools, increasing digitation of text, and heightened demands for critical and creative thinking, communication, and collaborative problem solving. To succeed in our rapid pace global society, our learners must develop a high level of skills, attitudes and responsibilities. All learners must be able to

"The mission of the school library media program is to ensure that students and staff are effective users of ideas and information. The school library media specialist (SLMS) empowers students to be critical thinkers, enthusiastic readers, skillful researchers, and ethical users of information by:

- collaborating with educators and students to design and teach engaging learning experiences that meet individual needs
- instructing students and assisting educators in using, evaluating, and producing information and ideas through active use of a broad range of appropriate tools, resources, and information technologies
- providing access to materials in all formats, including up to date, high quality, varied literature to develop and strengthen a love of reading
- providing students and staff with instruction and resources that reflect current information needs and anticipate changes in technology and education
- providing leadership in the total education program and advocating for strong school library media programs as essential to meeting local, state, and national education goals."

(AASL 2009a, 8).

access high quality information from diverse perspectives, make sense of it to draw their own conclusions or create new knowledge and share their knowledge with others. (AASL 2009b, 5)

Such a perspective places information acquisition, dissemination, and use in the broader context of social responsibility. It is not enough to be a good locater and evaluator of information; it is the responsibility of all to continue to learn and to contribute what they have learned to society in a beneficial manner. To meet these demands, the AASL has developed learning standards that focus on the learner and expand the definition of information literacy to include multiple literacies, such as digital, virtual, textual, and technological, that are crucial for all learners to acquire to be successful (AASL 2009b). Following are the four learning standards:

1. Inquire, think critically, and gain knowledge.
2. Draw conclusions, make informed decisions, apply knowledge to new situations, and create new knowledge.
3. Share knowledge and participate ethically and productively as members of a democratic society.
4. Pursue personal and aesthetic growth.

Within each standard are the four strands of skills, dispositions, responsibilities, and self-assessment strategies that identify the goals for the learner (see figure 5.1).

Dealing with Declining Funds in Schools

Adequate school funding continues to be a challenge at the national, state, and local levels and is the primary challenge school libraries are facing today. As noted in 2012, "school libraries are some of the most underfunded classrooms in the United States because struggling local, state and federal budgets combined with the fact that No Child Left Behind (NCLB) ignores a direct correlation between school libraries and increased student achievement" (Ballard 2012, 15). There is little doubt that some citizens have limited confidence in their school systems. This, coupled with a general feeling among taxpayers that they have been taxed enough, has led to a resistance to increasing their tax burden for the public schools. The damage to schools from this trend is magnified by the need for additional monies to accommodate the rapid changes in learning technologies and the proliferation of excellent print materials published today for young people.

The State of America's Libraries 2014 (ALA 2014), an analysis of data from 2011 to 2012, projects a stormy horizon for our nation's school libraries. The report shows that funding for school libraries in 2013 was more uncertain following sequestration, which began on March 1, 2013. The full effect of sequestration on school libraries and student education will become more apparent as time passes, but some effects are already clear. Under sequestration, funding to the Department of Education was cut more than

FIGURE 5.1

AASL Learning Standards

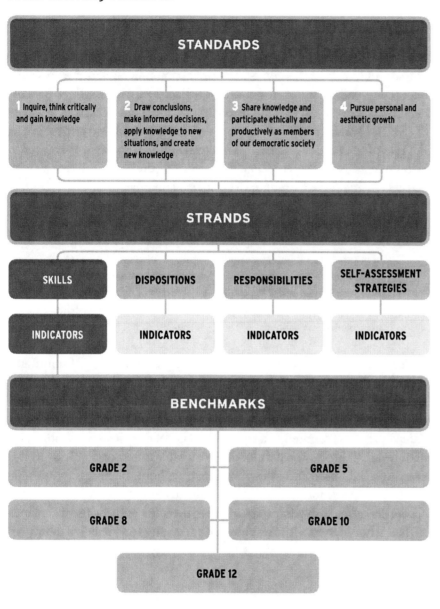

Source: AASL 2009b, 7.

5.2 percent. This is likely to have a direct impact on grant programs that provide school library funding. One example is the Innovative Approaches to Literacy program. The Library Services and Technology Act (LSTA) was also cut by more than 5.2 percent. This is the only federal funding that is exclusively set aside for libraries (Sullivan 2013). Some urban school districts have been hit particularly hard. Because schools are undergoing financial strains, there is an understandable temptation to place existing resources directly into teaching along with classroom materials and activities. Such a reallocation merely increases the drain on dwindling school library media

> "School librarians offer students much more than access to books. They serve as a vital component of the education teams found in today's schools. Librarians teach essential skills of inquiry, critical thinking, digital citizenship and technology. They foster a love of reading. Their efforts to educate our children are recognized by the National Board for Professional Teaching Standards. They are understood to be educators whose instruction can be measured to meet standards for professional teaching excellence. . . . It has been proven time and again that school librarians are essential to effective learning throughout K-12 education. More than 60 education and library studies have produced clear evidence that school library media programs staffed by a qualified school librarian have a strong and positive impact on student academic achievement."
>
> (Sullivan 2013)

center financial resources and diminishes the opportunity for the libraries to effectively assist teachers in the learning process.

Addressing the Shortage of Certified School Librarians

The school library profession is at a critical point, being faced with severe budget cuts and positions eliminated or replaced with noncertified personnel. Unfortunately, it seems the school library profession has been in a state of crisis for some time, but this has gotten more serious and critical just as the role of the school librarian has become more important than ever to help students use the Internet and electronic resources and collaborate with teachers to attain the Common Core State Standards:

> *The Pew Research Center's Internet & American Life Project Online Survey of Teachers* found that although the Internet has opened up a vast world of information for today's students, their digital literacy skills have yet to catch up. Twenty-four percent of those surveyed stated that students lack the ability to assess the quality and accuracy of information they find online. Another 33 percent reported that students lack the ability to recognize bias in online content. (Sullivan 2013)

For some years, it has become clear that the labor force of librarians, including those working in schools, is aging. The library profession is now seeing the results of the study from 2002 that stated by 2014, approximately 68 percent of school librarians will have left the profession (Everhart 2002). Already, this has resulted in a severe shortage of certified school librarians nationwide. If professional programs are unable to respond quickly to this pressing need, more and more individuals without the necessary training will be hired by school systems that are already tempted to replace certified school librarians with paraprofessionals to meet the pressing fiscal demands of their school systems. The resulting loss in quality and vitality of the school library would be a disturbing result.

Dealing with Increases in Technology

Schools have devoted considerable resources to educational technologies. In many ways, they are leaders in this area. The number of computers per school continues to rise, as does the connectivity to school libraries, thanks to an increase in networked computers in schools as well as remote access to school library databases. "Although the average number of computers in school libraries in 2012 (29.3) is comparable to the number in 2011 (27.9), the average number of school computers outside the library with networked access to library services has increased significantly" (ALA 2013, 30). Schools continue to struggle to keep up with the rapid pace of technological change. Although classroom access to computers is increasing rapidly, the most frequent and creative uses of computer technology are not being completely linked to curricula, and there are many factors influencing the use of computers in schools. For computers to become an integral tool for learning, continued improvements are needed in both the quantity and quality of computers available.

The impact of access to the Internet has been dramatic and rapid. As technologies and technological use increase, the school library will have to respond in kind, meaning increasing demands in terms of costs, staffing, training, equipment, and physical facilities. In addition, as students increasingly view the web as the most common channel to obtain information, librarians play a special role in identifying the many resources that are available in the web environment, and in training and educating both students and teachers on how to locate and evaluate websites. Similarly, school librarians must be able to organize websites for local access.

A continuing concern in most schools nationwide is the "filtering of legitimate, educational websites and academically useful social networking tools" (ALA 2013, 30–31). Schools report that "overly restrictive filters have a negative impact on student learning, and findings indicate that they also impede curriculum development and collaboration activities" (ALA 2013, 31).

Schools are beginning to use more digital content, such as test books and e-books, as well as the BYOD (bring your own device) approach, which allows students to bring their own electronic devices to school to use in their education. Though this brings many satisfactory results, it also brings a new set of concerns to the school system. School librarians must continue to develop and enhance their skills to provide the necessary leadership to enable students and teachers to effectively use these resources.

> "From 2006 to 2011, the number of school librarians declined more than the number of other educators, with the exception of instructional coordinators and supervisors, according to data from the National Center for Education Statistics. The total number of school librarians increased by less than one percent from school year 2005-2006 to 2006-2007; then decreased less than 1% in 2007-2008, 1.1% in 2008-2009, 2.3% in 2009-2010, and 4.3% in 2010-2011. . . . A comparison of school library staffing from 2007-2008 and from 2011-2012 reveals that the number of school library staff who hold only a classroom teaching certificate decreased by 5.2%. The number of staff holding a master's degree in a library-related major remained steady, decreasing less than 1%. Of note: The numbers of school library staff who hold a state library media certificate increased by 14.3%, according to the NCES."
>
> (ALA 2014, 31)

Conclusion

While there are many challenges facing school libraries and school librarians in the coming years, the overall picture remains optimistic. With the increasing use of technology in the classroom and dependence on sources such as the Internet for curriculum enhancement, there is an ever increasing need for the skills that the school librarian brings to the school setting.

To make sure that the school library remains an integral part of the educational operation, it is imperative that school librarians continually work to upgrade their skills and work collaboratively with teachers and administrators to see that all information resources are used to their fullest extent in the instructional process. To further the understanding of their role, school librarians need to actively advocate for their profession within their school communities as well as within their states and nationally.

Further Reading

Ingersoll, Richard, and Mei Han. *School Library Media Centers in the United States, 1990–1991*. Washington, DC: US Department of Education, 1994.

Martin, Ann. *Seven Steps to an Award-Winning School Library Program*. Westport, CT: Libraries Unlimited, 2005.

Minkel, Walter. "The Year in K–12 Libraries: School Librarians Redefine Themselves." In *Bowker Annual Library and Book Trade Almanac*, 48th ed., 10–15. Medford, NJ: Information Today, 2003.

Snyder, Timothy. *Getting Lead-Bottomed Administrators Excited about School Library Media Centers*. Westport, CT: Libraries Unlimited, 2000.

Stein, Barbara L., and Risa W. Brown. *Running a School Library Media Center: A How-To-Do-It Manual for Librarians*. 2nd ed. New York: Neal-Schuman, 2002.

US Department of Education, National Center for Education Statistics. *Digest of Education Statistics, 2004*. Washington, DC: US Department of Education, 2005.

References

AASL (American Association of School Librarians). 2009a. *Empowering Learners: Guidelines for School Library Programs*. Chicago: American Library Association.

———. 2009b. *Standards for the 21st-Century Learner in Action*. Chicago: American Library Association.

———. 2012. "Position Statement on the Role of the School Library Program." Revised January 21. American Library Association. www.ala.org/aasl/advocacy/resources/statements/program-role.

ALA (American Library Association). 2013. "School Libraries." In *The State of America's Libraries 2013*, 28–33. www.ala.org/news/sites/ala.org.news/files/content/2013-State-of-Americas-Libraries-Report.pdf.

———. 2014. "School Libraries." In *The State of America's Libraries 2014*, 28–33. www.ala.org/news/sites/ala.org.news/files/content/2014-State-of-Americas-Libraries-Report.pdf.

Ballard, Susan. 2012. "ALA Presidential Task Force: Focus on School Libraries." *School Library Monthly* 28 (6): 15–17.

Board of Education, Island Trees Union Free School District no. 26 v. Pico 457 U.S. 853 (1982).

Everhart, Nancy. 2002. "Filling the Void." *School Library Journal* 48 (June): 44–49.

Lau, Debra. 2002. "Got Clout?" *School Library Journal* 48 (May): 40–45.

Martin, Ann M. 2009. "Preface." In *Empowering Learners: Guidelines for School Library Programs*, by the American Association of School Librarians, 5–6. Chicago: American Library Association.

Morris, Betty J. 2004. *Administrating the School Library Media Center*. Westport, CT: Libraries Unlimited.

NCES (National Center for Educational Statistics). 2007. *School Library Media Center Questionnaire: Schools and Staffing Survey 2007–08 School Year*. Published May 11. http://nces.ed.gov/surveys/sass/pdf/0708/LSIA.pdf.

Sullivan, Maureen. 2013. *State of America's School Libraries*. *Huffington Post Blog*. Posted April 15. www.huffingtonpost.com/maureen -sullivan/state-of-americas-school-_b_3063055.html.

Wikipedia. 2014. "School Library." Accessed May 19. https://en.wikipedia .org/wiki/School_library.

Part II

Administration in the Small Library

Budgeting

John A. Moorman

A budget takes the library's planning and converts it into revenue and expenditures, and it is also the operating plan for allocating resources among priorities within the library. Before discussing the budget process, it is necessary to make general comments about budgeting in libraries. While the information presented in this chapter describes the budgeting process and gives pointers on how to prepare and present budgets, each library's situation will be different. The budget that a library prepares may not deal with all aspects of library service. For example, libraries may have personnel funding as a part of an institution's or government's general personnel budget, or they may have certain building functions, such as maintenance and utilities, coming under another part of the same entity's budget. Some libraries may not know the total expenditures for library services, as they are not separated out of the general budget of the entity that funds them.

Be proficient in the software system(s) used by the library's funding entity. If at all possible, use the same system that your funding entity employs in its budget preparation and reporting process. Work with your funding entity to enable you to have quick access to financial records relating to library operations and services.

Budget Types

There are two main types of budgets: capital budgets and operating budgets.

Capital Budgets

A capital budget is for major, nonrecurring items that have long life spans and may require multiyear planning. Capital budgets may be projected out over a period of three to ten years or more. Many libraries or the institutional entities providing funding have a threshold dollar amount before an item may be considered for inclusion in a capital budget; that is, anything over $50,000 is considered for inclusion in a capital budget. What goes into

> If the expense is major and nonrecurring, it is a capital expense. If the expense is normal and reoccurring, it is an operating expense.

a capital budget? Major equipment purchases, such as vehicles, heating and air-conditioning equipment, building renovation, new building planning, construction and furnishing, automation upgrades or migration, are included in a capital budget. Any item that is not a normal operating expenditure or normal maintenance of equipment and building is a candidate for the capital budget.

A planning document is an important tool in selecting items for a capital budget. What does the library's plan indicate will be done for the next several years? What needs are implied that do not fit into an operating budget? To prepare for a capital budget, examine current buildings and operations to see what items have a limited expected life span or will likely need replacement in the near future. Working with staff and appropriate governing entities, gather information on costs, decide when in the budget time frame this item or project best fits, and then place it there. Remember that, like an operating budget, a capital budget is a plan and a proposal of accomplishment. It will likely change over time but serves as a planning tool for expenditures that are major in nature and have a higher initial cost than what is normally placed in the operating budget.

Operating Budgets

The most common way of developing an annual operating budget is the line item budget. Other approaches to budget preparation include the zero-based budget, the program budget, and the performance budget.

Line Item Budget

The line item budget focuses on what is bought, whether it is staff services, equipment, supplies, books, materials or electronic databases, or utilities. See figure 6.1 for a sample work form.

Each major expenditure and revenue category receives a line in the budget. Depending on library needs or the requirements of funding entities, the line item budget may have more or fewer lines within it. When a line item budget is the basis for library operations, the annual budget process is based on suggested changes in each line item within the budget and requests for changes must be justified accordingly.

Zero-Based Budget

The zero-based budget is a totally different approach to the provision of library services. Unlike the line item budget that uses as its base the previous year's budget, zero-based budgeting is a process of preparing an operating budget that starts with no authorized funds, thus the name for the process. Each activity to be funded must be justified in its totality. In the preparation of a zero-based budget, each major area to be funded becomes a decision unit and decision packets are prepared. Library decision units could include these:

- Circulation
- Adult services

> The line item budget is the most-used budget process in libraries.

- Children's services
- Technical services
- Facilities
- Administration

These packets usually contain several alternatives for achieving service objectives. The selection is made between alternatives within each budget unit and the budget is put in its final form for consideration.

The zero-based budget is a more time- and resource-consuming process than either line item budgeting or program budgeting. To work properly, it requires a detailed consideration of the mission and goals of operations, identification of decision units and decision packages, analysis of decision packages, development of measurable performance and service objectives for each decision unit, and monitoring performance accordingly. This method is seldom used by library or governmental units for ongoing annual budget preparation. What is more common in practice is that some aspects of a library's service may be selected on an annual basis for this approach, or the library as a whole will be considered for zero-based budgeting on a regular basis, such as every five to ten years.

Program Budget

A program budget defines library services by what service is being given. All aspects of that individual service—circulation, young adult, and so on— are presented in a budget for that service. The library's budget becomes a series of program statements combined into a total budget reflecting library operations.

Performance Budget

The goal of performance budgeting is to describe in measurable units the outcomes desired for the funding expended. Performance budgeting is possible using any of the budgeting methods just described. What is unique about this type of budgeting is that the budget is directly connected to the specific goals of the organization. An example of this would be if one goal of the library were to have one-day return of materials to the shelf after check-in. The total costs of this objective would be directly related to the goal in the budget preparation.

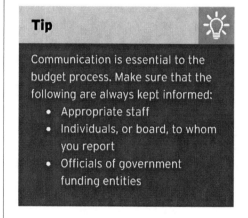

Tip

Communication is essential to the budget process. Make sure that the following are always kept informed:
- Appropriate staff
- Individuals, or board, to whom you report
- Officials of government funding entities

Budget Preparation

Budget preparation and development are ongoing processes. Work on next year's budget is beginning as approval is received for the current year's budget. A library director is continually looking at library operations and discussing library needs with staff, the board of trustees, academic deans, provosts, company leadership, and local officials. Awareness of library services and needs is essential to budget development and approval. This awareness is not accomplished by an annual presentation to a board or governing body but by continual exposure to library services, programs, and needs.

In preparing a budget, the following elements are essential:

- Have accurate and detailed information on library operations and services.
- Have in-depth and accurate information on the library. Without it, success with any request for increases in services, staff, or programs is highly unlikely.
- Have a plan for what is desired to be accomplished with the budget. A plan is essential to the preparation of an effective, easily understood budget, one that stands a chance of approval by the library's governing board and funding entities.
- Understand the political situation in which the library operates.
- Know the plans and goals of the funding entity(s) for the coming year:

  In academic and special library settings, what is the library's position within the institution and how do faculty, business associates, and administration view it?
  In the public library setting, how strong politically is the library board and support base?

- A year with tight resources or when the entity is looking at a tax rate reduction may not be the year to ask for a substantial increase in library funding. Know when it is good to be a team player for long-term benefits or when it is opportune to ask for new programs or services. Sometimes it is time to fight no matter what, but at least be aware of what the library is facing.
- Know and follow the time frame of the funding entity(s) for budget preparation and submission. There are few things worse than missing deadlines for budget submission. Make sure that there is knowledge of all deadlines. If, due to circumstances beyond control such as conflicting deadlines from other funding entities or lack of information on resources due to legislative slowness in determining state aid monies, deadlines cannot be met, notify the appropriate officials immediately. Generally, they will be accommodating.

In presenting a budget request to any group, the following points are important:

- Keep the presentation clear, short, and simple.
- Avoid the tendency to use library jargon and to have too many charts, graphs, or PowerPoint examples. Present highlights only and give emphasis to those areas that are proposed for changes from the current budget.

Tip

It is good to have a separate page in monthly budget reports to highlight unusual occurrences in spending or revenue.

FIGURE 6.1

Line Item Budget

Revenue

Item	Current Fiscal Year	Next Fiscal Year	Dollar Change from Current Fiscal Year	Percentage Change
Local Government				
State Government				
Federal Government				
Library Sources				
Other				
Total Revenue				

Expenditures

Compensation

Item	Current Fiscal Year	Next Fiscal Year	Dollar Change from Current Fiscal Year	Percentage Change
Salaries and Wages				
Retirement				
Health Insurance				
Workers' Compensation				
Other				
Total Compensation				

Collections

Item	Current Fiscal Year	Next Fiscal Year	Dollar Change from Current Fiscal Year	Percentage Change
Books				
Audiovisual				
Databases				
Other				
Total Collections				

(continued)

FIGURE 6.1 (continued)

Operations

Item	Current Fiscal Year	Next Fiscal Year	Dollar Change from Current Fiscal Year	Percentage Change
Building Maintenance				
Communications				
Contractual Services				
Insurance				
Maintenance				
Supplies				
Miscellaneous				
Postage				
Printing				
Travel and Training				
Utilities				
Total Operations				

Total Expenditures				

- Give one individual the responsibility for overall budget presentation. It is easier for individuals to understand a presentation when they are dealing with one individual rather than three or four. Have others available to answer questions, but do not employ a team approach to the basic presentation.
- Have a thorough understanding of the budget and be prepared for questions on all aspects of it. There will always be unanticipated questions. Be knowledgeable in all aspects of the budget, and have others (e.g., the faculty/staff/board of trustees/Friends of the Library/higher administration) available as needed to elaborate on sections of the budget where appropriate.
- Go into each session with a positive attitude. This is as important as any of the previous points.

Budget Tracking

An important element of the budgetary process is budget tracking, which is an ongoing process. It is an expected part of library operations that the library's governing entities, or administrative units to which the library reports, will require monthly reports on how the budget is being spent. These reports should include what revenue has been received, what has been spent, what has been encumbered, and the percentage of the total year's budget that has been used to date. An encumbrance is simply the anticipated cost of items for which purchase authorization has been given to a supplier but the product or service has not yet been received. Such information enables the library to have a more accurate picture of where its expenditures stand at any one time. See figure 6.2 for a condensed example of the form used to present this report.

In its completed state, the form would also indicate what percentage of the total budget had been spent during this time period. There would also be as many line items on the form as there are line items in the budget.

Budget tracking is also an important component of budget preparation because it serves to indicate areas where expenditures are exceeding expectations, and line items must be accordingly increased in next year's budget, or where expenditures are not as high as expected, line items could be decreased in next year's budget.

FIGURE 6.2

Budget Report Form

	Budget	Actual	Encumbered	Total	Percentage Spent and Encumbered
Compensation	1,200,000	395,250	-0-	395,250	32.9
Collections	220,000	105,324	15,443	120,767	54.9
Supplies	43,000	19,342	4,249	23,591	54.8
Percentage of Budget Year Completed	41.6				

Conclusion

Budgeting is the process whereby a library's resources are distributed to provide the services and programs approved by the institution's governing body. How it is accomplished varies from library to library. Many factors play a role in the process; these include the type of library, its governance structure, and, in the case of academic and special libraries, how the parent institution allocates resources.

Further Reading

Kirk, Rachel A. *Balancing the Books: Accounting for Librarians*. Santa Barbara, CA: Libraries Unlimited, 2012.

Miller, Gerald J., W. Bartley Hildreth, and Jack Rabin. *Performance Based Budgeting*. Boulder, CO: Westview Press, 2001.

Moran, Douglas. *Handbook on Public Budgeting*. Salem, OR: Oregon State Fiscal Association, 2002.

Smith, G. Stevenson. *Accounting for Libraries and Other Not-for-Profit Organizations*. 2nd ed. Chicago: American Library Association, 2002.

Policies and Procedures

John A. Moorman

Policies and procedures are at the heart of any library's operation. Without properly developed policies and procedures, an institution will flounder and both users and staff will be unclear as to what they are to do and how they are to respond to everyday questions and situations.

The *Concise Oxford English Dictionary* defines policy as "a course or principle of action adopted or proposed by an organization or individual." It defines procedure as "an established or official way of doing something." The core difference is that policy is a statement approved by the governing body of the organization that indicates how the organization will respond to a certain situation or event whereas a procedure is a statement that describes how a certain activity or function is to be carried out. Procedure is often tied to policy in that it describes how a specific policy is to be carried out. It, unlike policy, does not require action from a governing body to be in effect.

Policy Development

In developing policy, the administrator and staff play an important role. While it is the governing entity, whether board of trustees, school board, county or city government, or the organization's board of directors, that has the final say in the development and approval of any policy statement, as much input as possible must be brought into the development of each policy statement. Good policy is the result of much thought, examination of the library's experience, knowledge of the community in which the library operates, and examination of how other libraries in similar settings have dealt with the situation being considered. The more minds that can be brought to bear on the matter, the better the end policy will be. However, it is not the role of the library administrator to make policy. The library administrator only recommends policy to the governing board of the institution or to the person to whom he or she reports. If the library administrator does not agree with the policy developed by his or her governing entity, then he or she has choices to make as to his or her future with the organization.

> **Players in Policy Development**
>
> - Staff
> - Director
> - Individual to whom director reports
> - Governing body

Procedure Development

Procedure development is a different matter. This is the responsibility of the library staff. While it is good to let governing boards know about library procedures and even to share procedure documents with them, it is not their area of responsibility.

In procedure development, the more minds employed, the better, particularly those who will be in the direct line of its implementation. Procedure should be written in simple language, without nuances, covering the *major* points of how a specific policy or activity is to be accomplished.

Policies Needed

The policies needed to operate a library properly depend on the size of the library, its relationship to the larger units of which it may be a part, and whether it has any contractual relationships with other entities. For example, if your library is part of a corporate business entity or a division of a city or county, then you may not need a personnel policy because personnel will be covered by the policies of the larger unit. Look at your operations and determine what authority you have over them. The areas where you have operational control are candidates for policy statements. See figure 7.1 for a list from *A Pocket Reference Manual for Public Library Trustees* (South Carolina State Library 2010) that describes major areas to consider when developing a policy manual for your library. Figure 7.1 is not an all-inclusive list but an example of the many areas where policies will be necessary for the successful operation of the library.

How do you go about developing successful policies? The first step is to look at what you currently have, what has worked, what is not working, and where you see gaps. The readings at the end of this chapter include some books that contain sample policy statements. Examining these and contacting librarians in like institutions and asking for copies of their policy statements, many of which are now available on library websites, can aid in policy development. It is advisable in any policy development to run your policy past an attorney before finalizing it. It may be common sense to you and your board, but the law may think differently and a little legal advice up front can save a large amount of legal time and cost later.

Tip

In policy development, look at the following:
- What you currently have
- What has worked
- What is not working
- Where you see gaps

Remember, you are not the first institution to deal with this issue. Take advantage of what others have done and modify it to fit your specific situation or need.

Writing Good Policy

A good policy is succinct and clear yet gives room for staff to interpret. Good policy, like good literature, is hard to write. It is also open to continual revision and examination. See figure 7.2, for example.

FIGURE 7.1

Policy List for Public Libraries

Every library does not necessarily require every policy on this list. The list is provided here to help boards check their policy accomplishments and needs. The list is arranged in the form of an outline to underscore how policies relate to one another. Listed under each policy are items that may be considered and covered when making policy.

I. Library Mission and Role Statement

II. Library Board Bylaws

III. Public Service Policies

A. Customer Eligibility for Borrowing and Services (Resident and Nonresident)

B. Collection Development Policy

1. Restatement of library mission and goals, and a description of the service population
2. Scope and priorities of collection
3. Library staff responsibility for materials collection
4. Formats to be included in collection
5. Selection criteria for each format
6. Selection procedures and vendor relations
7. Evaluation, weeding, and collection maintenance
8. Censorship, access, and challenged materials procedures
9. "Intellectual Freedom Statement," "Library Bill of Rights"
10. Gifts and donations

C. Circulation Policy

1. Loan period and renewal
2. Confidentiality of patron information
3. Reserved material
4. Fines, damages
5. Interlibrary loan
6. Special collections
7. Audiovisual materials and equipment
8. Cooperative borrowing policy

D. Reference Policy

E. Facilities Policy (in Terms of Public Service)

1. Hours of operation
2. Americans with Disabilities Act compliance
3. Security
4. Meeting room use

(continued)

FIGURE 7.1 (continued)

5. Exhibits and displays
6. Copiers and other equipment use

F. Community Relations Policy

1. Relations with local government
2. Relations with schools
3. Volunteers
4. Friends groups

G. Patron Behavior Policy

1. Unattended children
2. Respect for staff, users and library property

H. Internet Use Policy

IV. Management Policies

A. General

B. Responsibility and Authority

C. Budgeting and Purchasing

D. Personnel

1. Responsibility and authority
2. Job descriptions and classifications
3. Salaries and benefits
4. Hours, annual and sick leave, overtime, holidays
5. Hiring, termination, resignations, and nepotism
6. Performance evaluation and promotion
7. Continuing education/professional development
8. Discipline and grievances
9. Americans with Disabilities Act compliance
10. Fair Labor Standards Act compliance
11. Sexual harassment
12. Personnel records

E. Facilities

1. Responsibility and procedure for maintenance
2. Acquisition and ownership
3. Insurance and liability
4. Emergency preparedness
5. Use of equipment, vehicles, etc.

Source: South Carolina State Library 2010, 51–53; used with permission.

FIGURE 7.2

Public Library Policy Sample

Behavior

The Williamsburg Regional Library is committed to providing excellent facilities and emphasizes courtesy and respect. Consequently, the Library does not permit:

1. Willful damage to or unauthorized removal of library property
2. Disorderly conduct
3. Smoking
4. Extreme body odor or other strong smells
5. Animals other than service animals
6. Open food or beverage containers or the consumption of food or beverages without authorization from the Library (Beverages in bottles, cups with lids, or cans are acceptable unless otherwise posted.)
7. Insufficient attire. Shirts and shoes are required.

Any person failing to abide by this policy may, in the discretion of the Library Director or designee, be removed from the Library for the day or, depending on the seriousness of the violation or in the case of repeated offense, have his or her Library privileges revoked.

[Approved by WRL Board of Trustees May 11, 1994. Approved as amended by WRL Board of Trustees October 19, 1999. Approved as amended by WRL Board of Trustees March 27, 2002. Approved as amended by WRL Board of Trustees October 23, 2002. Approved as amended by WRL Board of Trustees April 28, 2004. Approved as amended by WRL Board of Trustees March 28, 2007. Approved as amended by WRL Board of Trustees June 25, 2008. Approved as amended by WRL Board of Trustees February 23, 2011.]

Source: Williamsburg Regional Library 2015, "General Policies—Behavior."

Figure 7.2 shows a policy that deals with the use of a public library. It gives general guidance to staff and the public as to what is permitted in library facilities, but it is not detailed in its description of what is or is not permitted. For example, there can be different interpretations of what constitutes "extreme body odor or other strong smells" or "loud or obscene language." This gives staff latitude to deal with each situation in its context rather than being held to one strict standard. Figure 7.3 is an example of an academic library policy.

The public library policy (figure 7.2) was first approved in 1994 but has had seven amended versions since then. This indicates that it has been examined on a regular basis and hopefully refined at each examination. The governing body of your library should regularly examine policy statements for two reasons. The first is that regular reviews enable all board members to become familiar with library policies and with the reasons for their

FIGURE 7.3

Academic Library Sample Policy

Ladd Library Food Policy

Snacks and beverages in spill-proof containers are allowed. No meals or dinnerware may be taken out of New Commons. Enjoy snacks—but leave no trace.

In order to maintain a clean and inviting library for all to use, please follow the guidelines below.

- Be considerate and respectful of other library users and help prevent damage to library materials and facilities
- Clean up after yourself
- No sticky, smelly, greasy foods
- Empty liquids into bathroom sinks
- Report spills to the library staff
- Recycle when possible

The use of tobacco products is prohibited in Ladd Library.

Rollerblades and skateboards are prohibited.

Pets are not allowed in the library, with the exception of guide/therapy dogs for patrons with special needs.

Source: Bates College 2015; used with permission.

existence. The second is that it requires the library to regularly examine its policies to see if changes are needed.

Figure 7.4 is an example of a policy dealing with a specific situation. The policy states the reason it is needed and outlines what is permitted and what is not permitted. Again, it indicates that it has been examined on a regular basis.

Writing Good Procedure

Writing procedures is similar to writing policy in that good procedures are clear and able to be easily followed. While procedures should be as concise as possible, they should be long enough to describe adequately what is desired. As figure 7.5 demonstrates, any procedure should also cover the basic steps of how an activity, or action, should be accomplished.

In writing a procedure, the first step is to examine what it is that you are describing. The next step is to break it down to its component parts, indicating what steps or actions are first, what comes second, and so on, through the completion of the task or action. Procedures are not a place to tell you why you are doing something, but only what you are doing and the order

FIGURE 7.4

Specific Situation Sample Policy

Animals in the Library

To prevent possible damage to library facilities and property, and possible injury to library users and staff, animals (as defined in § 3.2-6500 of the Code of Virginia, 1950, as amended) are not permitted in any Williamsburg Regional Library facility, except for:

1. Use or exhibition for a valid purpose, as determined by the Library Director or designee, only when such use or exhibition has been pre-approved by the Library Director or designee, who shall provide such approval on a case-by-case basis; or

2. Service animals in accordance with the Americans with Disabilities Act of 1990 and accompanying regulations. See 28 CFR § 35.104 for definition of a service animal.
   - Control of Service Animal;
     A service animal must be under the control of its handler. A harness, leash or other tether should be used unless;
     i. A disability prevents the handler from use of a harness, leash or tether; or
     ii. The harness, leash or tether would interfere with the work of the service animal.
   - In such cases, voice control, signals, etc. must be used.
   - Removal of Service Animal;
     The Library may request that a service animal be removed from the facility, and further deny access, if the animal;
     i. Is out of control and the handler cannot regain control of the animal;
     ii. Is not housebroken; or
     iii. Poses a direct threat to the health and safety of others.

[Approved by WRL Board of Trustees February 14, 1990. Approved as amended by WRL Board of Trustees March 27, 2002. Approved as amended by WRL Board of Trustees December 1, 2004. Approved as amended by WRL Board of Trustees October 24, 2007. Approved as revised by WRL Board of Trustees September 28, 2011.]

Source: Williamsburg Regional Library 2015, "General Policies—Animals in the Library."

in which it should be accomplished. Notice in figure 7.5 that procedures do not have to be specific to individuals; for example, the procedure notes that the finance office does this and the program services department does that but does not name specifically who in each area is responsible for performing the work.

There is a tendency in writing procedures to be too specific and too detailed. While sufficient specificity and detail are needed to enable individuals to perform what is desired, too much of either can have a countereffect and hinder efficient library operations.

Conclusion

Policies and procedures are an essential part of any library operation. However, there is the tendency to overdo both. Not every action needs a policy statement, nor does every step in your operation need a procedure outlining how it is to be performed. A second problem in this area is the tendency to make procedures into policy statements. Before making a policy statement, examine it thoroughly. Will the document state a course of action or a principle by which the library will operate? If so, it is policy. Does the document describe a way of doing a task or an operation within the library? If so, then it is procedure.

FIGURE 7.5

Sample Procedure

A. Accounts Receivable

Any monies due to the library are billed and accounted for by the finance office. This includes funds to be reimbursed by the Friends of the Library, Williamsburg Regional Library Foundation, and grants; meeting room and theater usage fees not collected; cosponsored program expenses with other agencies and credits for returned materials.

1. Procedure

    a. Send the original and a duplicate copy of any invoices or paid receipts to the finance office. The finance office will match invoices with any purchase orders and reconcile monthly expenditures. The finance office will prepare a bill and send it to the individual or group responsible for payment. When a check is received for payment, the bill will be dated and marked paid by the finance office.

    b. Theater and room use fees are typically paid in advance. If overtime charges or additional expenses are incurred, program services staff will provide an invoice to the finance office. This invoice will include a summary of hours and facilities used, the date and amount of any prepaid credits, and the balance due.

    c. The finance office will bill the patron and file a copy in the Finance Office accounts receivable file. The Program Services department will submit invoices to the Finance Office at month's end.

    d. When payment is received, the check will be given to program services staff to ring into the cash register, mark paid in full on the room reservation form and the duplicate invoice, and forwarded to the finance office with the daily cash register reconciliation.

    e. Other: Credits in lieu of a check reimbursement on some accounts, such as regular book vendors, simplifies the accounting process and is acceptable. The finance office handles credits of an unusual nature such as inadvertent overpayment credits and monies due from limited use vendors.

Further Reading

Brumley, Rebecca. *The Academic Manager's Forms, Policies, and Procedures Handbook with CD-ROM.* New York: Neal-Schuman, 2007.

———. *Electronic Collection Management Forms, Policies, Procedures, and Guidelines Manual with CD-ROM.* New York: Neal-Schuman, 2009.

———. *The Public Library Manager's Forms, Policies, and Procedures Handbook with CD-ROM.* New York: Neal-Schuman, 2004.

———. *The Reference Librarian's Policies, Forms, Guidelines, and Procedures Handbook with CD-ROM.* New York: Neal-Schuman, 2006.

Mid-Hudson Library System. "Topics—Trustee Resources" (sample public library policies and development tips). www.midhudson.org.

References

Bates College. 2015. "Library Building Policies." Accessed January 5. www.bates.edu/library/about/library-building-policies/.

South Carolina State Library. 2010. *A Pocket Reference Manual for Public Library Trustees.* Columbia, SC: South Carolina State Library.

Williamsburg Regional Library. 2015. "Library Policies." Accessed January 5. http://www.wrl.org/about-us/library-policies.

Staffing

John A. Moorman

Staffing deals with individuals who are paid employees of the library. A good staff is the core of any library operation. Personnel administration, which covers all of the topics in this chapter, is an area where knowledge of current laws is essential. If the library is part of a larger unit, such as a school district, corporation, or entity of local government, that organization will have a human resources or personnel department. This department will work with the library and handle, or coordinate, most of the activities discussed in this chapter. If this is not the case, it is essential that the library staff working in these areas have a detailed knowledge of personnel law and have an attorney skilled in this area on retainer or on call for consultation and advice.

IN THIS CHAPTER

- ✓ Hiring
- ✓ Training
- ✓ Scheduling
- ✓ Supervising
- ✓ Evaluating
- ✓ Dismissing
- ✓ Conclusion
- ✓ Further Reading
- ✓ References

Hiring

The employment of individuals to fill positions within the library is the most important part of the staffing process. If it is done poorly, or without proper attention being paid to what the law requires, it can cause tremendous waste of staff and money and lead to legal difficulties.

The first step in the hiring process is to determine exactly what is needed. This step is often overlooked amid the rush to hire that librarian, shelver, cataloger, or even library director. Before beginning the process, there must be agreement on what the new employee will do. Examine in detail the current job description, or if a new position, make sure that a job description is developed that accurately reflects the tasks and duties that will be expected of the person in this position. There are many types of job descriptions, but all should cover the basics: what employees are expected to do, where they are expected to do it, to whom they report, necessary qualifications for the position, and any requirements such as drug testing and background checks that will be necessary before employment. The job description for a circulation services assistant that is presented in figure 8.1 is a good example of what should be found in a job description.

> Do not start the hiring process until you know exactly what you need.

FIGURE 8.1

Sample Job Description

Circulation Services Assistant   813

Department Division: Williamsburg Regional Library/Circulation Services

Nature of Work

Under the supervision of the Circulation Services Director, the Circulation Services Assistant performs a variety of tasks to support the activities of the circulation services division, including complex procedures involved with the computerized transactions of library materials to the public. Also answers circulation and directional questions, collects money for late and lost library materials and sale items, and assists in opening and closing of the library.

Essential Functions of the Job

- Provides public services at the circulation desk, performing all related tasks.
- Uses library automated system for transactions in the charging out of library materials, processing user records, determining materials status, locating resources within the system, arranging for transfers of library materials, placing reserves, registering new users, and performing additional procedures as needed.
- Learns new computer procedures for each upgrade and software release in a timely manner; runs computer reports as required.
- Answers circulation and directional questions; refers other questions to appropriate person or division.
- Operates cash register, transfers funds from the cash register to the safe, and reconciles daily receipts.
- Verifies and sends overdue notices; resolves problem files; receives and records overdue fines; sends related correspondence as needed; processes lost/damaged library materials to technical services; resolves user records; and processes user refunds.
- Assists in opening and closing procedures of library.
- Assists in checking in, sorting, and shelving library materials as needed.
- Assists in training new employees; may schedule and supervise circulation services volunteers.
- Monitors user activities in the library, and may handle problems as they occur.
- May participate in library-wide committees or projects, or attend staff development programs, workshops, or conferences.
- Performs other duties as required.

Job Location and Equipment Operated

The job is located in Williamsburg Regional Library buildings. Administers work typically at a public service desk. Work involves bending, reaching, lifting up to 25 pounds, walking, and other limited physical activities. Frequent operation of computer keyboard, barcode scanner, and cash register is required; other office equipment as needed. Regular contact is made with staff members and the general public.

(continued)

FIGURE 8.1 *(continued)*

Required Knowledge, Skills, and Abilities

- Ability to learn and operate library automated system with high degree of efficiency.
- Ability to independently organize work, set priorities, use time effectively, and meet deadlines.
- Excellent written and verbal communication skills.
- Must have desire and ability to serve the public with friendliness, tact, and diplomacy.
- Ability to follow through on numerous details and maintain records in a standard, orderly, systematic fashion and work well under pressure.
- Basic knowledge of personal computer operations.
- Accuracy in clerical skills, including typing and filing.
- Ability to compare names and numbers quickly, resulting in working knowledge of the Dewey Decimal System.
- Ability to sort/shelve fiction collections alphabetically by author's last name.
- Desire and ability to work with enthusiasm and initiative.
- Ability to establish and maintain effective working relationships with supervisor, division directors/managers/officers, staff members, and the general public.
- Ability to lift up to 25 pounds.

Minimum Qualifications

- Bachelor's degree or combination of higher education and/or two years library or bookstore experience to provide the necessary knowledge, skills, and abilities as cited above.
- Experience working with the public.

Necessary Special Qualifications

- Requires the ability to travel among various library sites.

Work Schedule

Full-time or part-time, non-exempt position. Full-time position is 40 hours per week; part-time position is minimum 12 hours per week. Varied schedules include mornings, afternoons, evenings, and weekends.

Division

Circulation Services

Supervisor

Circulation Services Director

DATE PREPARED: January 2, 1991

REVISED: March 1993; March 1993; March 1994; April 1996; October 1998; April 1999; July 2001; October 2001; August 2002; September 2002; May 2003, April 2006; June 2006; August 2009; December 2009

Source: Williamsburg Regional Library 2015b; used with permission.

FIGURE 8.2

Interview Questions for Circulation Assistant

1. Why do you want to be a Circulation Services Assistant with the Williamsburg Regional Library? What interested you in applying for this position?
2. Having reviewed the job description, if a friend asked you what you would be doing in this job, what would you say?
3. This job requires working the circulation desk serving users, maintaining records, taking payments, answering the phone, and moving library materials quickly and accurately. The job also requires working a rotating schedule between the Williamsburg Library and the James City County Library with varied days, evening and weekend hours. Can you perform these tasks and work this schedule? All part-time staff is expected to help fill in shifts. Would you be able to adjust your weekly work schedule on short notice to accommodate short-term needs of the division including but not limited to staff training, staff illness, or staff vacations?
4. Describe your experience helping customers of all ages.
5. Describe the types of confidential records in which you have had access. What steps did you take to ensure their safekeeping?
6. Describe a project you have done where you worked with minimal supervision. What did you have to do to get started? What was the outcome?
7. This job requires you to apply library policies and procedures fairly. In Circulation Services, that may include charging someone a fee for a damaged item, telling a minor she cannot check out an R-rated movie, or explaining to someone that he or she needs different identification in order to get a library card. Do you have any experience in applying policies and procedures to different situations fairly? When do you feel comfortable making an exception to the written procedures?
8. Give an example of a time when you had to come to a decision quickly. What was the outcome?
9. Do you have a customer service philosophy? How would you describe it?
10. Tell us about a time when you had a customer who was angry because he or she was not satisfied with an answer to a question. How did you handle the situation, and what was the outcome?
11. What are your expectations of your coworkers? Your supervisor?
12. If you were asked to evaluate your own performance, what factors would you consider most important?
13. How would your colleagues describe working with you?
14. If you were the successful candidate for this position, what skills or characteristics do you have that you feel would be especially useful in this position?
15. What do you want us to remember about you that would make you stand out from the other interested candidates?

Source: Williamsburg Regional Library 2015a; used with permission.

The job description should contain requirements only for what is needed, not what is desired. As an example, it should specify only the amount of education needed for the position in question.

Once the job description is completed and approved, then the process of seeking applicants begins. Where it should be advertised—locally, regionally, nationally, or only through in-house sources—depends on the job and whether there are in-house candidates who would adequately fill the position. If serious consideration will not be given to candidates outside of the general area, then advertise in only local sources.

The job advertisement is important. It should be a summary of the duties and requirements of the position with either a salary range or beginning salary indicated. Give enough information so that only those who are qualified or willing to work for that salary will apply (no guarantee here). If forms have to be filled out by all applicants, indicate so and where they can get these forms. Note if only online applications are being accepted. Indicate if a résumé is required. Make sure that a closing date for the receipt of applications is included; if there is none, indicate "open until filled." If a drug test is required before hiring, this, too, should be included in the ad.

Once the applications have been received, it is good practice to acknowledge to the applicants that they have been received. In deciding which candidates to interview, first examine all applications to make sure that necessary qualifications are met. In most cases, several applications can be winnowed out at this time.

Hopefully, there will be at least three individuals who meet enough of the job criteria to be seriously considered for the opening. Generally, it is good to interview no more than five to seven individuals for any single opening.

Prior to the interview session, develop a list of questions to ask of each interviewee. The questions should be the same for each person interviewed. Figure 8.2 shows a set of interview questions used in circulation assistant job interviews.

Make sure all interview questions are legal.

Make sure that the questions asked are legal and will give enough information about the individuals, their skills, and experience, to enable a wise final selection to be made. Have questions vetted by the personnel department or attorney. It is important to check references for finalists for positions. Although most references have been preselected to tell nothing but the best about the individual in question, there are times when voice and response can give insights that would not have been able to be obtained otherwise.

Before making a job offer, make sure that the final choice understands what the job requires, what benefits and salary he or she will receive, what schedule he or she will work, and when and where he or she is expected to report. If a drug test is required before a job offer can be made, this is the time for it. Ask the candidate if there are any final questions and be sure to let him or her know whom to contact if additional questions occur prior to the start date. A written letter should follow up any job offer so that there are no questions about the job offer. Request a written acceptance from

FIGURE 8.3

New Employee Checklist

Name: _____

Job Title: _____

Supervisor: _____

Important Dates

Effective Date: _____

Introductory Period Review Due to Human Resources: _____

Introductory Period Expected to End: _____

Annual Performance Evaluation Date: _____

Required Training

Training	Location	Date	Time
New Employee Benefits Orientation	HR Office		9:00 a.m.

Department Information   Date Completed   By

Please review with new employee and initial.

Review county mission, vision, and values _____

Tour of work location _____

Introduction to coworkers _____

Work hours/lunch times _____

Time/leave accrual sheet completion _____

Reporting absences/lateness _____

Organizational structure of department _____

Expectations of new employee _____

Telephone usage _____

Employee performance/development _____

Overtime policy _____

Internet usage _____

E-mail usage _____

Access/usage of myJCC _____

County property/equipment use _____

Uniforms (if applicable) _____

Tool/clothing allowance (if applicable) _____

Outside employment _____

Emergency Conditions and Unexpected Closings Policy (AR-10) _____

Supervisors

Please send a copy of this checklist back to Human Resources within one (1) week of employee's start date.

_____   _____

Supervisor's Signature   Date

Revised 08/13

Source: James City County, Virginia 2015; used with permission.

the individual. It is good practice for a member of the interview team to personally call all those interviewed to let them know of the employment final decision.

Training

See figure 8.3 for a sample of a new employee checklist. As this example indicates, the employee checklist should provide a thorough introduction to the job and the entity for which the individual now works.

Continued job training is a mixture of on-the-job experience, in-house workshops conducted by library staff or individuals brought in from the outside, and attendance at outside workshops and conferences. Excellent resources for these training opportunities are regional, state, and national library associations and library-related organizations such as WebJunction. Other sources for excellent training opportunities are state library agencies and their respective library development divisions. A list of these resources is included at the end of this book.

Scheduling

Scheduling of staff is always a challenge. Factors involved in scheduling include hours of operation; number of staff, including how many are full time and part time; needs of the institution; any limitations placed upon scheduling by previous practice, agreements, or labor contracts; and how many locations are involved. This does not include factors such as illnesses, maternity and family leaves, and educational class or workshop attendance.

There are basically two ways to create a good work schedule. The first is to prepare a grid chart with times needed and then place individuals in the chart until the schedule is filled. The second is to purchase scheduling software. With this software you can input names, hours of employment, and other factors and the software will come up with a work schedule. The way to locate good scheduling software is to check with other libraries, place informational requests on an electronic discussion list, or contact the library development division of your state library agency.

Factors to remember in developing any work schedule are these: be fair, be consistent, follow all regulations imposed by personnel policies or labor contracts, and schedule according to library needs, not staff desires. It is important to communicate regularly with staff during all phases of work scheduling.

Supervising

Employees need supervision to see that tasks are accomplished in a timely and appropriate manner and policies and regulations are followed in the performance of their work. Good supervision is an art as much as it is a science. It involves knowledge of human behavior, good communication skills, knowledge of the work that is to be accomplished, flexibility, a good sense of humor, and the ability to control ego and feelings. The best supervisor is one who appears not to be supervising, but simply observing and encouraging his or her employees in their daily activities.

The following are the ten *be*s of good supervision:

- Be available.
- Be aware.
- Be clear.
- Be concise.
- Be fair.
- Be flexible.
- Be firm.
- Be patient.
- Be supportive.
- Be understanding.

These are easy to say but hard to accomplish. All individuals are good at some of them, but few, if any, are good at all of them. How are skills improved in this important and essential area? There are books and articles that assist in focusing attention on aspects of good supervision, some of which are included in the readings at the end of this chapter. Other sources are workshops put on by various associations, including chambers of commerce, community colleges and universities, and state library agencies, or by consultants who specialize in this area.

Remember that in supervision, as in other areas of work, whether dealing with staff, a board, governing officials, or the general public, people like to be treated with respect and fairness. Before acting as a supervisor, always ask, "Is this the way I would like to be treated?" If the answer is no, then take a different course of action.

Evaluation is a yearlong process, not done in just a week before the evaluation is due.

Evaluating

Regular evaluation is an essential part of effective personnel management. All individuals need regular feedback to know if they are performing tasks at the expected level. Supervisors need to communicate to those they supervise about successes or failures in job performance. Evaluation often becomes a chore when communication about job performance is not done on a regular basis and there is not an ongoing flow of information from supervisor to employee as well as employee to supervisor about work and the setting within which it is accomplished. A good evaluation process is a summary of conversations held during the time period since the last evaluation and holds no surprises for either party.

The most often used time frame between evaluations is one year. Some institutions conduct evaluations on a six-month basis or when problems are occurring for which correction is needed if employment is to continue.

Evaluations come in all shapes and sizes. There are check-the-box evaluations whereby individuals are rated on a variety of workplace behaviors and job performance standards. There are modifications of this approach that also give room for comments. There are written evaluations involving specific job performance questions. There are also as many variations of these types as there are evaluators. Use what works best in your situation and serves the purpose of recording job performance and giving expectations for future performance or about what is required by your governing authority.

Another important aspect of the evaluation process is whether the evaluation is directly linked to any pay adjustment or is separate from any consideration of employee pay. Each approach comes with its advantages and problems. If an evaluation is linked to pay, there may be an immediate positive reinforcement of work accomplishments. However, it may also be a negative factor if good performance is not sufficiently rewarded from a financial standpoint. If the evaluation is not linked with any pay adjustment, it might not be given sufficient weight by either the employee or the individual giving the evaluation.

No matter what form of evaluation is used, there will always be a subjective element involved. The goal of any evaluation will be to remove, as much as possible, any subjectivity from the evaluation process and to provide each employee with as fair and objective an evaluation as possible. A good evaluation has these qualities:

- Is fair
- Is objective
- Reflects actual performance during the time covered by the review
- Measures work performance against job expectations
- Allows for employee input
- Gives expectations for the next evaluation period

Sufficient time should be set aside for discussing the evaluation with the employee. It is advisable to share a copy of the evaluation with the employee prior to this meeting so that the employee comes prepared to discuss the evaluation. Points of disagreement can be noted in the final review. It is general practice to have the employee sign an acknowledgment that he or she has seen the evaluation and has discussed the evaluation with the supervisor.

Dismissing

Dismissing an individual from employment is never an easy task and is a step that should be taken only after all other measures have been tried. It is vitally important that the library, or the entity to which it reports, has a detailed personnel policy that includes thorough disciplinary policy sections outlining what offenses will result in personnel actions being taken. Generally, a personnel policy will have step penalties for various job offenses, with most offenses resulting in warnings and suspensions. However, for some serious offenses, the immediate penalty is dismissal from employment.

The goal of any employer is to keep employees in employment. Much time and effort have been spent in hiring, equipping, and training these individuals, and the best course is to work with individuals to see if their work performance or job behavior can be brought up to an acceptable standard. Thus, in most cases, it is important to work with the individual, using whatever personnel resources available to counsel the individual, prior to seeking to dismiss the individual from employment.

The importance of documentation in the employment process cannot be emphasized enough. In dismissing an employee, there will need to be sufficient documentation of the work performance or behavior in question to pass muster with any agency to which the employee might go for redress in the case of dismissal. This is vitally important. This documentation should be substantial, indicate that the performance in question arose over a period of time, and outline what steps were taken to correct the work performance/behavior prior to dismissal taking place. It should also indicate that the library's personnel policy has been followed and that there are no special exceptions in the case under consideration. It is important here to consult with the library's governing body's human resource department or attorney to make certain that no steps have been omitted or not properly followed.

When the time comes to dismiss an employee, make sure that another individual is present as a witness to the dismissal. This person can be another staff member or a member of the human resource department of the city, county, or larger entity of which your library is a part. Make the presentation brief, stating only the reason for the dismissal. Do not get into an argument with the individual being dismissed. Make the person aware of what benefits will be coming to him or her and how he or she will receive them. Have someone observe the individual as he or she takes personal belongings from the library, and make sure that the person has turned in all library property before leaving. Notify library staff that the individual is no longer an employee of the library and is not to be allowed in nonpublic areas of the library.

Dismissing an employee from the library is never an easy task, nor should it be. However, it is one that a library administrator will do more than once during his or her career. The rules to remember are these: do it fairly, do it firmly, and do it with consideration for all involved.

Conclusion

Staffing is one of the most challenging aspects of library operations. In hiring, training, scheduling, supervising, evaluating, and dismissing library employees, the librarian is dealing with individual human beings and all that they bring to the table. To be successful, the librarian needs to make sure that actions are legal, follow policy and procedure, and are done fairly and in a consistent manner.

Further Reading

Giesecke, Joan, and Beth McNeil. *Fundamentals of Library Supervision.* 2nd ed. Chicago: ALA Editions, 2010.

Mayo, Diane, and Jeanne Goodrich. *Staffing for Results: A Guide to Working Smarter.* Chicago: ALA Editions, 2002.

Munde, Gail. *Everyday HR: A Human Resources Handbook for Academic Library Staff.* Chicago: ALA Editions, 2013.

Smallwood, Carol. 2011. *Library Management Tips That Work.* Print/ebook bundle. Chicago: ALA Editions, 2011.

Stewart, Andrea Wigbels, Carlette Washington-Hoagland, and Carol T. Zsulya, eds. *Staff Development: A Practical Guide.* 4th ed. Chicago: ALA Editions, 2013.

Tunstall, Patricia. *Hiring, Training, and Supervising Library Shelvers.* Chicago: ALA Editions, 2010.

References

James City County, Virginia. 2015. "Human Resources Forms" (internal document). Accessed January 5. www.jamescitycountyva.gov.

Williamsburg Regional Library. 2015a. "Interview Questions" (internal document). Accessed January 5. www.wrl.org.

———. 2015b. "Job Description" (internal document). Accessed January 5. www.wrl.org.

Planning

Nelson Worley
Revised by John A. Moorman

Planning is the process by which the library determines its course. Planning results in a time-specific plan document that is used as the basis for library operations. Planning is an ongoing, cyclical process of assessment, forecasting, goal setting, implementation, and evaluation. The planning process typically asks four questions:

- What is the library's current condition?
- What do you want the library to be?
- How does the library get there?
- Did the library get there?

The planning process offers several opportunities for the library:

- Considers the needs of the community
- Identifies trends
- Identifies options and possibilities
- Encourages creative thinking
- Provides direction to library services
- Sets priorities
- Focuses attention on effectiveness and efficiency
- Provides feedback for learning, adapting, and improving library services
- Encourages library and individual accountability
- Orients the library and library staff members toward the future

For all these opportunities that the planning process presents for the library, it is likely that the most important reason for planning is that it is a requirement of the library's governing body, the locality, and/or the state. In fact, it is quite likely that having an up-to-date plan is a requirement for receiving funding on the local governing level as well as any state or federal funding available to the library. This chapter discusses the different approaches, models, and methodologies for developing a plan as well as the key components of the plan and the steps in the planning cycle.

Planning Approaches

The Public Library Association (PLA) and the American Library Association (ALA) have developed manuals and tools to help libraries assess the needs of communities and set goals and objectives for future development. Although the models and tools cited in this chapter are designed for public libraries, elements may be adapted to other types of libraries. Also, other types of libraries may have their planning process dictated by how the larger unit plans as a whole. In any case, the principles discussed in these models apply to planning in all types of libraries. John Ulmschneider, Executive Director of Libraries at Virginia Commonwealth University, prepared the following summary of academic library planning, which will be of assistance to librarians in the small academic library.

Strategic Planning in Academic Libraries

Libraries at academic institutions, like libraries everywhere, face a "perfect storm" of challenges that will converge in the near to medium-term future. Chief among those challenges are these:

- **Changes in funding:** Higher education institutions, especially public colleges and universities, are in the midst of a long-term, permanent decline in public funding support, growing pressure to develop other revenue streams, and skepticism about tuition levels and how universities use their funding. Consequently, academic libraries must themselves develop new funding sources, demonstrate tangible benefits from parent institution investment by planning carefully for maximum impact from every new dollar, and highlight their efforts to operate efficiently and deliver public benefit. The deep and long-standing tradition of collaborations among libraries, public and academic, powerfully displays the commitment of libraries to making the best use of every dollar. For that reason, consortia arrangements and collaborations of all kinds will strengthen and expand in the coming decade.
- **Accelerating changes in the publishing environment:** The transition to digital publishing has now been under way for two decades or more. Years of slowly evolving business practice in the publishing industry have given way to increasingly rapid changes. The consolidation of publishers through mergers and acquisitions continues to drive up the cost of published material for the academy, in print and digital forms, at a pace far higher than other inflation measures. At the same time, emerging alternative publishing venues have introduced new sources of material for

library collections, such as open access publishing, viable self-publishing (through Amazon.com and other sources), and open educational resources. The result: increased costs for academic libraries, but also a complex new environment that holds promise for reducing costs in the future but requires greater expertise to navigate and understand.

- **Recruiting and retaining staff:** All libraries share the challenge of recruiting and retaining the best library talent. One abiding concern over the past decade—that the career pipeline might prove insufficient to keep up with retirements of librarians—has largely abated, but it remains difficult to meet the demand for highly skilled librarians. Large applicant pools do not always yield strong finalists, and the combination of skills needed in contemporary academic settings remain hard to find. Consequently, academic libraries must continue their individual and collaborative efforts to support training and development of librarians and staff and encourage rigorous preparation at the graduate level—and not always through an MLS degree program—for careers in academic librarianship.

- **The abiding but misleading image of libraries:** While very few libraries anywhere fit the stereotypical image of a quiet place for reading books, academic libraries perhaps have departed furthest from such a traditional model. Contemporary academic libraries are abuzz with group study, coffee shops, computers, snack food, and conversation (although all still provide some places for quiet study and intellectual retreat). They also focus increasingly on emerging areas of urgent need among faculty, serving as the chief campus resource on matters related to copyright, authors' rights, open access publishing, research data management, and assessing the impact of a scholar's work using alternatives to traditional metrics, among others. To help convince academic leaders to resource these vital operations, academic libraries require more sophisticated and aggressive marketing and publicity to displace stereotypical concepts held by students and faculty with the reality of libraries' very active role in the academic and social lives of their institutions.

How should academic librarians approach planning in this challenging environment? First and foremost, it is no longer sufficient to conduct occasional planning exercises that lay out long-term internal goals. Formal planning exercises must be more frequent, and the focus must be on results that are visible to constituencies and advance overall institutional goals in teaching and learning, research, and student life. Furthermore, the pace of change in higher education is such that long-term planning has questionable value. Planning horizons should be scaled back to no more than two to three years, which also encourages more frequent planning cycles. Longer-term goals should be relegated to a mission/vision/values statement, development of which forms the essential first step and foundation for near-horizon strategic planning. Planners should adopt formal methodologies for planning that concentrate institutional efforts and speed up the planning process. An important emerging element in such methodologies is integrating a focus on evidence-based results as captured through quantified measures.

The overall result of new planning practices increasingly resembles a framework document rather than a detailed plan. The need for agility and flexibility to respond to opportunities and changes in the environment has emerged as a paramount virtue for all libraries. Plans with richly articulated strategies/objectives/tasks often prove inadequate when confronted with the rapidly changing circumstances that characterize contemporary academic environments. Instead, leaders should favor plans that identify broad areas of investment and focus and are coupled with evidence-based metrics that can drive assessment.

Those charged with initiating or leading a planning effort in an academic library have easily at hand the most valuable of resources: examples! Many academic libraries place their strategic plans on their websites and will readily share internal planning documents on request. The methodologies and processes in these examples provide invaluable guidance for nearly any academic library. Furthermore, examples of powerful alternative planning methodologies that are relatively new to academe and to academic libraries, such as balanced scorecard and compact planning, have outstanding exemplars on the web. Librarians can consult excellent plans at libraries ranging from Association of Research Libraries (ARL) institutions to libraries at elite, undergraduate-focused institutions for instructive examples.

Smart planners at academic libraries will start with three fundamental steps. First, if the library does not have one, a mission/vision/values statement must be developed that expresses and captures the culture of the library. Many examples of such statements from academic libraries are available on the web. Second, leaders of the planning effort will carry out a rapid but rigorous review of plans and planning methodologies at peer institutions and other related institutions. The result will be a clearly defined planning discipline but, more important, a discipline that accelerates the planning process and creates quantifiable goals or targets. Finally, every aspect of the plan will be tied to the parent institution's goals and ambitions and demonstrate bottom-line value to the parent institution through quantifiable evidence as well as quantifiable results. Only a library plan that advances the academic institution as a whole will have a compelling place in the institution's vision of its future.

Planning Models

Since the publication of *A Planning Process* in 1977, the PLA has issued other models. *Planning and Role Setting for Public Libraries: A Manual of Options and Procedures* (McClure et al. 1987) and *Planning for Results: A Public Library Transformation Process* (Himmel and Wilson 1998) each introduced new aspects to the planning model. These titles are no longer in print but are included here to give a historical perspective on library planning. *Planning and Role Setting* introduced the notion of role selection for the public library, defining eight representative role profiles that could be used by library planners to describe the essential priorities of the library and to guide the allocation of budget, staffing, and energies.

Planning for Results, among other changes, introduced the idea of "visioning"—a concise expression of what is envisioned for the community or how the community will benefit from having a successful library. Previous planning models had been institution centered, whereas this new step in the process sought to create a stronger connection between the library and its community. *Planning for Results* also recast the eight role profiles from the previous planning model into thirteen responses. This change incorporated libraries' experience in using the original roles and reflected the growing application of technology in the library environment.

Planning for Results, originally published in two volumes, provided very detailed information on planning steps, tasks, and service responses. Feedback from librarians who used the process in the original version led to the publication of a more simplified revision, *The New Planning for Results: A Streamlined Approach* (Nelson 2001). *The New Planning for Results*, with a different format, retained the basic elements of *Planning for Results* while simplifying many of the steps in the planning process (e.g., the planning tasks were reduced in number from twenty-three to twelve, and the time line was decreased to four to five months instead of eight to ten months).

In 2008 came the publication of *Strategic Planning for Results* (also by Nelson). This book contained two significant differences from previous planning material. First, the term used to describe the planning process changed from *long-range planning* to *strategic planning*. This is more than a semantic change; it acknowledges that the future is too uncertain to make firm long-range plans. Strategic planning accepts this view of the future and stresses that planning is an ongoing process. The second difference is the emphasis on implementing the changes indicated in the library's strategic plan.

This emphasis led to the publication of Nelson's *Implementing for Results* in 2009, which contains the following:

- Tips to help determine which activities effectively support goals and objectives
- Fourteen easy-to-follow tasks, presented in order
- The tools needed for staff to prepare and effectively communicate changes
- All the necessary tools for reviewing current and potential library activities

In addition to this implementation-specific text, several other companion volumes, part of the PLA's Results Series, for *Planning for Results* and *The New Planning for Results* are useful for more specific planning activities:

- *Managing for Results: Effective Resource Allocation for Public Libraries* (Nelson, Altman, and Mayo 2000) is a resource allocation model based on the service responses in *Planning for Results*; however, it may be used with other planning models. The primary topics are managing staff, collections, facilities, and technology. Work forms are included. (One word of caution: some librarians consider some of the activities and tasks very labor intensive.)
- *Staffing for Results: A Guide to Working Smarter* (Mayo and Goodrich 2002) provides more in-depth coverage of staffing issues. *Managing for Results* assists in identifying staffing required and the abilities needed for the library to accomplish identified service goals, objectives, and tasks. If the library's planning process indicates that large-scale staff adjustments are needed, *Staffing for Results* provides tools to decide what changes to make and what the possible implications of the changes might be. Worksheets are included.
- *Creating Policies for Results: From Chaos to Clarity* (Nelson and Garcia 2003) is a tool to assist library directors and trustees in adopting policies that support the library in its efforts to achieve its goals in meeting the needs and priorities of the community. Changes in the library priorities as a result of the planning process will have an impact on library policies. As a result of the planning process, it is necessary to review, revise, and develop policies, regulations, guidelines, and procedures that support the library's efforts to implement its plan. Worksheets are included.
- *Technology for Results: Developing Service-Based Plans* (Mayo 2005) builds on the proven process outlined in *The New Planning for Results*. It provides a step-by-step guide to assist librarians and administrators in creating a dynamic technology plan. Work forms are included.

Other Planning Methodologies and Resources

The models just discussed have been developed over the years by PLA specifically to provide tools and training for public library planners in their efforts to improve planning and implementation of public library services. There are other planning methodologies, models, or techniques that may be used. Planning activities are known by numerous terms—long-range planning, short-range planning, strategic planning, reengineering, and crisis management, among others—that have varying definitions. Management trends such as total quality management and continuous improvement initiatives are also used in planning.

Types of Planning

- **City/county planning processes:** Depending on your library's governance structure, the library's planning process may be a part of the broader framework of the local jurisdiction's planning. While these processes can and do work, the challenge is to ensure that whatever the planning process used, it is meaningful and useful as it pertains to the library.
- **Scenario planning:** As outlined in *Scenario Planning for Libraries* (Giesecke 1998), scenario planning focuses on the uncertainty of the environment and urges library planners to take a flexible approach to viewing the future. By asking "What if . . . ?" questions, different futures are developed. For example, What if a new library branch is planned and . . .

  > the branch opens with additional staff and resources?
  > the branch opens without any additional staff and resources?
  > the branch's opening is delayed and additional staff have been hired and resources have already been purchased?
  > the branch is delayed and there are no additional staff or resources?

  Considering such scenarios helps planners design strategies to help the library move forward regardless which scenario occurs. An additional benefit of scenario planning is that it helps prepare the library staff psychologically for various possibilities.
- **Peer comparison:** While assessing the library's current situation and creating a vision and goals are important, an equally important aspect of planning may be comparing the library to peer libraries. Peer comparison enhances effective planning by providing an opportunity to see the library's strengths and weaknesses vis-à-vis comparable libraries in size, type, locale, and so on. In comparing the library with neighboring ones, areas of cooperation and collaboration among libraries may be identified. Peer comparison is aided in some states through the adoption of standards, sometimes in formats by levels or profiles that assist in comparison activities. The state library agency may be helpful in providing comparison assistance. A number of states provide access to the statistical collection and analysis tool Bibliostat (discussed in more information detail later).

Other Planning Aids

- **State library requirements, standards, and guidelines:** Many state library agencies have established requirements, standards, and/or guidelines for libraries to use in planning. Often the state agency dictates that requirements and standards must be

For Further Information

The Chief Officers of State Library Agencies (COSLA) maintains a website at www.cosla.org that provides basic information about COSLA and the individual state library agencies.

included in the library's planning document, and must be met, in order to receive state funding. Some states also provide tools to assist libraries in planning. Contact your state library agency to identify what requirements, standards, and guidelines are applicable and to determine what planning tools may be available. Additionally, planning information and tools from other states may also be helpful.

- **Edge Initiative:** Developed under the leadership of the Urban Libraries Council, with funding by the Bill and Melinda Gates Foundation, Edge is a suite of tools that support continuous improvement and reinvestment in public technology and can be used by all sizes of libraries. Materials include the Edge Toolkit and Edge Benchmarks. There are eleven benchmarks in three categories against which a library can assess its technology-related services, and each benchmark has a set of indicators.

- **Public library performance measures:** Currently under development by the PLA, this Performance Measurement project, when completed, will provide surveys that libraries can use to collect customer outcomes. Related training and support tools will also be available and will assist libraries in using outcome data for advocacy, planning, and decision making.

Library Statistical Information

- **State and national statistical information:** There are more than 9,000 public libraries in the fifty states and the District of Columbia. Each state has a designated state data coordinator, usually appointed by the state librarian or head of the state's library agency, to gather data on its public libraries for submission to the National Center for Educational Statistics (NCES). The state data coordinator can be an invaluable resource person by providing more information about the annual Federal-State Cooperative System (FSCS) data collection and by using the data more effectively in the library planning and evaluation process. The Institute of Museum and Library Services (IMLS) provides data analysis tools on its website (www.imls.gov/research/library_services .aspx) that enable academic and public libraries to make data comparisons with other libraries throughout the country.

- **Bibliostat Collect and Bibliostat Connect:** A number of state library agencies maintain subscriptions to these Internet-based data collection and data analysis tools. Bibliostat Collect is a customized tool that allows for a more complete, accurate, and timely data collection process for annual public library reports. State library agencies that have a subscription for Collect use this tool to collect data for the FSCS survey as well as state-specific public library data. The companion application, Bibliostat Connect, allows libraries to conduct quick and easy, statistical and graphical comparisons. A current Bibliostat Connect subscription provides access to the most current versions of FSCS, PLA, and state data. In addition to using Connect for planning purposes, such as identifying strengths and weaknesses, the peer comparisons can be used in budget proposals and presentations to protect existing, or to secure additional, resources. Statewide subscriptions to both tools include unlimited software access, toll-free technical support, online help, tutorials, and documentation. To find out if these tools are available, contact your state library agency.

- **Public Library Data Service (PLDS):** The PLA collects data from participating public libraries and makes the data available in two forms. The first is an annual overview of data collected on operating finances, output measures, interlibrary loaning, and technology provisions, published in *Public Libraries*. The second is PLAmetrics, the online portal to PLDS. Available through subscription, this service enables users to access not only PLDS data (2002–2013) but also public-use IMLS data (1998–2011). Data can be employed for peer comparisons, benchmarking, and/or trend analyses as well as to meet local, custom needs.

Other Information Resources

- **Federal resources:** Additional useful data may be available from the US Bureau of the Census (www.census.gov) and the US Bureau of Labor Statistics (www.bls.gov).
- **State and local resources:** At the state and local levels are a number of sources of data that you might find useful in your planning process:

  o Employment and workforce commissions
  o State and local departments of education
  o Economic development departments
  o University centers for public service
  o State and local chambers of commerce
  o Planning commissions

Key Components of the Plan

Regardless of the planning model used, there are several key components that you will need to include in your plan:

- **Mission statement:** The purpose of the mission statement is to inform the community about the library's priorities. Mission statements should be clearly written and concise, using terms that

> **For Further Information**
>
> To learn more about the Edge Initiative, visit the website at www.libraryedge.org. To check the progress of the PLA's Performance Measurement project, go to www.ala.org/pla/performancemeasurement.

are easily understood. A brief, to-the-point mission statement is more easily conveyed and remembered.

- **Vision statement:** This statement describes what the library is to be: What will the future look like? How will the library's future contribute to the community's vision? By comparing the library's vision statement with the existing situation of the library, planners can determine what steps need to be taken. The library's strategic plan provides the guide to fulfilling the vision.
- **Goals:** These are general statements that describe desired long-term (usually three to five years) achievements. These may be service goals or management goals. Service goals directly reflect the roles or service responses selected in the planning process. Management goals that may support service goals are concerned with resources, staffing, funding, or other management issues. Goals should logically follow the library's vision and mission and provide a framework for developing objectives.
- **Objectives:** These are more specific statements that describe measurable results to be accomplished in a specific period of time. Objectives are written for each goal, although some objectives may overlap goals. Types of objectives include those which

  o develop new services or management operations,
  o maintain or improve the quality of a service or management operation, and/or
  o reduce or eliminate a service or management operation.

- **Strategic directions:** These are the areas that the library will emphasize during the plan period.
- **Activities and tasks:** These are the specific actions that the library will carry out to achieve its goals and objectives.

Another key component of the plan is determining the level of effort to be used in the planning process. This is an extremely important decision, one that is usually made by you and/or the library board/governing authority. The level of effort required—basic, moderate, or extensive—will depend on the library's current situation and the effectiveness of the plan already in place:

- **Basic:** This level of effort may be appropriate if a good plan already exists that can be adapted and if there are no major external or internal factors affecting the library.
- **Moderate:** This level of effort may be appropriate when a library senses that a complete reworking of its plan is needed and/or the library faces internal or external changes (e.g., funding increases or reductions, community growth or decline).
- **Extensive:** This level of effort may be appropriate if the library desires to conduct an extensive planning process, the library is

faced with a crisis, the previous planning effort was not successful, and/or the library is facing significant community change.

The Planning Cycle

Regardless of the planning model or methodology chosen, the process is cyclical in nature. The basic steps are these:

- Planning to plan
- Determining where the library is currently
- Deciding where you want the library to be
- Setting strategic directions
- Setting goals, objectives, and activities
- Implementing the plan
- Evaluating the plan's effectiveness

Planning to Plan

Deciding upon the planning model or approach and the level of effort are two of the more important decisions in planning to plan and basically answer the questions "What?" and "How?" The answer to the question "Who?" is influenced by the level of effort. Moderate and extensive planning efforts call for more community and stakeholder participation. Staff and the library board should give careful consideration when deciding which community representatives and stakeholders are asked to join the planning effort. A collaborative approach to selecting the planning committee is preferable. The answer to the question "When?" will be determined by the library's situation. Requirements to submit a planning document and updates to the state library agency will be a factor in determining when to initiate the planning process. A library facing a crisis or significant change in the community will be more pressured to initiate the planning process sooner rather than later. If possible, the planning process should be scheduled to allow for maximum participation. The summer months may not be the best time for planning activities.

Levels of Effort in the Planning Process

Basic
- **Process:** Informal
- **Indicators:** When a good, adaptable plan is in place and no major external or internal factors are affecting the library
- **Who:** Library director, library board, library staff
- **Decisions:** Based on the committee's working knowledge and review of existing demographic and library data
- **Activities:** Most of the planning work completed within the committee
- **Time line:** Weeks

Moderate
- **Process:** More formal
- **Indicators:** When a complete reworking of the library's plan is needed and/or the library faces internal or external changes
- **Who:** Library director, library board, library staff, community representatives
- **Decisions:** Based on a thorough review of demographic and library data as well as information from surveys, focus groups, and similar activities
- **Activities:** Community input through focus groups, surveys, and so forth
- **Time line:** Months

Extensive
- **Process:** Very formal
- **Indicators:** When the library wants to conduct an extensive planning process, is faced with a crisis, recognizes that the previous planning effort was not successful, and/or is facing significant community change
- **Who:** Representatives from all identified stakeholders and additional consulting and/or project support staff as needed
- **Decisions:** Based on extensive review of library and demographic data and information from surveys, focus groups, interviews, and so on, with stakeholders and with nonusers
- **Activities:** Extensive data collection and stakeholder input through surveys, focus groups, interviews, public hearings, and review by other governing bodies
- **Time line:** Several months to a year

Determining Where the Library Is Currently

Library planners must address several important issues as they begin this phase of the planning process:

- What information about the library needs to be reviewed?
- What information about the community should be reviewed?
- What current library services focus on community needs and with what success?
- Which libraries should be identified as peer libraries?
- Who will be responsible for reviewing the information and how will it be presented to library planners?

SWOT (strengths, weaknesses, opportunities, threats) analysis is a planning tool for examining internal and external conditions: What are the current strengths and weaknesses of the library? In the community, the region, the state, and perhaps nationally, what are the opportunities and threats that may affect the library? SWOT analysis is a technique that can also be used with other groups, such as library staff, Friends of the Library, focus groups, and community groups.

Deciding Where You Want the Library to Be

When deciding where the library should be, give consideration to the community's vision and that of the library:

- Where is the library compared to the community vision?
- What are the community needs?
- Specifically, which community needs will the library help meet?
- How will the library through its selected roles, service responses, or strategic directions connect with the community needs?

Setting Strategic Directions

If you use this approach in your planning process, you will need to determine directions that you will emphasize during the plan period. You will need to include brief statements after each direction to indicate how these strategies will be accomplished. Figure 9.1 provides an example of this approach from the Williamsburg (VA) Regional Library's strategic plan for the years 2012–2015.

Setting Goals, Objectives, and Activities

The purpose of stating goals, objectives, and activities is to provide a guide to get the library from its current status to where you want the library to be. Goals, objectives, and activities should address selected roles, service responses or strategic directions, and community needs that the library has chosen to help meet. Again, goals are general statements of a desired

FIGURE 9.1

Strategic Directions

The Williamsburg Regional Library will focus its efforts on the following areas throughout the years of this plan. These directions are based upon knowledge of the community and its demographics, information gathered through the planning process, and the mission, vision, and values statements. The library will continue to build upon its reputation for excellence in collections, programs, and services.

Provide excellent service

- Put users' needs and expectations first.
- Treat all users with courtesy and respect.
- Use technology where appropriate to enhance users' experience.
- Expand services for teens.

Provide excellent collections

- Ensure collections are up-to-date, well-used, and available in formats that meet users' expectations.
- Expand offerings of digital content.
- Enhance collection access and use through technology.

Provide excellent outreach services

- Continue to provide Mobile Library Services to our community.
- Develop a comprehensive communications plan (including social media) to promote library collections, programs, and services.
- Explore options for delivering outreach services electronically.

Provide excellent programs

- While emphasizing programs for youths, offer programs that promote lifelong learning.
- Offer programs that advance the library's function as a community center.

Provide excellent facilities

- Ensure that meeting spaces and the Williamsburg Library Theatre are well maintained, equipped with appropriate technology, and available to all groups.
- Rearrange spaces in both library buildings to maximize their effectiveness for users and staff members.
- Ensure that library vehicles are reliable and equipped to provide efficient, effective service.
- Maintain clean, attractive, and safe library facilities.

Provide for excellence in daily operations

- Provide regular opportunities for staff members to develop and improve knowledge and skills.
- Collaborate with community groups and organizations to enhance service delivery.
- Adapt organizational structures to address library priorities.

The library's priorities are creating a comprehensive communications plan, expanding offerings of digital content, rearranging spaces in both library buildings, providing opportunities for staff development, and expanding services for teenagers.

long-term achievement, objectives describe measurable results to be accomplished in a specified period of time, and activities are specific actions that identify how the library will achieve its goals and objectives.

Implementing the Plan

The basic components in implementing the plan are writing, communicating, and utilizing. In writing the plan, it might be advisable to have a smaller, select number of planners to do the drafting. Keep the audience in mind. If the audience includes the general public, extra effort is needed to be sure the plan is clear, concise, and logical. Library terms that may be unfamiliar should be defined. As the written plan progresses, it is advisable to have the drafts reviewed by the planners, the library staff, and the library board. The final document should be accepted by all the planners and presented to the library board and/or other governing bodies for approval.

In communicating the plan, decide to whom and why. When communicating with internal audiences such as the library staff, the intent may be to persuade and/or direct. With external audiences, be sure to match the communication to the audience. A particular audience may be interested in specific goals and objectives rather than the plan as a whole. When communicating to an audience, give consideration to the amount of information needed, how the message might be tailored to that individual or group, the format to be used (electronic, print, or presentation), and the right language.

The plan needs to be used, not placed on a shelf to collect dust. A plan should be the foundation for all library activity—strategic planning, technology planning, business plans, budgeting, employee work plans and evaluations. The planning process involves a major investment of time and resources; use the result effectively.

Evaluating the Plan's Effectiveness

Just as planning is an ongoing process, so is evaluation. Periodic evaluation of the plan's effectiveness is desirable and useful both in keeping the library on track with the plan and in making any course adjustments. Things change, and as things change, it may be necessary to adapt the library plan. Flexibility may be needed. In addition to scheduling formal evaluations through numbers gathering, surveys, focus groups, interviews, and observation, it may be desirable to schedule periodic informal assessments with key individuals from the library board, library staff, and the community.

Conclusion

There is no best way to plan. Differences in communities, libraries, and types of libraries will be reflected in the process, in the strategies and techniques used, and in the final written document. Some libraries will undertake a rigorous planning process; others will pursue a simpler one. An individual library can set its own pace for the planning process. The process is flexible, so all libraries can plan for improved services. Each user community deserves the good service that results from effective planning. All libraries, regardless of size, must plan in order to be effective in today's world.

Further Reading

Applegate, Rachel. *Practical Evaluation Techniques for Librarians.* Santa Barbara, CA: Libraries Unlimited, 2013.

Bryan, Cheryl. *Managing Facilities for Results: Optimizing Space for Services.* Chicago: ALA Editions, 2007.

Garcia, June, and Sandra Nelson. *Public Library Services Responses 2007.* Chicago: ALA Editions, 2007.

Matthews, Joseph R. *Library Assessment in Higher Education.* 2nd ed. Santa Barbara, CA: Libraries Unlimited, 2014.

————. *Research-Based Planning for Public Libraries.* Santa Barbara, CA: Libraries Unlimited, 2013.

Matthews, Stephen A., and Kimberly D. Matthews. *Crash Course in Strategic Planning.* Santa Barbara, CA: Libraries Unlimited, 2013.

References

Giesecke, Joan, ed. 1998. *Scenario Planning for Libraries.* Chicago: American Library Association.

Mayo, Dianne. 2005. *Technology for Results: Developing Service-Based Plans.* Chicago: ALA Editions.

Mayo, Dianne, and Jeanne Goodrich. 2002. *Staffing for Results: A Guide to Working Smarter.* Chicago: ALA Editions.

Nelson, Sandra. 2001. *The New Planning for Results: A Streamlined Approach.* Chicago: ALA Editions.

————. 2008. *Strategic Planning for Results.* Chicago: ALA Editions.

————. 2009. *Implementing for Results: Your Strategic Plan in Action.* Chicago: ALA Editions.

Nelson, Sandra, Ellen Altman, and Diane Mayo. 2000. *Managing for Results: Effective Resource Allocation for Public Libraries.* Chicago: ALA Editions.

Nelson, Sandra, and June Garcia. 2003. *Creating Policies for Results: From Chaos to Clarity.* Chicago: ALA Editions.

Buildings

Frederick A. Schlipf

This chapter is concerned with how libraries occupy space and with how to ensure that the spaces created for libraries to occupy truly meet the needs of the libraries and their communities. The chapter covers the steps in the library planning and construction process, technical requirements of library buildings, typical library contents, and some common errors in library design. It also provides an example of a successful floor plan for a small public library.

Providing proper space is a problem for most libraries. Many libraries are too small, and many librarians struggle also with ineffective room arrangement, poor lighting, inadequate air-conditioning, insufficient wiring, poor security, annoying acoustics, and other common problems. Library buildings are not as important to long-term success as are friendly, competent staffs or strong collections, but bad buildings can totally hamstring library operations, alienate users, damage collections, and cost far too much to operate.

Buildings are also a problem because of their initial cost. Librarians can undertake many projects piecemeal. Collections and computer services can be developed over many years, but buildings usually require one-time expenditures of large sums of money, far more than most libraries can set aside from operating funds.

Due to their cost and permanence, buildings also require extremely careful planning. Badly chosen books and equipment can usually be replaced fairly easily, but buildings are so expensive that they usually must be used for many decades, if not centuries. The architectural choices of one generation are visited upon successive generations like family blessings or curses.

Although planning and building new library spaces is a complex undertaking, it actually consists of a number of individual steps. If you do not skip essential steps, if you spell out your needs clearly, and if you take time to learn what works and what does not work, everything should turn out well.

Steps in Planning and Constructing Libraries

Good library construction is a very straightforward undertaking. The major steps include the following:

1. Decide what kinds of services your library needs to provide.
2. Determine the kinds of spaces you need to provide those services.
3. Hire an architect.
4. Find a place to build the library.
5. Design a library with the spaces you need.
6. Find the money to construct the library.
7. Build the library.

Decide What Kinds of Services Your Library Needs to Provide

It is difficult to design a library until you have made a number of decisions about services. Some decisions have little impact on buildings, but it is surprising how many decisions have a direct impact on the kind of structure you need. For example, the maximum size of your collection and the formats of materials in your collection will determine the number of shelving sections and other storage units. How your customers use your library (or *would* use your library if it had the correct space) will affect the number and sizes of study tables, armchairs, computer workstations, and study rooms. The types of programs and other events you want to house in the library will affect the size and placement of meeting rooms. The decision to let people drink coffee in the library will affect your choice of carpeting. All of these decisions—and often hundreds of others—will directly determine the spaces, room arrangement, and finishes of your library.

Deciding on the services you need to offer is primarily a job for you and your board or administrator. Often you can do this by working your way through a comprehensive list of decisions, but you will need to decide how to be sure that you have paid attention to your users' needs and interests.

When planning services, lots of libraries simply rely on input from staff and users. If you listen to the people who use the library or simply watch them at work, you can learn a lot about what they want and do not want. The danger, of course, is that people have a tendency to unconsciously filter out things they do not really want to hear. For example, if I am personally opposed to coffee in libraries, I may simply ignore such suggestions from my patrons.

Carefully constructed surveys offer a chance to gather more unbiased data. It is fairly easy to survey library users. This is particularly true for most small academic, school, and special libraries, since they have limited user groups.

In the case of public libraries, things get much more difficult because a substantial number of residents in many communities almost never use the library. When public libraries survey users in the library, they do not learn anything about the people who *don't* use the libraries and the services those people would like to see. To learn about the entire community's interests, you may have to talk with people who never use your library or who use other libraries in preference to their local public library.

One easy way to find out what your citizens find lacking in your public library is to survey them when they use neighboring libraries. (Obviously, this can take place only in situations where nearby libraries honor one another's borrowers' cards.) Finding out what leads your citizens to prefer other libraries will show what can be improved in your library. An example of such a survey appears in appendix 8 of the Illinois Library Association's *Serving Our Public: Standards for Illinois Public Libraries* (see the readings at the end of this chapter).

Once you try to survey the entire user population of a public library, things can get a great deal more difficult. Most librarians who think this is essential will want to consult a professional (and ideally evaluate at the outset whether the cost of the survey justifies its findings). Of course, by surveying every possible user, a library may end up being inappropriately influenced by the opinions of people who never use libraries under any circumstances.

Unfortunately, one of the main reasons for undertaking surveys is to prove to the people who are providing the funds that what you have been saying all along is correct. In situations like this, librarians sometimes end up doing surveys just to demonstrate by acceptable methods what it is that citizens want. Because of the difficulty of conducting usable surveys, a better option may be to rely on focus groups instead.

In much planning these days, one of the most frequent problems is dealing with campus planners or civic leaders or school administrators who contend that the digital revolution has made libraries obsolete—usually because they have other plans for the money. You will need to be prepared for this contention and know how to deal with it.

Determine the Kinds of Spaces You Need to Provide Those Services

This step is called *programming*. When you are finished with this step, you should have a very detailed list of all the spaces you need in your new library, the physical characteristics of those spaces (such as square footage, ceiling height, and so on), the contents of those spaces (such as the number and types of shelving units or tables), and the physical relationship between the spaces (adjacencies). For example, the description of a quiet reading room for adults might specify the number and types of seating, whether parts of the collection will be stored in the room, the type of atmosphere, special features like fireplaces, the room's location with regard to the rest of the library, lighting needs, acoustic separation, and so on. The size estimate should reflect the amount of space required for each item in the room to ensure the room will be neither too large nor too small. Programs can be surprisingly detailed and correspondingly long, ranging from about fifty to 400 pages, single-spaced.

If you have experience with programming or have taken an extensive course, you may want to prepare your own building program, but most libraries are better off hiring building consultants. In hiring a consultant, hire a librarian with considerable experience in library design. An architect should be employed, as his or her skills and talents become essential to the programming process. Hiring a separate architect will give your planning team greater depth. (This is a point on which librarians and some architects tend to disagree, but the librarians are right.) In addition, if your programmers work for you rather than for your architect, they are much more likely to give you the unbiased second opinions you need as your architect develops proposed designs. For this reason, hiring a team consisting of an architect and consultant can be a much poorer choice than hiring the two separately.

When you hire a library building consultant, look for someone with work experience in real libraries and a track history of consulting on other projects, as well as someone whose company you enjoy. You will spend a great deal of planning time with your consultants and architects, and if they drive you up the wall socially, you are in for a number of seasons of discontent.

If you can find a good consultant, you will be better off keeping that person on your project until construction is ready to begin so that someone who knows how libraries occupy space and who has a lot of experience with good and bad buildings can react to design ideas. This person can look out for the library's interests by speaking up for the needs of the library and sometimes disagreeing with powerful people on the library's behalf—for example, when you need someone to point out that a stupid idea is in fact a really stupid idea, like when your architect wants to place your school library next to the band practice room or the weight training room, or when your architect proposes a new college library based on the principle of the chambered nautilus.

Hire an Architect

Public libraries almost always hire their own architects, and most academic libraries are large enough to justify hiring architects for library projects alone. But in a corporate or school library, someone else may hire the architect for an entire building. When you cannot pick your own architect, having a building program and making sure the proper administrators are familiar with it are tremendously important.

Public libraries are usually independent agencies and hire their own architects. Such a situation leads to a much better chance of having a library design that responds to the library's specific needs. Still, there are a lot of badly designed public libraries out there. For this reason, it is important to select an architect with a track record of designing functional and effective library buildings.

Laws concerning the hiring of architects by public agencies vary from state to state, but generally speaking, you will have tremendous leeway

Tip

Proactive programming is extremely important. Get your needs into print before someone else decides either to do it for you or to just proceed without a program.

in picking the firm you want. One thing you may be barred from doing is picking a firm by low bid, but that is a very bad practice for projects as complex as libraries.

Most libraries begin looking for an architect by sending out Request for Information (RFI) letters to likely firms. (Other common terms are Request for Qualifications, or RFQ, and Request for Proposal, or RFP.) Architects who are interested in the job will respond with elaborate submissions, including lists of key personnel, information on prior work, and so forth. In soliciting information, it is important to require unambiguous detail on the number of completed library projects and the specific scope of the architect's work on each project. Before selecting a group of three or four architects to interview, always talk with people in the libraries the architects designed to ensure that they are happy with the relationship and the resulting library. And, if possible, visit sample libraries.

Tip

When the time comes for interviews, be sure to specify that each firm's proposed project architect (the person you will work with most of the time) should make the presentation for the firm, and that you are aware of that person's specific expertise. Some architectural firms practice "bait and switch," sending to interviews charming and inspiring sales architects you may never see again.

Find a Place to Build the Library

Designing a building without a specific site in mind is extremely difficult, as most buildings are fitted to available space. For a new public library with on site parking, a good first estimate of necessary site size is four times the gross square footage of the library. (A detention basin will increase the necessary site size.) If you do not have the money to construct your building right away, another possible approach is to purchase an option on the site, giving yourself a chance to back out if funding does not materialize.

Finding a good site can be surprisingly difficult. In some cases, you will be pressured to use badly located sites, undersized sites, polluted sites, sites far from utility hookups, or other problem areas. Any site decisions should involve both the project architect and the consultant.

Sometimes tremendous political pressure exists for public libraries to purchase ancient, empty buildings and convert them to libraries. This can sometimes be done, but many buildings that stand empty are standing empty for extraordinarily good reasons, and converting buildings to libraries can be surprisingly difficult and expensive. Some of the most successful conversion projects have involved former big box stores in excellent condition, but as a general rule, buildings should be converted only because they are handsome and worth preserving. The perils in conversions are many, so you need to involve your programming consultant to ensure that conversion would not result in a seriously dysfunctional structure.

Design a Library with the Spaces You Need

The standard contract of the American Institute of Architects (AIA) specifies five stages in the design and construction process. The first is schematic design. In this stage, the architect and client review a wide variety of design options, select the one the client prefers, and create a basic building design. In most cases, you will want to have your architect develop the schematic design for your library before you begin a major fund-raising campaign or

Tip

When you are contracting with an architect for schematic design work, be sure that it includes furniture layouts. Without furnishings, libraries can be pretty much big square rooms. Drawings without shelving and furniture and desks will not help you judge space effectiveness or sell other people on the project.

schedule a bond referendum. By the end of the design process, you should know how the library will be laid out (floor plans) and what it will look like viewed straight on (elevations). You should also have a preliminary budget. To raise money for construction, you need the information in the schematic design, so you can show donors or voters what the completed library will look like and tell them how much it is likely to cost.

In architectural terminology, your written building program defines the problem to be solved and the architect's plan is the solution to the problem. Usually everything goes well, but occasionally architects ignore or reject your building program. Having the library programmer review proposed building designs can counter this, as will asking architects to accompany their proposed designs with tables comparing the square footages of spaces in the program with those of spaces in the design.

Find the Money to Construct the Library

For many library construction projects, this is the crucial step and sometimes the hardest one. It is an old saw in the architecture business that the single most important construction material is money.

Schematic designs and the cost estimates that accompany them are essential for fund-raising, but in many cases, you will also need renderings (attractive pictures of the completed building) or models. The production of renderings has been vastly simplified by the use of computers for the design of library buildings. Elegant renderings and models, however, require the work of artists and are expensive. Before choosing this option, you will need to decide what level of investment is best for your library.

Fiscal pressures frequently tempt libraries to save money through cut-rate construction. However, throughout the life span of a building (twenty-five to one hundred years), initial construction costs are a very minor component of total lifetime operating costs. A small savings effected during construction can cost a library many times that amount in extra costs over the life of a building.

Build the Library

The remaining stages from the architectural perspective come after you have located the money for the project and include the following:

- **Design development:** In this stage, the general schematic designs are refined and expanded to provide information on how the entire building will work, including heating, lighting, and other essential mechanical systems. (Some architects contend that furniture placement is part of design development, but you must have these decisions made as part of schematic design. At the end of schematic design, it is essential that your floor plans show all furniture placement.)

- **Bid documents:** These are the incredibly detailed drawings and specifications necessary to construct a high-quality building by low bid. Even for a small library, they can run to dozens of large sheets of drawings and hundreds of pages of specifications.
- **Bidding:** Your architect will manage the bidding process for you. Obviously, you hope that the low bid is within your projected cost. If bids are lower than you expect, this provides the opportunity to improve your library with "add alternates," which are included in the bid requirements. If bids are too high, depending on your contract, your architect may be required to redesign and rebid the project at his or her cost. It is important to be sure that individual construction firms—in addition to providing attractive bids— have the necessary "horsepower" to do the job. To be sure the firms have good reputations, require that all bidders be bonded.
- **Construction:** Typically, constructing a small library building takes about nine months to a year, although remodeling and expansion can take twice as long if you do not move out during the period of work. If your library is part of a larger structure, construction time may depend on the schedule for the entire building. Larger projects may use the services of a construction management firm that acts as an agent of the library, bidding out the work in many small parts and supervising construction on a daily basis.
- **Ground breaking and ribbon cutting:** Most libraries—particularly public libraries—benefit from ceremonies to celebrate the beginning and completion of work. Be sure to invite all the right people, including politicians, who are always seeking photo opportunities. Get the media to attend, keep speeches short (and audible), involve cute children, and feed everyone. Provide amplification for weak voices, and know what you will do if it rains. Hold events when the weather is likely to be nice (midwinter in Minnesota is a bad choice) and plan times of day (such as 2:00 p.m.) when people from out of town can travel to the events and get home again.

This is the briefest possible review of the construction process. For much more detail, check out the sources listed in the readings at the end of this chapter.

Basic Requirements of Library Buildings

All small libraries have somewhat similar architectural requirements, whether they are located in separate buildings or in rooms in larger buildings. Some of the most important requirements include the following:

- **The right amount of space of the right type in the right arrangement:** This is where a building program is essential, for it gives you a yardstick for evaluating proposed designs.
- **Strong floors:** Books are extremely heavy, and floors designed for typical office use are seldom strong enough for book storage. For this reason, many small corporate libraries end up in basements, where floor strength is less of a problem. Libraries are usually designed to hold a minimum of 150 pounds of contents (live load) per square foot. Compact shelving running on rails requires substantially more floor strength.
- **High-quality light:** Libraries require bright, even low-glare lighting. Usually this means careful control of daylight (north light is best and west light worst) and the use of lighting systems specially designed to reduce glare. As a general rule, the best results are obtained by using primarily reflected uplight, bouncing all light off white ceilings. Some workable quick specifications include (1) fluorescent fixtures using four-foot T-5 or T-8 tubes with a CRI (color rendering index) of at least 85 and a color temperature of 3500 K, (2) electronic ballasts, (3) strip fixtures directing 70 to 100 percent of light upward, and (4) fixtures spaced to provide at least 60 footcandles of illumination at tabletop and at least 20 footcandles on the vertical surfaces of all books. (Enthusiasm for green building design has led to recommendations for dim lighting. Stick with the numbers given here.) Unfortunately, bad lighting is common in even new libraries. Among the things to avoid are recessed downlights (can lights), skylights, and architecturally mounted task lighting. At the time of writing, LED lighting appeared to be the wave of the future. Problems with miserable color rendering appeared to have been largely solved, but light sources were still far too direct for good library lighting, which requires soft, uniform illumination.
- **High-quality HVAC (heating, ventilating, and air-conditioning) systems:** HVAC systems should meet current standards for air exchange and efficiency of operations. They should keep the meeting room comfortable when it holds twenty people and when it holds one hundred. HVAC systems also need to control relative humidity. Humidity in libraries should not greatly exceed 50 percent. Except in old buildings, where condensation from humidification can be a problem in very dry weather, humidity should not fall below 30 percent. Because relative humidity changes as temperatures fluctuate, HVAC systems designed to lower temperatures at night can lead to destructive levels of humidity if they do not include humidity sensors. For example, if temperatures are lowered from 70°F to 60°F—just ten degrees—and the moisture content of the air does not change, relative humidity can increase from a book-friendly 50 percent

For Further Information

For detailed explanations of lighting technology, see the paper "Let There Be Half-Way Decent Light," by the author of this chapter and the editor of this book, in the readings at the end of this chapter.

to a mold-friendly 70 percent. Far too many libraries have seen mold develop on books when temperatures are lowered. Mold also flourishes happily in school libraries when carpets are steam cleaned just before buildings are shut down for the summer.

- **Good electrical supplies:** In the midst of the computer age, it's nearly impossible to have too many electrical outlets. If your designers ask, "Where will you need to place computers?" the correct answer is, "Anywhere we want." Just because you have scheduled book shelving for an area today does not mean that you will not want to relocate the shelving and need to plug in something there tomorrow. Adding extra outlets after the fact can be extraordinarily expensive, particularly with slab-on-grade construction. Kitchenettes in meeting rooms or staff lunchrooms require multiple twenty-amp circuits to allow microwaves, coffee brewers, slow cookers, Dutch ovens, and other equipment to be operated simultaneously.

- **Pleasant acoustics:** Libraries that echo or reverberate are unpleasant to occupy. Library rooms that transmit sound easily can lead to serious compromises with user confidentiality. Library offices that fail to provide a place for private conversations also can cause major problems. Among the worst sources of acoustic problems in libraries are hard-surfaced ceilings and floors, large areas of glass, and office walls that do not continue past suspended ceilings. Cathedral or barrel vault ceilings (or any other shapes that are not flat) often transmit sound in impressively distressing ways, but they are usually acceptable if they have acoustic surfaces. If your suspended ceilings are installed before partitions between rooms are built, conversations in one room can frequently be heard in the room next door. Architects seldom hire acoustical engineers to review designs, and clients sometimes need to insist that they do.

- **Adequate ceiling height:** Most book shelves are high (typically seven or seven and a half feet), and eight-foot ceilings are almost always too low. Suspended uplights (the only satisfactory way to light small libraries) usually hang down at least two feet from the ceiling, so ceilings need to be an absolute minimum of ten feet high to keep the lights eight feet off the floor. Most libraries do better with ceilings that are eleven or twelve feet high.

- **Good sight lines:** The easiest way to maintain good security in libraries is to maintain good sight lines. If a single staff member at the service desk can see all areas of the library (including the front door and the entrances to the restrooms), operating the library will be far easier. (In an effort to provide the best possible sight lines, a number of libraries have been designed with stack aisles radiating from service desks like the spokes of wheels. This has proven to be a disastrous idea.) One of the best ways to

For Further Information

The list of readings at the end of the chapter includes an excellent review of library acoustics, by Denelle and John M. Wrightson.

improve sight lines is through internal windows and glass walls. It helps to provide windows between offices and public areas and to create study rooms that are essentially fish tanks. (It is also a good idea to watch out for unfortunate sight lines, particularly when restroom doors are opened.)

- **Clear internal arrangement:** As libraries grow larger and more complex, keeping their floor plans simple and straightforward becomes more and more difficult, but small libraries should be easy to understand. The floor plan discussed later in this chapter provides an example of a clear and straightforward design.

- **Pleasant internal spaces:** Most libraries want to encourage users to stay in the library to read, use computers, consult library staff, and (increasingly) socialize with other library users. To be successful, therefore, libraries need comfortable, well-lighted spaces with good acoustics and, wherever possible, views of the outside world. One of the great challenges in library design is providing cozy spaces that do not lead to supervision problems. One of the most successful solutions has been to install a few diner-style booths, which appeal to people who come to the library in pairs or groups and which feel far more private than they really are. Another extremely popular design is small study rooms, for four to eight people, with glass walls but with effective sound insulation.

- **Parking:** School libraries and corporate libraries usually rely on parking provided for the entire building, and libraries on small residential campuses may expect students to arrive on foot, but all public libraries need to be concerned about where people will park. Local codes may specify minimum off-street parking. A good first rule of thumb is that your parking lot should be at least as large as the floor area of your library.

- **Provision for after-hours return of materials:** Every library needs to provide a way for users to return books and recordings when the library is closed. A wide variety of return bins is available. Library users particularly like bins that they can reach from the windows of their cars; this requires one-way driveways, heavy bollards to protect bins from collisions with cars, and a long, straight run that allows drivers to pull up closely to the bins. Return slots can also be built into walls, but the receiving bins must be in fireproof spaces. The big problem with all drive-through return bins is the height of the return slots from the ground because vehicles vary so greatly in height. Another possibility is a return slot with a rain canopy next to a very short-term parking space. (In many new libraries, return bins or wall slots are located on driveways that curve too much to allow users to pull sufficiently close.)

- **Provision for external pickup of materials:** Many new libraries have external boxes that can be opened by using keypads. Books can be checked out on request and kept in the boxes until users pick them up. Although the original idea was to serve people who could not stop by when the library was open, the heaviest users appear to be parents with children in car seats.

- **Good sites:** All libraries need convenient sites. For public libraries, this means sites next to other destinations, such as stores. Most campuses seek central locations for their libraries. For corporate and school libraries, this means sites in the middle of buildings, not in remote locations. There are also sites you may not want. If you build a new public library across the street from a homeless shelter, you can expect that all the library's comfortable chairs will be occupied by sleeping nonreaders much of the day. If you build a school library next to the gym, you can expect to have problems with noise. Most good sites, of course, are sought after by other organizations or departments in addition to the library, and you may need to be aggressive to protect workable turf.

- **Provision for expansion:** No matter what people say, all libraries run out of space sooner or later. For this reason, all separate library buildings should be designed for later expansion. However, for corporate libraries that require more space, it may be easier to relocate to larger areas in the building than to expand within their original quarters.

- **Inexpensive maintenance:** Some buildings can be extraordinarily difficult (and therefore expensive) to maintain. Keep life simple (and inexpensive) by avoiding light fixtures you cannot reach (or that fill with visibly dead bugs), wall surfaces that are hard to clean, light-colored grout in ceramic tile floors (when requesting "dark grout," be sure your designer does not decide that this means "pastel grout"), cut pile (rather than tightly woven loop) carpeting, high maintenance exteriors (such as wood or EIFS [Exterior Insulation and Finish System] rather than brick), highly complex mechanical systems, and so on. See the later section Major Design Problems to Avoid, under Difficult Maintenance, for detailed suggestions.

- **Good security:** Security needs vary with the type and size of library, but all libraries have security concerns. Among the issues you will need to confront are limiting the number of entrances, providing alarms with time delays on fire exits, installing appropriate systems for fire detection and control, supervising restrooms, controlling who can open windows, providing panic buttons for staff members at service desks, and determining whether you need a theft control system. Each of these issues has design and space implications. For example, the security gates for magnetic theft control systems cannot be directly adjacent to door hardware, computers, or bookshelves, and all security gates must be staffed.

Typical Library Contents

Almost all libraries have similar needs for interior contents:

- **Service desks:** Most small libraries have single, multipurpose desks. Even if several people must be on duty at busy times, there will be other times when a single person is sufficient to meet users' needs. By limiting your library to a single desk, you can correspondingly limit the number of people it takes to operate the library. Service desks need extraordinarily good sight lines. As this chapter's sample plan demonstrates, it is possible to set up a 6,000-square-foot library so a single person can oversee the entrance to the building, the entrances to the restrooms, reader seating, stack aisles, and people using the program room. To avoid problems with desks, use modular construction, so desks can be decreased or increased in size or easily repositioned. For the same reason, avoid matching soffits over desks. Standard high-pressure laminates are too flimsy for the tops of lending desks, but plastic products like Corian work well.
- **Shelving:** Most libraries use steel cantilever shelving with decorative end panels. Cantilever shelves hook onto support posts. They are far more sturdy and reliable than shelves supported by pins at their ends and vastly better than shelves that slide into slots. Cantilever shelving for libraries is made by half a dozen specialty manufacturers, and you are always better off sticking with one of them. Libraries that purchase low-cost shelving designed for other purposes quickly regret the decision. Many libraries purchase shelf end panels with slat wall sections to enable displays of books at the end of stack ranges.
- **Storage for other parts of the collection:** Hardbound books are easy to store if they are not too large, but everything else is challenging. Library furniture and shelving catalogs are full of special equipment for storing atlases, unabridged dictionaries, newspapers, paperbacks, children's picture books, graphic novels, CDs, DVDs, kits (book/CD sets and all sorts of other combinations), and so on. Librarians tend to have strong opinions on much of this equipment, so you will be better off watching it in use in other libraries before making a selection.
- **Reader seating:** Most libraries provide a mixture of seating at tables and in upholstered chairs. Tables come in a variety of sizes. I prefer four-person tables because they work for both groups of

> **Tip**
>
> In a small library, a work counter behind the service desk, facing the entrance, will allow staff to work off desk and simultaneously supervise the library.

students and individual users who like to spread out their work, but some libraries purchase smaller tables for two readers or even for one. (Single-person tables are often called carrels, particularly if they have high sides.) Upholstered furniture is essential if you want to encourage people to linger in the library, but avoid couches in any area except children's departments. (Adults are not comfortable sharing couches unless they know each other, teenagers are occasionally too eager to share, and you probably have some adult users who are eager to turn your couches into beds.) Furniture varies tremendously in quality, and library furniture is more expensive primarily because it is sturdier. Reading tables and chairs purchased from a discount furniture store may not last out the seating. Placement of furniture also matters. By and large, for example, users do not like sitting with their backs to the action.

- **Program rooms:** Most libraries have spaces for programs or for meetings. In a public library, a program room will be much more successful if it and the restrooms can be reached directly from the entry foyer, enabling the program room to be used when the rest of the library is closed. Restrooms will also need to be accessible from the foyer. For this arrangement to take place, it must be part of building planning from the very beginning. Probably the single greatest error made in the design of program rooms is the omission of necessary storage closets for furniture, program equipment and supplies, book sale books, and so forth. There is also a temptation to provide overly elaborate lighting controls.

- **Study rooms:** Among the most successful developments in library design in the past twenty years or so has been study rooms, small rooms large enough for perhaps four people, used for quiet study, taking examinations, tutoring, meetings of community committees, student group projects, and any other uses where the elimination or containment of sound is important. To be successful, study rooms must be glass boxes (for user security and staff oversight) with excellent sound isolation and individual thermostats.

- **Restrooms:** Public restrooms are essential in many libraries, but they can be a royal pain. Restrooms should have floor drains and all surfaces should be easy to clean. It helps if the entrances to the restrooms are clearly visible from the service desk. Unless you plan to keep restrooms locked at all times and issue keys to users as needed, you will be better off with restrooms with individual stalls and with outer doors that do not lock. For all but one-person restrooms, be sure that the fixtures and their users are not on proud display to patrons of the opposite sex who happen to be walking by when the door opens. (Check your plans for both direct views and views reflected in mirrors.) Many larger libraries

Tip

Be sure that fire exits from the program room lead to the outside world and not into other areas of the library, or your plan to separate programs from the rest of the library will be defeated.

have installed airport-style restrooms, with zigzag entry passages rather than doors. Due to security issues, some libraries have one-person restrooms with stalls and with doors that do not lock.

- **Staff workrooms:** All libraries need staff workrooms with doors that lock. Even if staff members do most of their work at the service desk at slow moments, they still need a place to store materials in process, leave complex projects spread out, keep purses and coats, and so on. One of the sad mistakes many libraries make when money is tighter than they hoped is to begin space reduction by eliminating staff workspaces.

- **Staff restrooms:** All but the tiniest public libraries need staff restrooms. (You are not allowed to disagree with this if you are not an experienced librarian.)

- **Storage:** Most libraries have massive quantities of stuff that needs to be stored somewhere. If you build a new library without a good-sized storeroom, you will be in the market for a large garden shed within a few months.

- **Circulation space:** In architectural language, *circulation space* is walking around space, not space for lending and receiving books. (To avoid confusion when you speak with your architect, you may want to use the term *lending* for the latter.) All libraries need open space for people to move about. Just fitting in all the tables and chairs and desks is not enough.

- **Support spaces:** All libraries require hallways, entryways, electrical rooms, mechanical rooms, and custodial spaces, and two-story libraries devote a substantial amount of space to stairways and elevators. For many school and corporate libraries, these spaces are not part of the library itself, but almost all academic and public libraries need to plan for them.

Common Design Problems

- Too many entrances
- Bad lighting and glare
- Bad security
- Inadequate staff workspace and storage space
- Dangerous features
- Funny-shaped buildings
- Too many built-ins
- Radial stacks
- Remodeling ugly buildings
- Atria
- Difficult maintenance

Major Design Problems to Avoid

The library world is full of bad design decisions. This section covers some of the most frequently encountered bad ideas (see sidebar).

Too Many Entrances

The only way to keep an eye on the contents of your library is to have a single entrance near the service desk. You will frequently be under pressure to maintain more than one entrance, but if you let this happen, you will tie up expensive staff members watching doorways. If people push them on you, remind them of how having to watch more than one door will drive up your staffing costs and ask them if they are prepared to provide the extra operating money every year.

The following are some very common situations leading to multiple entrances:

- **Public libraries in converted commercial buildings on town squares, with front doors facing the square or courthouse and back doors (*far* to the rear) facing parking areas:** In addition to being almost impossible to watch, back doors will spook your staff when they hear unknown people fumbling around after dark.
- **School libraries with entrances from more than one part of the school:** This concept may appeal to people who want the convenience of multiple entrances or who want to funnel different age groups through different entrances, but you may have major supervision problems.
- **Historic libraries with inaccessible front entrances:** Buildings of this type (which include most Carnegie-era buildings) can be made accessible only by providing a new entrance and an elevator connecting the basement and upper floor or floors. Unless you are lucky enough to have a library built on sloping land, where people entering a new addition can simply walk into either the basement or main floor, you will end up with many ways into the building. Such buildings are also a problem because their architecture frequently indicates the location of the historic main entrance. If you close the main entrance and bring everyone in through a new, accessible entrance, you will destroy part of what you are trying to save.

Bad Lighting and Glare

More libraries suffer from bad lighting than from almost any other problem, but avoiding it is fairly easy. The worst sources of glare are skylights (which are always a bad idea), western windows without blinds (modern glass helps, but you still need blinds), and highly direct artificial lights. Small libraries should always stick with high-quality fluorescent uplight. Strips of suspended fluorescent uplight fixtures (without "perforations," which display all the dead bugs) work extremely well. Tell your designer you want neither can lights (recessed downlights) nor task lights. Never accept a light source with a CRI of less than 85. In the future, LED illumination will almost certainly become standard, but problems with odd colors and excessive directionality will need to be solved.

Some states require motion sensors for restroom lighting or even for all library lighting. These are not acceptable in reading rooms, and you need to reject them. For smaller rooms, insist that motion sensors be activated by the motion of the door and not require people to enter dark rooms to turn on the lights.

Bad Security

A wide variety of situations can undermine security. For example, if users can open the windows in your library (or have access to "reading terraces"), they can pitch your books into the bushes outside and retrieve them later. If book aisles have dead ends, people can be cornered by users they are not eager to meet. The sources of security problems in libraries are many and are frequently not understood by architects who do not specialize in libraries. Ask your consultant to list the features you need and then to review your plans.

A common source of bad security in school libraries is when libraries act as passageways to other parts of the building. Another major problem occurs when school libraries have two stories but no internal elevators, so that students can enter unsupervised levels of the library from other parts of the school.

The standard basic rule of small library design is that the number of public entrances to a library cannot be more than one.

Inadequate Staff Workspace and Storage Space

When cost becomes an issue (as it almost always does), the first things superintendents or corporate managers or mayors or library boards want to cut are staff workspace and storage space. Doing so produces some unwelcome consequences:

- Many libraries are planned to handle twenty or more years of growth in collection sizes, but they have no space for even one additional employee.
- Many libraries have virtually no place to store anything.

Dangerous Features

A number of clever architectural design features have caused problems in libraries. These are some of the most common ones:

- **Balustrades with horizontal bars:** Bars (balusters) are vertical for good reason; small children can climb horizontal bars and be up and over the barricade in seconds.
- **Indoor water features:** Libraries with indoor water features have trouble with users falling in, kids dropping books into the water, leakage into lower floors, coins clogging drains, and staff members constantly running to the restroom in response to the encouraging sound of running water. They also harbor Legionnaires' disease.
- **Staircases without risers:** A riser is the vertical panel that connects two treads. Some designers like to omit them to create an open and airy look, but users with acrophobia panic when they can see through stairs, and objects can fall through the openings.

In general, libraries work best with as few steps as possible, and they should never (ever) have "cute" steps.

Funny-Shaped Buildings

Some designers love curved and diagonal walls. Unfortunately, all too often such walls lead to high construction costs and to interior spaces that are difficult to use. Almost everything libraries own is rectangular and fits into rectangular spaces. Diagonal walls lead to funny corners, and curved walls are expensive. (Years ago, promoters of round or even hemispherical buildings talked about how such shapes used the least amount of surface to enclose the maximum amount of space, but most of them were practical failures because so much of the space was unusable and construction cost per square foot was very high. Rectangular buildings are easier—and much cheaper—to build. And it is difficult to hang pictures in an A-frame, let alone in a geodesic dome.)

Too Many Built-Ins

Long before library buildings wear out, their owners change their way of doing business. The more that spaces are designed to work in only one way, the sooner librarians find they do not work at all. Libraries are full of abandoned niches for card catalogs that no longer exist, special provisions for 16 mm film projectors, and other well-designed places for long-forgotten gadgets. They also have service desks that were envisioned as monuments and are now obsolete. The way to avoid this is to never send architecture to do the job of furniture. If your spaces are clean, open, well-lighted, and heavily wired, you stand the best possible chance of having them work for decades to come.

One bad idea in the same family as built-in furniture is so-called "task lighting," lighting carefully positioned to light specific work areas or objects. The trouble with task lighting is that—long before the light fixtures wear out—librarians move the things the lights illuminate, and too many libraries end up with special light fixtures lighting not much of anything.

Radial Stacks

Some libraries have been built with stacks arranged like the spokes of a wheel, usually to allow someone seated at a service desk to see down multiple aisles at the same time. This is an unbelievably awful idea, but for some reason, people keep reinventing it.

Remodeling Ugly Buildings

Remodeling is surprisingly expensive, about two-thirds the cost of new construction per square foot. Some libraries buy secondhand buildings thinking they can save money by remodeling them, but usually the only way to save much money is to purchase the building for about the value of the land or to use it just as it comes. If the building does not meet all the criteria listed in the earlier section Basic Requirements of Library Buildings, and it cannot be easily converted to meet these criteria, run away. Remember also that the costs of remediating issues regulated by the Environmental Protection Agency, like asbestos, lead paint, and buried fuel tanks, can be incredibly high, and that any library that requires ramps or steps to enter will always cause accessibility problems. Unfortunately, it often seems that when a town needs a new public library, someone who has been trying for years to ditch a dog of a building suddenly sees rescuers riding over the horizon like the Seventh Cavalry, with bugles blaring in the afternoon and public money fluttering like guidons.

Atria

Atria are large open spaces that connect two or more floors. Often they are topped with skylights. Atria look elegant, and in large buildings, they sometimes help people get their bearings, but they have a number of drawbacks. They take up immense amounts of expensive space, transmit noise, encourage children on upper levels to experiment with gravity, create temperature control problems, interrupt traffic flow, and usually have light fixtures that are difficult to maintain. Few small libraries have enough space for designers to suggest atria, but it is worthwhile being forewarned.

Difficult Maintenance

Libraries, by and large, receive extremely heavy use, and a building that looks elegant and handsome on opening day may be difficult to keep that way over the years. Some designers are very conscious of which materials are the easiest to keep looking good, but others are motivated more by vogues and costs. Among the most important questions to ask at the beginning of planning are these:

- What is the life span of the carpeting? Many kinds of carpet (such as cut pile) are too fragile for institutional use.
- If carpet tile is chosen to allow replacement of stained or damaged areas, how many years will pass before the replaced tiles stand out prominently from the older, faded tiles?
- How will you change your lamps (light bulbs)? Lots of fixtures are almost impossible to reach once construction scaffolding has been removed. Although librarians have been aware of the problem for years, new libraries open all the time with lights no one can reach.
- Will your light fixtures quickly fill with visible handfuls of deceased insects? Chandeliers shaped like hanging bowls pose particular problems. This is one additional strong argument for uplighting—dead bugs do not show.

- Are your wall surfaces sufficiently washable? Latex paints are very much in vogue now because they do not emit solvents while they dry, but they are harder to keep clean. Ask your designers to provide names of heavily used institutions with the kind of paint they are recommending. Instead of paint, many libraries use vinyl wall coverings.

- Where will you store your ladders? Many public libraries find they have no place for ladders, but so do academic libraries, which may find that campus operations and maintenance departments expect every building to provide spaces for its own ladders.

- Where will you store your lawnmower and snow blower? This is a particular concern of public libraries, which frequently find they have no legal space to store gasoline-powered equipment.

- How will you maintain resilient flooring? Many standard types of flooring, such as vinyl tile, require frequent stripping, waxing, and buffing. Other types, such as rubber tile, can be maintained by damp mopping.

- How will you maintain ceramic tile flooring? Actually, washing tile is easy. The problem is the grout, which is virtually impossible to clean. Unless you start out with very dark grout, most of the grout, but unfortunately not all, will soon be permanently dark. There are lots of pastel colors that do not qualify as dark but are frequently suggested.

- Is your furniture easy to maintain? Upholstery needs to withstand 100,000 or more "double rubs" (a person sitting down and then leaving a seat). Tabletops need to be made of strong laminates; wood is far too fragile, no matter how elegant it looks when it is new. Service desk tops, in turn, need to be made of materials stronger than everyday laminates; try solid-core laminates, Corian, or stone. (Some libraries with fragile tabletops or countertops end up covering them with glass, which is fragile, causes glare by reflecting light, and breaks at awkward moments.)

- Is the exterior of the building sheathed in durable material, such as brick or stone? Wood, EIFS, and some other materials may be initially attractive, but they tend to lead to very high long-term maintenance costs. (EIFS, which stands for Exterior Insulation and Finish System, is very popular for commercial storefronts these days, but it consists of just a skim coat of stucco over plastic foam. EIFS is easily dented or damaged, has to be repainted, and costs nearly as much as brick, and when water gets in behind it, tremendous structural damage can result.)

- Do doors have colored metal handles? With anything except chrome or stainless steel finishes, the color eventually starts wearing off.

An Example of an Effective Library Floor Plan

The floor plan that accompanies this chapter was developed for the public library of Tolono, a small town in central Illinois. The library was completed in 1997 and measures about 6,000 square feet. The architect was Gary Olsen of Champaign, Illinois, who has an extensive track record designing successful small public libraries. The floor plan illustrates a number of excellent design features.

- **Oversight:** A single staff member standing at the service desk can see almost the entire building by simply looking around. He or she can see people arriving and leaving, including people entering the program room and the restrooms; can see down all the book aisles; can see what is going on in the program room by looking through the windows; and can see children on the reading structure by looking through the two glass walls in the director's office. About the only thing hidden is the adult reading area with soft seating because the view is blocked by shelving.
- **Wayfinding:** People entering the library find it easy to orient themselves. The service desk is the first thing they encounter, enabling them to ask for help immediately. Children's services are located on one side of the desk and adult services on the other, which means that collections can be grouped logically. The same good sight lines that serve the staff serve users, who can see almost everything in the library when they are standing at the service desk.
- **Program room usable after hours:** The library is designed so that the program room can be used when the building is closed. People using the room have necessary access to the restrooms, but not to the rest of the library.
- **Quiet reading space:** By isolating adult soft seating in one corner, the library has protected adults who want to be as far as possible from the noise of children. The seating also offers north light and a view of the main street in front of the library.
- **Computers:** Computers are high-maintenance devices. Patrons using computers need more help than patrons reading books, and some libraries want to oversee the use of the Internet. Of all library furniture and equipment, computers need to be closest to service desks. In this library, computers are clustered near the service desk. To make this work, the library needed space, electrical wiring, and data connections.

The following three points are important ones, but they are not revealed by the floor plan.

Desirable Design Features

- Oversight
- Wayfinding
- After-hours program room
- Quiet reading space
- Computers
- Indirect lighting
- Attractive architecture
- Modest cost

Snappy Rules for Small Library Buildings

- Good looks do not ensure functionality. As someone once said, "It's always tempting to impute unlikely virtues to the cute."
- For any new structure larger than a bicycle shed, you need an architect.
- Creating excitement with light in a library is like creating excitement with steps in a nursing home.
- Even if your proposed library is no larger than a Porta-Potty, someone will call it a Taj Mahal.
- The right number of public entrances to a library is one.
- Skylights are too dark by night and too bright by day, but they make up for all of that by leaking.
- Basements in new library buildings cost nearly as much as extra floors, but they offer the additional advantages of subterranean darkness and moisture infiltration.
- Always insist that your architect show you how your proposed building can be expanded.
- Remodeling old buildings to create libraries is frequently a very bad idea because libraries have such specific structural requirements.
- All windows that can be exposed to direct sun must have some kind of adjustable shading (there is no such thing as "modern glass" that makes shades unnecessary). High windows that are out of reach can be a particular source of trouble. Watch out for so-called "monitor" structures—raised portions of roofs with glass on all four sides—and shun cute little windows halfway up sloped roofs.
- When selecting an architectural firm, pay limited attention to awards. Architectural awards are not given for comfort and functionality.
- When you are planning a new library building, people with other plans for the money will insist that the Internet has made libraries obsolete. They are wrong, but be prepared to refute them.
- Although the people who approve building expenditures frequently understand the need to open new libraries with empty shelving, they simultaneously have a skittish fear of opening new libraries with unoccupied staff workspaces. Most libraries still have lots of available collection space long after most staff members are tucked cozily on one another's laps.
- Share the good information with your community yourself, but get your architects and consultants to deliver the bad news, since they can go home afterward.
- Delay means a smaller, cheaper building. Construction costs always increase faster than the value of money in the bank.
- A contemporary addition to a historic building may eventually become a painfully dated addition to a historic building.
- Exposed steel ceiling beams, naked electrical conduit, and raw concrete floors do not constitute "truth."
- Always make sure that your programmers and designers are different people. If your programmer is a librarian with a wide knowledge of library architecture rather than an architect, you will end up with a far more balanced source of input on your project.
- When you ask your architect how to change the lamps (light bulbs), he may say, "Use a lift." This is about as helpful as being told to "use a screwdriver" when you ask how to rebuild a carburetor.

- **Indirect lighting:** Almost all of the library's lighting is bounced off the ceiling.
- **Attractive architecture:** The building is a handsome structure with interestingly complex cathedral ceilings.
- **Modest cost:** Because the architect was able to create a striking design while employing standard construction techniques, the building was constructed of durable materials at a very reasonable cost.

This library was the result of extensive staff input, a carefully written building program, and an architect who had the skill and library knowledge to combine function and good design.

Getting Help

If all of this sounds complex, that is because it is. Unless you already have two or three library building projects under your belt, you will be a lot better off if you start out with experienced assistance. If you are a public librarian, try your state library development office. If you run a school library or corporate library, talk with your facilities managers, but do not expect them to understand the special space needs of libraries without indoctrination or outside assistance. Similarly, expect campus architects to bring great strengths in terms of planning, campus standards, and quality construction but sometimes to have little knowledge of the practical needs of library buildings.

Hiring an experienced building consultant to prepare a program (and preferably to stay on the design team to forestall bad design ideas and to walk you through the steps of the process) will always help and will frequently prevent serious errors. Also, be sure the architect selected for your specific project has a track record of designing libraries that work.

Remind your employer that building libraries is exhausting for librarians, and that you will need all kinds of special consideration and loving care during the entire process.

Ask me for free assistance (in moderation) at fschlipf@illinois.edu or 217-898-1393.

Further Reading

American Library Association, Library Administration and Management Association, Buildings and Equipment Section, Functional Space Requirements Committee. *Building Blocks for Planning Functional Library Space.* Lanham, MD: Scarecrow, 2001.

Dahlgren, Anders C. *Planning the Small Library Facility.* 2nd ed. LAMA Small Libraries Publications Series. Chicago: American Library Association, Library Administration and Management Association, 1996.

Illinois Library Association. "Sample Surveys." In *Serving Our Public: Standards for Illinois Public Libraries*, 74–88. Rev. ed. Chicago: Illinois Library Association, 1997.

McCarthy, Richard C. *Managing Your Library Construction Project.* Chicago: American Library Association, 2007. (I strongly disagree, however, with his belief that architects should do the programming.)

Sannwald, William W. *Checklist of Library Building Design Considerations.* 5th ed. Chicago: American Library Association, 2009.

Schlipf, Fred. "The Dark Side of Library Architecture: The Persistence of Dysfunctional Designs." *Library Trends* 60 (2011): 227–55.

———. "Expanding and Remodeling Carnegie-Era Library Buildings." *Library Trends* 62 (2014): 556–80.

Schlipf, Fred, and John A. Moorman. "Let There Be at Least Half-Way Decent Light: How Library Illumination Systems Work—And Don't Work." Unpublished paper. Available at www.fredschlipf.com/presentations.html.

———. "The Public Library Construction Process: From Problem Recognition to Ribbon Cutting." Unpublished paper. Available at www.fredschlipf.com/presentations.html.

Wrightson, Denelle, and John M. Wrightson. "Acoustical Considerations in Planning and Design of Library Facilities." *Library Hi Tech* 17 (1999): 349–57.

Governing Boards and Governmental Relations

John A. Moorman

A *governing board* is the entity responsible for the operation of the library. The term *governmental relations* refers to the process whereby the library deals with entities that have funding or governing relationships with it. This chapter defines the types of governing boards, explains the roles of the governing board and director in operating a library, and discusses what is necessary for a good director-board relationship.

Types of Governing Boards

Libraries have many different types of governing boards:

- School librarians generally report to the principal of the school they serve. In turn, the school board governs the school.
- Special libraries usually report to someone within the hierarchy of the entity of which they are a part. This individual, in turn, reports to the entity's board. It could be a for-profit company's board of directors, a legal firm's partnership board, or a hospital's board of directors.
- Public libraries have a wide variety of governance. Some libraries report directly to the governmental entity, be it a city or county, without any sort of an advisory board. Other libraries have a board of trustees, which may have full or partial governing authority for the operation of the library. These boards may be appointed or elected. A third type of public library governance is the district library where the library serves a legally defined area and the board is elected and has taxing and full governing authority.
- Academic libraries generally report to an institutional administrator who, in turn, reports to the board of the institution.

Role of the Governing Board

- Set policy
- Hire director
- Determine budget
- Other duties as specified by company policy or law

Roles of the Director and the Governing Board in Library Operations

The relationship between the library's governing body and the director of the library is a major determining factor in the successful operation of the library. It is important that each party understands its role in the operation of the library and adheres to that role in library operations.

A good board member will have a working knowledge of all laws applicable to the library, be well acquainted with the community, have a working relationship with those who serve on municipal and county councils, and regularly attend meetings of the board and participate in regional and national conferences and workshops to enhance his or her knowledge and skills.

The director's role is to operate the library under the guidance of the policy established by the board. He or she should have final authority over who is hired to staff the library, set procedures based on board policy for library operations, and represent the library on local, state, and national levels. A good director, like a board member, should know the local and state officials with whom he or she needs to liaise in the course of operating a library. The director should actively seek out opportunities through workshop and conference attendance to upgrade and enhance his or her skills.

Any successful library operation requires a partnership between the director and the board. While policy determination is the role of the board, the director and staff need to play an advisory role in the setting of any board policy. Good policy is the result of staff experience and knowledge, coupled with the board's understanding of and appreciation for the community the library serves.

To be effective, the library board needs to understand library operations and procedures. When a new member is appointed to the library board, it is essential that he or she receive an orientation session on his or her new responsibilities. This session can be conducted by the library director and the chair/president of the board. The orientation session should cover the following:

- Bylaws and format of library board meetings
- Expectations for member participation
- Library's planning document
- Library's budget and current financial situation
- Presentation of the *Trustee Handbook* developed by the state library/library association
- Any legal documents relating to library services
- Library policies
- Library Friends/Foundations organizations
- Introduction to library staff
- Tour of library building(s)

Essentials for a Positive Board-Director Relationship

Six factors are core to establishing and maintaining a good relationship:

- Hiring process
- Trust
- Respect
- Honesty
- Communication
- Accountability

In hiring a director, the board must take the time to make certain that the individual chosen for the position is the one who best fits the needs of the institution and the community that the library serves. Sometimes, in the desire to complete the search process, the board may select an individual who does not quite fit the needs of the library or with whom the board does not have a level of comfort. The concept that he or she will "grow into the position" is a very dangerous one and usually does not work.

Likewise, before accepting an offer to become director of a library, the individual needs to look closely at the board as well as at the institution, its staff, and the community it serves. If there is doubt that the board is one with which the individual can work, the individual should heed his or her instincts and look elsewhere for employment.

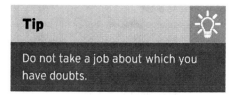

Tip

Do not take a job about which you have doubts.

Trust is the key to any successful board-director relationship. There has to be trust by both the board and the director that each will act within acceptable boundaries, that each has the best interests of the library in mind, and that each can be counted on to act wisely when any situation arises.

How is trust established? It is the end result of the final four factors listed previously. There must be respect by each party for the other party. The board must respect the director for his or her skills and knowledge and, likewise, the director must respect board members for what they bring to their role as board members. Respect is shown by how each is addressed, both in public and in private, and by how well ideas and concerns are received, listened to, and acted on.

Without honesty, no successful board-director relationship can endure. Sometimes honesty is painful, but it is essential to establishing and maintaining any successful relationship, and the board-director relationship is no different. Both parties need to be honest about their perceptions of library operations, services, relationships with the community and its leaders, and how they perceive each other. Both the board and the director need to be able to accept that neither is perfect and acknowledge when mistakes are made (as they always will be). Sometimes the hardest thing to say is, "I made a mistake on this one," but that acknowledgment is an essential part of any successful relationship.

FIGURE 11.1

Evaluating the Board

1. Do we as a library board meet regularly and have a written agenda distributed in advance?
2. Do all of our board members attend the meetings regularly?
3. Does each member actively participate in the discussion and decisions?
4. As a board do we plan an orientation program for new members?
5. Has the library adopted a written statement of clear and specific objectives, which serves as a basis of services and activities?
6. Is there a written policy manual?
7. Are the statements of objectives reviewed every year and revised if necessary?
8. Is our librarian included in board meetings and expected to present a monthly report to the board, either written or oral?
9. Does our board report regularly to the appropriating body and to the community with statistical, financial, and human interest facts?
10. Do members of the board and staff attend system and state library meetings?
11. Does the library provide funds to pay expenses of such meetings?
12. Are you familiar with the state statutes and city ordinances that govern your library operation?
13. Are you familiar with local library history?
14. If all the other trustees were to resign tomorrow, would you be prepared to take over, at least temporarily, as president?
15. When visiting another town, do you ever go to its library to look around?
16. Do you attend all meetings of the board?
17. Do you do your library homework?
18. Are you courteous to fellow trustees, even when you disagree with them?
19. Does the librarian, after gathering the appropriate information, meet with the board or a committee of the board to determine needs?
20. Is our budget estimate based on the current year's expenditures plus cost changes, expanded service, standards of good services, and the library's objectives?

21. Does the board formally adopt the budget at an official meeting before submitting it to the governing body?
22. Do members of the board participate in the presentation of the budget to the governing body?
23. Do you have a policy for accepting gifts, monetary as well as real property?
24. Are you taking full advantage of all existing funding programs—local, system, and state?
25. Is a systematic accounting of funds maintained by the librarian or someone delegated to this particular job?
26. Do all board members receive monthly financial statements that include the budget, current, and year-to-date expenditures with balances for each line item?
27. Do you have written, up-to-date job descriptions for all positions?
28. Are your salaries comparable to those paid in your community for comparable work, and also to the scale of other libraries of comparable size?
29. Does your staff have vacation and sick leave with pay, and an opportunity to participate in Social Security, retirement, and health insurance?
30. Does your staff have comfortable working conditions such as adequate light, heat, ventilation, and work- and restrooms?
31. Is your staff encouraged and helped to get in-service training through paid time and travel expenses to attend professional meetings and workshops?
32. Does your library service all parts of the community: geographic, economic, educational, occupational, social, retired, etc.?
33. Is the library dedicated to real service rather than to mere storage of books?
34. Does your collection meet the needs of the entire community?
35. Does the library take full advantage of the services offered by the library system?
36. Do you visit your library regularly?
37. Do you let your librarian administer the policies you make?

Source: Swan 1992, 37–39; used with permission.

FIGURE 11.2

Director Performance Appraisal

Board of Trustees
Annual Performance Appraisal
Library Director

Colleagues:

Please complete this form with a numerical rating and comments that support your rating:

> **5 = Outstanding.** Performance exceeds performance standard to a significant degree.
>
> **4 = Exceeds Performance Standard.** Performance goes beyond performance standard to some degree.
>
> **3 = Fully Meets Performance Standard.** Performance completely meets performance standard.
>
> **2 = Partially Meets Performance Standard.** Performance needs improvement to meet performance standard.
>
> **1 = Below Performance Standard.** Performance fails to meet performance standard.

Ongoing Responsibilities:

1. Administers the library according to approved Board policies.
2. Provides an adequate number of highly qualified staff members necessary to meet the needs of library patrons in a professional manner.
3. Prepares the budget in consultation with the Board and regularly updates the Board on current expenditures.
4. Communicates his/her vision for the development and improvement of the library to his/her staff, the Board and the community through the establishment of short- and long-range strategic planning goals for the library.
5. Oversees the library's program of public relations, including, but not limited to, active participation in community groups, such as Rotary, Chamber of Commerce, local newspapers, willingness to speak to community groups, etc., to inform and promote library services and activities.
6. Keeps abreast of advances in library service, is active in library organizations, and attends appropriate meetings, workshops, and conferences.
7. Develops and maintains professional working relationships with city and county officials and staff and local state legislators that are beneficial to the operation of the library.

Board Relations:

8. Facilitates open and honest communication between administration, staff, and Board.
9. Regularly reviews and updates policies for adoption/revision by the Board.
10. Implements Board decisions in a timely manner.
11. Acts as technical advisor to the Board and keeps them informed of changes in library legislation and standards.

(continued)

FIGURE 11.2 (continued)

Staff Relations:

12. Delegate's responsibility and authority to staff members in a way that empowers them to do their jobs well and is perceived as fair and equitable.
13. Encourages and offers regular opportunities for training and development.
14. Sets an example for the staff by exhibiting integrity, honesty, dependability in dealing with staff, public, and Board.

Specific Goals for Current Year:

List goals developed at the last evaluation with space for individual comment after each goal.

How would you rate the overall job performance of the Library Director (taking into consideration your own assessment and the assessment of his/her performance by his/her department heads)?

What suggestions for improvement would you offer?

Please consider the following question that we will discuss in CLOSED MEETING:

What suggestion would you make for a salary adjustment (e.g., count cost-of-living increase)? An amount or percentage beyond that?

Source: Williamsburg Regional Library 2005; used with permission.

Communication is at the core of developing and continuing this positive relationship. There are many means of communication, some better than others. Good communication contains several core elements: it is regular, operates through agreed-upon channels, is done in a respectful manner, and takes into consideration the needs of the institution and the time needs and expectations of both the board and the director. Both the board and the director should work diligently to see that neither is caught by surprise over any action or event. If either is blindsided by something, then it is time to seriously examine the channels and methods of communication. The ability to disagree civilly and with respect for each other is a skill that is often lacking but is an essential part of the communication process.

Accountability, the final factor in the establishment of a good board-director relationship, has two elements. The first is that the board and the director both must accept accountability for their actions. It is easy to blame the other party for what went wrong, and it might work for a short time, but in the long run, it is fatal for the relationship. The second is that both parties must continually look at themselves and evaluate their performance and progress.

I believe that it is just as important for the board to evaluate itself as it is for it to evaluate the librarian. A good tool for a board to use to evaluate its members is presented in figure 11.1, which offers a list of questions that will help you focus on how well your board is doing.

This document should be looked at on an annual basis and the results of the evaluation used in planning board activities and training. The director is the hire of the board and should be evaluated by the board on an annual basis. Several approaches can be used for this evaluation; see figure 11.2 for an example. Whatever approach used should be consistent, fair, and useful and a tool for further growth and development.

What causes a board-director relationship to go sour? Usually it is the result of one or more of the six core factors becoming absent. Communication is poor, respect nonexistent, trust lacking, honesty gone or expressed in counterproductive ways, and accountability for actions absent from the scene. How can the situation be corrected? Depending upon the severity, several steps are possible. If it is minor, the board and director can sit down and work through their differences and hopefully reestablish a good working relationship. However, in many cases, the rupture is beyond simple repair and other remedies are needed. These vary from calling in local individuals skilled in conflict resolution to work with the board and director, to hiring special consultants who have experience working with boards and directors in such settings, or to requesting the help of outside agencies with experience in board-director relationships. One good source for locating assistance is the library development department of your state library. This entity should have a variety of resources available to consult.

If all else fails, then there are two options, neither one easy nor pleasant. The director is the employee of the board and usually serves at its pleasure, particularly in the public library setting. However, the director may have a contract that specifies certain obligations on the part of both parties and outlines how the contract may be terminated. Thus, the first option is that the director is fired or asked to resign. The second is that the director resigns, as he or she cannot fire the board. Sometimes, one or the other is the only result possible. If either happens, it should be handled in a respectful manner by both parties, although this is often not the case.

Governmental Relations

The secret to establishing a successful working relationship with local government entities is much the same as that for working successfully with a library board. There must be trust, respect, and good communication for the relationship to succeed.

The working relationship between the board and local government is a cooperative venture between the board and the director. Hopefully, the library board contains individuals who have friendships or good working relationships with members of the local governing boards, whether they are city or county. Always make good use of these relationships and understand whether difficulties exist between certain board members and certain members of either city or county governing bodies.

The library director should work to establish good working relationships with the administrative heads of local government. In some instances, the relationship will, of necessity, be closer than others, as the library director may be considered a head of a department of the local entity while the library board operates in only an advisory capacity. Again, the skills to work on are good communication, respect for each other, and honesty. A good understanding of the local political scene and how it operates is essential to working with local government. Without that, any library director will never be successful in his or her relationship with local government. The library director is a participant in the political process and, to be successful, must acknowledge this and develop the skills necessary to operate successfully in this arena.

In working with library directors, boards, local government, and administration at all levels, it is essential that the individual or the entity as a collective body give whomever they are dealing with the same respect, honesty, trust, and communication that they expect to receive. The whole of this chapter can be summed up succinctly in the phrase "Do unto others as you would have them do unto you." All the rest is but icing on the cake.

Conclusion

There are three essential elements to any successful working relationship, including the ones discussed in this chapter. These elements are respect, trust, and good communication. While good communication can begin at the start of any relationship, trust and respect must be earned, which takes time and effort, but their accomplishment is at the core of good library relationships.

Further Reading

Minow, Mary, and Thomas A. Lipinski. *The Library's Legal Answer Book.* Chicago: ALA Editions, 2003.

Owen, Patricia. *A 21st-Century Approach to School Librarian Evaluation.* Chicago: American Association of School Librarians, 2012.

Reed, Sally Garner, and Jillian Kalonick. *The Complete Library Trustee Handbook.* New York: Neal-Schuman, 2010.

Tucker, Virginia, and Marc Lampson. *Finding the Answers to Legal Questions: A How-To-Do-It Manual.* New York: Neal-Schuman, 2010.

References

Swan, James. 1992. *Working Together: A How-To-Do-It Manual for Trustees and Librarians.* New York: Neal-Schuman.

Williamsburg Regional Library. 2005. "Director's Evaluation Form" (internal document). Williamsburg, VA: Williamsburg Regional Library.

Friends Groups and Foundations

John A. Moorman

Friends of the Library groups and Library Foundations are organizations that exist to support the library with which they are affiliated. They are 501(c)(3) nonprofit entities, as recognized by the Internal Revenue Service (IRS).

If the funds available to the small library from its funding sources were adequate to cover all library needs as well as provide for special programs and services, there would be no need for either Friends groups or Foundations. However, this is not the case. While there are a lucky few small libraries with ample resources, they are the rare exception. For the rest, dependence on Friends groups and/or Foundations are necessary if a special or enhanced program is to be provided, a new or renovated facility is to have all the furnishings desired, or new or innovative programs or collections are to be possible. While there are Friends groups in special and school libraries and Foundations from which they may draw assistance, these are the exception rather than the rule. In discussing Friends groups and Foundations, this chapter reflects the public and academic library experience.

Friends Group Formation

Friends groups, commonly referred to as Friends of the Library, are entities whose sole purpose is to support the activities of the library of which they are a part. Through a variety of fund-raising activities, to be discussed later, they raise monies that are then made available for library programs, services, or projects.

How are Friends groups formed? While there may be a group of citizens, or students and faculty, with interest in the library who come to the director or governing board with the desire to assist the library, in most cases, the library director takes the initiative and works with the board of trustees, interested citizens, and the academic community to initiate a Friends group. Before a Friends group is formed, each of the following questions needs to have a positive answer:

IN THIS CHAPTER

✓ Friends Group Formation
✓ Friends Group Fund-Raising
✓ Friends Group Role
✓ Library Foundations
✓ Care and Feeding of Friends Groups and Foundations
✓ Conclusion
✓ Further Reading

- Is there sufficient interest in forming the Friends group?
- Are there individuals who are capable of taking a leadership role?
- Do those interested in forming the Friends group know the role and limitations of a Friends group?
- Does the formation of the Friends group have the active support of the board of trustees or the library's governing body?
- Does the library have projects in mind for the Friends group?
- Is there sufficient seed money to start the Friends group?
- Is the library director willing and able to take the time necessary for the formation of the Friends group?

Once all these questions have been answered in the affirmative, the group is ready to be formed. A Friends group, to be effectively organized, needs incorporation papers, a set of bylaws, and 501(c)(3) status with the IRS.

The first step toward getting organized is to get the group of interested citizens together, explain to them the purpose and role of the Friends group, and solicit initial volunteers to serve on the organizing board. Generally, the library director, working with the board of trustees, will hand select this first board. The board members then become those listed in the incorporation papers filed with the office of the secretary of state. This is a simple process with only a small cost involved.

While the library director can manage this step and the other steps of starting a Friends group, it is best to involve an attorney in all steps of the process. This is where seed money comes in. It is wise to have on hand $1,000 to get the Friends group started. Some groups will have a local attorney who is willing to do the work involved pro bono. However, even with this assistance, the process will cost either $400 or $850 depending on anticipated income over a four-year period to get 501(c)(3) status determination from the IRS.

Once the incorporation papers have been received from the secretary of state's office, the next step is to develop bylaws for the Friends group. Figure 12.1 provides a template for Friends bylaws developed from the author's thirty years of experience with Friends groups.

Once the bylaws have been approved, next is the process of obtaining 501(c)(3) status with the IRS. This can be a lengthy process. In most cases, the Friends group will obtain a preliminary certification from the IRS that is good for a certain number of years. At the end of this time, paperwork must be filed to show that the Friends group is doing what was stated in the initial request to obtain permanent certification.

Paperwork for the initial certification is substantial. As mentioned earlier, it is best to have the assistance of an attorney in completing the paperwork and communicating with the IRS during the process. Information required for this step includes the group's incorporation papers and bylaws, information about the parent organization, and a fund-raising plan and budget for several years' operation. The IRS charges for 501(c)(3) certification, as mentioned earlier. However, this is an essential step for, without it,

For Further Information

Besides local attorneys, use the following source to assist you in filing 501(c)(3) papers with the IRS: www.501c3.org.

FIGURE 12.1

Friends Bylaws

Bylaws of Friends of Anytown Library

Article 1   Name

The name of this organization shall be Friends of Anytown Library.

Article II   Purpose

The purpose of this organization is to create public interest in and greater use of the Anytown Library, to provide financial support to the Library, and to sponsor cultural and related programs. The intention is to supplement and encourage the work of the staff of the Library with the Friends, a separate group, supportive rather than authoritative.

Article III   Membership

Membership in this organization shall be open to all individuals, organizations, businesses, and clubs in sympathy with its purposes. Each organization or individual member shall be entitled to one vote.

Article IV   Officers

The officers of this organization shall be a President, Vice President, Secretary, and Treasurer.

Officers shall be recruited and nominated by a committee chosen by the Board defined in Article VI. The nominations shall be submitted in writing to the membership two weeks prior to the annual meeting. Additional nominations may be made from the floor at the annual meeting with the consent of the nominee.

Officers shall be elected by a majority vote of those members in good standing present at the annual meeting. The term of office shall be for one year and shall begin on the first day of January following the annual meeting.

Vacancies shall be filled by appointment by the Board until the next regular election.

Article V   Duties of Officers

The officers shall have the usual duties and authorities customarily exercised by officers of a nonprofit organization.

The President shall be an ex officio member of all committees.

The Vice President shall succeed to the President's position upon the inability of the President to serve in that office.

The elected officials shall set up the necessary standing committees. The chairs of the committees and at-large members of the Board shall be appointed by the President. Each chair shall select that committee's members.

Article VI   Board

The Board shall consist of the elected officers of the organization, the appointed committee chairs, and members-at-large. The Library Director and the Chair of the Board of Trustees shall serve as ex officio members of the Board.

(continued)

FIGURE 12.1 (continued)

Meetings of the Board shall be held at least four times a year. The President may call special meetings.

Members of the Board are expected to attend all regular board meetings. Any member of the Board who misses half of the meetings in any calendar year may be asked to resign by a majority decision of the officers of the Board.

One-half of the members of the Board shall constitute a quorum.

Article VII   Meetings

The organization shall hold at least one meeting a year.

The annual meeting shall be held on a date, to be determined by the Board, near the end of the fiscal year. Members shall be notified in writing at least one month prior to the date of the meeting.

The Board may call a special meeting of this organization at any time.

Only those members in good standing shall be allowed to vote at any meeting.

Article VIII   Dues

Dues shall be paid annually and are good for one year's membership from date of payment. The Board shall set the membership contribution schedule and categories.

Article IX   Fiscal Year

The fiscal year shall be from January 1 to December 31. All funds shall be deposited to the account of Friends of Anytown Library and shall be disbursed by the Treasurer as authorized by the elected officers or the Board.

Article X   Disposition of Assets Upon Dissolution

In the event that this organization is terminated or dissolved, all assets belonging to the organization will be transferred to the Anytown Library to be disposed of as recommended by the Library Board of Trustees; however, if the named recipient is not then in existence or is no longer a qualified distributee or is unwilling or unable to accept the distribution, the assets of this organization shall be distributed to a fund, foundation, or corporation organized exclusively for purposes specified in Section 501(c)(3) of the Internal Revenue Code.

Article XI   Amendments

Amendments to these Bylaws may be made at any meeting of the general membership by a two-thirds vote of those present and in good standing. Notification in writing of the proposed amendments shall be given to each member at least two weeks before the meeting at which voting is to take place.

Article XII   Parliamentary Procedure

Robert's Rules of Order, Revised, when not in conflict with these Bylaws shall govern the proceedings of this organization.

contributors to the Friends group will not be able to take a tax deduction for their contributions.

A solid connection between the Friends and the library is important in the establishment and operation of the Friends group. Some Friends groups can, due to board member interests, become disengaged from their purpose and seek to serve other roles, such as supporting groups other than the library, or become interested in day-to-day library operations. As indicated in the sample bylaws, it is important to have the library director and the president of the board of trustees as ex officio members of the Friends board. This gives the Friends information on wider library operations and helps them to feel more a part of the library's service to the community. The library director needs to work closely with the Friends board and serve as the point person for the presentation of library needs to the Friends.

> It is important that the library director be an ex officio member of the Friends board.

Friends Group Fund-Raising

To support library operations, the Friends group will need a source of income. Many Friends groups employ used-book sales as their primary source of income. Whether the sales are annual, semiannual, monthly, or combined with an ongoing Friends book sale in the library, these events need a core of volunteers to be successful.

Questions that need to be positively answered prior to conducting a sale include these:

- Is there a sufficient source of books and materials for the sale?
- Can weeded library materials be included in the sale?
- Is there adequate storage for materials between sales?
- How willing and able are library staff members to assist with sale setup and disassembly?
- If the plan is to host an ongoing book sale, is there adequate display space for books in the library?
- Does the Friends group have adequate volunteer labor to conduct the sale?
- Is there committed leadership among the Friends group to organize and conduct the sale?

Another question that must be faced before starting book sales as a source of revenue is whether this is a niche in your community that is already taken by another group. If so, can you work with this group to include the Friends as a part of the other group's operation? If not, it might be best to look at other fund-raising opportunities.

Other fund-raising opportunities are as many as there are libraries. One popular source is a Friends gift shop in the library. This can be a valuable source of revenue. However, before beginning such an operation, be sure to address the following questions:

- Is there space in the library for such an operation?
- Is this space in a prominent location and is there a long-term commitment to use this space for a Friends gift shop?
- Are there enough volunteers to keep the shop open on a regular schedule?
- Is there a niche in the community that the Friends gift shop could exploit so that it will provide a unique source of items for sale?
- Does the gift shop have the support of the library director and the board of trustees?
- Is there a business plan for the gift shop's operation that indicates its viability?

If these questions have positive answers, then this could be a good source of income as well as a way to inform the community about the Friends group and to garner additional members.

Friends Group Role

The sole purpose of the Friends group, as indicated in the bylaws in figure 12.1, should be to assist the library in improving its services and programs. It is important for the library director to have a strong voice in selecting the ways that the Friends group assists the library. The library director knows the library's needs and can prioritize them for the Friends group and suggest ways in which its funds could be best used.

Some Friends groups place limitations on what their funds may be used for while others do not. Limitations might include using funding only for collections and programs or for special areas of the library, such as children's materials and programming. Some Friends groups sponsor the library newsletter or special programs or an annual lecture series. However the Friends group supports the library, it is important that the rationale behind the decision is understood and agreed to by the Friends group, the library director, and the board of trustees.

Library Foundations

Library Foundations have a similar purpose to Friends groups in that their sole role is to obtain funds for the library. Where they differ is in their emphasis. Whereas Friends groups serve to assist the library on a short-term basis through support of programs and special events, a Library Foundation is more long-term in nature. It works to establish an endowment and manage that endowment to provide funds for projects that are more major in nature, such as building projects, major purchases like outreach vehicles, or long-term support of collection areas or programs. There will also be the need for expertise in financial management on the Foundation board.

A Library Foundation is set up similar to a Friends group. It needs incorporation papers, bylaws, and must file with the IRS for 501(c)(3) status. Without the 501(c)(3) designation, donors to the Foundation will not be able to claim their donations as tax deductible on their income tax returns. In addition, the Foundation will need to adopt an investment policy.

Before beginning a Library Foundation in a small library, be sure to ask the following questions:

- Is there a need for a Foundation or can the Friends group be expanded to serve in this role as well?
- Are there long-term library needs that would benefit from the formation of a Foundation?
- Are there community resources that can be tapped to provide funding for a Foundation (e.g., wealthy individuals or community businesses with donation possibilities)?
- Is there a sufficient source of capable board members for the Foundation and a commitment to serve from these individuals?
- Is there support from the library director and board of trustees for the establishment of a Foundation?

Once these questions are answered, the formation of the Foundation can proceed. The bylaws will be similar in nature to those for a Friends group. Many Library Foundations are closed groups with the membership being the board of the Foundation. In some libraries, the board of trustees of the library selects Foundation board members. In any case, the library director and president of the board of trustees should be ex officio members of the Foundation board.

Sometimes Library Foundations are set up as the result of a large donation through a bequest to the library. This is fine, but the earlier questions still need to be answered before a Foundation is established. There may be other ways of accepting a large bequest.

A Foundation, unlike a Friends group, needs to have plans in place for increasing its funding base. This means working with local attorneys, banks, insurance agents, and certified public accountants to make their clients aware of the Foundation's availability as a qualified recipient of resources for continued community growth and enhancement.

Care and Feeding of Friends Groups and Foundations

Both Friends groups and Library Foundations can wither on the vine. Like grapes, they need constant care and tending to produce successful results for libraries and their users.

Factors in the care and feeding of these groups include the following:

- Make sure that there is constant communication between the library and both the Friends group and the Foundation. Have joint meetings of all bodies on a regular basis to share programs and ideas.
- Provide both groups with fundable projects and programs so that they will continue to feel needed and a part of the library effort.
- Head off early any attempt to deviate from their established purpose of assisting the library.
- Have a commitment by the library director to be an active participant in the processes and work programs of both groups.

Another unstated role of the library director and Board of Trustees is working with local funding agencies to make certain that these bodies understand that funds from these sources are not to be considered a part of the library's normal revenue stream; that is, a Friends or Foundation dollar does not allow the funding agencies to drop their contributions to the library by that amount. This can be difficult but is essential if the Friends group and/or Foundation is to be successful in its role and mission in support of the library.

Conclusion

Friends groups and Library Foundations can be a vital component of the services that the small library provides to its community. Through being sources of additional funding beyond that available through governmental or parent body appropriations, they enable the library to increase and enrich the programs and services offered to library users. They may also make it possible to have new or expanded facilities years earlier than otherwise possible.

For a library director, either group can be a godsend. However, do not underestimate the time and commitment of a director's time that either group will take if it is to be successful. A library director will need additional skills as well as time because Friends groups and Foundations are made up of individuals with egos and agendas of their own, and for either group to work as a harmonious whole, diplomacy and tact will be needed on a regular basis. Do not hesitate to use praise and recognition (sometimes even more than is actually warranted), for these are the only payments these individuals will receive.

Does a small library need both groups? Not necessarily. Know your own community and know which individuals have the time and willingness to volunteer their services to the library. In many instances, the Friends group may be expanded to include the functions served by a Library Foundation.

The following Further Reading section includes material that is useful in working with both Friends groups and Library Foundations, resources that also are core background materials for this chapter's discussions. The development of the material for this chapter comes from the author's over thirty-eight years of experience with Friends groups and Foundations in four states. Chapter 14, "Development," goes into further detail about how libraries may raise additional funds to provide programs and services.

Further Reading

Dowd, Susan, ed. *Beyond Book Sales: The Complete Guide to Raising Real Money for Your Library.* Chicago: ALA Neal-Schuman, 2013.

Goldberg, Benjamin. *Forming and Funding Public Library Foundations.* 2nd ed. Chicago: Public Library Association, 2005.

MacKellar, Pamela H., and Stephanie K. Gerding. *Winning Grants. A How-To-Do-It Manual for Librarians with Multimedia Tutorials and Grant Development Tools.* New York: Neal-Schuman, 2010.

Maxwell, Nancy Kalikow. *The ALA Book of Library Grant Money.* 9th ed. Chicago: ALA Editions, 2014.

Thompson, Ronelle, and Ann M. Smith, comps. *Friends of College Libraries.* 2nd ed. CLIP Note #27. Chicago: Association of College and Research Libraries, 1999.

United for Libraries, a division of the American Library Association. www.ala.org/united.

Community Partnership Development

Janet L. Crowther and Barry Trott

Partnerships are formal, collaborative efforts between two or more community organizations that support the mission, vision, and goals of each of the participants. The phrase *library partnerships* generates hundreds of thousands of hits in a search on the Internet. Libraries of all sizes say that they are partnering to achieve their goals. However, when libraries describe their partnering efforts, there does not seem to be any consistent definition of what the word *partnership* means. Since developing a formal partnering program involves a commitment of staff and resources, it is especially important for small and medium-sized libraries to have a clear definition of what partnering means before they set out to establish collaborative ventures.

Partnerships and partnering have become important to libraries of all sizes for a variety of reasons. Businesses, nonprofits, and government agencies are all looking to establish collaborative efforts. It is useful to understand what drives these different sectors to look for partnerships. In many cases, these sectors will seek out partnerships for financial reasons. As budgets are cut or tightened at the local, state, and national levels, nonprofits and government agencies may seek out partnering opportunities to supplement declining revenues or to bolster decreased budgets. For all three of these sectors, partnerships offer the opportunity to increase visibility in the community and to establish leadership in the community on specific issues. At the same time, partnerships can also be a way for organizations to maintain a positive community image. Increasingly, grant funding organizations either require or reward collaboration, making partnering essential to organizations that operate with grant-based funding. All of these groups, businesses in particular, may look at partnering as a way to gain access to new customers and to expand the markets for their services.

For these reasons, and more, partnering is a strategic tool that can provide opportunities for libraries. Partnerships offer libraries a new way to connect with their communities. Rather than working at the grassroots level, trying to reach individuals one at a time, partnering works through gatekeepers in the community. The library establishes a relationship with these gatekeeper organizations and works through them to expand its reach into the community.

Libraries have every reason to be wary of faddish management trends, but partnering is a tool with an external focus on the community and the library's role therein. Since the mission of any library—public, academic, or special—is directed at serving its community and demands engagement with that community, partnership development will continue to be an important mechanism that libraries can use to fulfill their missions.

In this chapter, the authors explore partnerships for libraries using the Williamsburg Regional Library model and examine the issues, challenges, and opportunities that collaborative efforts afford for libraries. They conclude by assessing the realities of partnering for small libraries.

Partnership as a Strategic Tool

Partnering is a strategic tool used to achieve the library's goals. It is one of many tools that libraries can use as they seek to fulfill their missions. Many libraries would define partnering broadly, as simply working collaboratively with another institution to develop a program or service. However, a true partnership between organizations is one that involves shared goals, visions, and responsibilities as well as a long-term commitment by both partners.

Williamsburg Regional Library (WRL), a medium-sized public library in southeastern Virginia serving approximately 70,000 residents, has developed a partnership program that balances the needs of the library and its partners. To capture the variety of possible collaborative relationships with all parts of the community, WRL developed a tiered approach to partnering that includes one-time events with another organization as well as the more involved and expansive relationships that are true partnerships.

The WRL partnering model establishes four levels of partnership—glances, dates, engagements, and marriages—that take place between the library and a community entity:

- Glances are any form of contact between the library and an outside organization. A glance can range from a phone conversation or e-mail from an outside group to a visit or participation in a meeting. A glance is the most basic level of contact between two organizations.
- Dates are any one-time or shorter-term collaboration between the library and an outside organization. Most library outreach efforts would usually fit into this category. A date usually involves a specific event or program that the library puts on with some collaboration from a community partner.
- Engagements are more formal arrangements between the library and a community partner to pursue some longer term goals. Engagements, by their very nature, usually either evolve into

marriages or dissolve. The engagement is a way for the partners to try out a relationship without making an extensive, long-term commitment. Grant-funded collaborations, supported by soft money, can be an example of an engagement between the library and a partner.

- Marriages are longer-term collaborative agreements. They should include a formal, written agreement between the library and the community partner in which the partners agree to common goals, develop initiatives, and share in both the risks and the rewards of the relationship. Marriages are established where there is an opportunity for each of the partners to bring resources of similar value to the relationship and commit to an ongoing alliance.

Regardless of how your library decides to define partnering, it is essential that there be agreement within the institution about what a partnership is. This definition will be useful both internally and externally. Within the library, a clear understanding of partnering makes it easier for staff to see how partnership development fits within the mission of the library. Externally, a clear definition of what a partnership is means that possible partners will be better able to understand what the library needs to get out of a collaboration.

There are many tools that libraries can use to achieve their goals. Marketing the library's resources and services can bring new users into the library. Library outreach efforts take the collections, programs, and services of the institution out into the community, reaching users who may not be able to physically access the library buildings. Working with funding bodies and library boards to build the library's assets by adding additional internal resources is an essential ingredient to remain viable. All of these tools are important ways that libraries can advance their missions and goals and best serve their users. Community partnership development is simply another mechanism that libraries can use to achieve their vision. These tools are by no means mutually exclusive, and libraries should explore all of them as they plan for the future.

Partnering Scaled to Fit

It is important for libraries to understand that developing a community partnering program will require staff time and resources. This can be a particular concern for smaller libraries that may not be rich in either of these areas. It is important for smaller institutions to remember that it is possible to scale partnering programs to the needs and size of almost any library. In fact, partnering offers some particular advantages to smaller libraries that can make the time spent on developing a partnering program even more worthwhile:

The Williamsburg Regional Library Partnering Model

The partnering model developed by the Williamsburg Regional Library is based on several principles:

- Partnering needs to be done strategically and flows from the organization's strategic plan.
- To develop partnerships, a library must assess what it can offer to potential partners. By developing this list of assets and strengths, it will be better able to see what it is that the institution can bring to a collaborative effort.
- All segments of the community are considered as potential partners.
- Few other institutions in a community reach as broad a population as does the public library. This is one of the strengths that the library brings to any potential partnership.
- Partnering is a library-wide effort. To be successful, library partnering efforts need to be embraced by everyone in the organization, from the library board through administration to library staff.
- Partnering is a formal process that involves establishing structures.
- Successful community partnering requires establishing clear communication channels both within the library and between the library and its partners.
- The development and managing of partnerships need to follow directions established by the library.
- The library needs to periodically evaluate both individual partnerships and partnering as a tool.

Williamsburg-James City County Schools Partnership

For many years, the Williamsburg Regional Library (WRL) provided a variety of programs and services to the Williamsburg–James City County Public Schools (WJCC). These included classroom reading visits, library tours, author visits, and database training for media specialists and students. As the library began to explore the value of collaborative relationships, it became clear that the existing relationship with the schools provided the foundation for a more formal partnership to be developed. The partnership between the library and the schools is based on four principles:

1. The mission statements, core values, and goals of WRL and WJCC reflect common purposes to support the educational goals of students and their families and to work collaboratively through the community to achieve excellence.
2. Historically, WRL has been an active participant in enriching area schools' access to children's programming, library collections, student study space, and meeting room space for adult education. Formalizing this relationship acknowledges the value of the library's support. It also creates a strengthened framework that will enable the relationship to grow through system-wide planning and coordination.
3. While the partnership draws on the unique strengths of the two institutions, it also benefits from serving the same city-county population.
4. The community is best served by the library and school system working together toward common goals.

The goal of the relationship is "to (a) bring a love of reading and books to area students; (b) teach students to access and analyze information in all formats; and (c) support individuals in their goals for lifelong learning."

This partnership has brought all of the services and programs that WRL offers to the schools together under a single umbrella. In this fashion, the library has been able to make better use of library resources and staff time and avoid duplication of effort between library divisions. At the same time, WPL has also been able to offer these services and programs to schools in a more consistent way. Rather than simply reacting to an individual principal or teacher coming to ask for a program, library staff can now work through the communication mechanisms established by the partnership to offer programs and services more directly to all the schools, so that no school feels left out. In addition, this partnership has expanded the opportunities for the library to reach both students and teachers. WPL now reaches new teachers prior to the start of school through their orientation training and introduces them to the collections, programs, and services that the library offers. The library extends special privilege library cards to all classroom teachers and school system professionals who work directly with students. Working with the media specialists, the library has also been able to expand the promotion of its database collection to students and teachers. The library has seen significant increases in database use in the past few years, attributable in part to the relationship with the schools. The partnership with the schools has also allowed WRL to tap into student and faculty feedback on the library as well as information on community trends and demographics. This valuable range of information helps the library plan for the future. As part of a project to improve services to teens, the library worked through the schools partnership to survey middle and high school students about their needs and interests. During a recent round of strategic planning, the schools helped WRL to set up student focus groups to gain insight into what directions teens thought would be best for the library. An additional benefit that the library has gained from formalizing its relationship with the schools is the recognition that the library does a great deal to support the school system. Bringing all of the library's work with the schools under the partnership reinforces the two-way nature of the relationship between the schools and the library. Each institution has roles and responsibilities that it must take on for the partnership to be successful. Formalizing the collaboration ensures that neither partner is bearing all of the responsibilities, and that each partner is gaining what it needs to be successful.

- Choosing the right partner can actually save the library time by allowing small libraries to bundle initiatives together.
- By developing collaborative relationships, the library can reach out into the community in a more focused fashion. For instance, rather than working with each of the individual schools in your community, your library can partner with the school system and combine all of its school-related projects under a single relationship.
- By working through organizations that are community gatekeepers, the library can reach a broader audience than it could on its own.

How does the library scale its partnering efforts? It is essential to ensure that whatever partnering efforts take place are closely tied to the library's mission and vision. Partnering must be strategic, that is, tied to where the library is trying to go. Partnership development should not be adopted simply because it is a trendy topic. There have to be clear goals that the library is trying to achieve and that can be addressed through collaborative efforts. So, a clear mission and vision are crucial first steps to successful partnership development.

Once your library has an understanding of where it wants to go, then you can begin to look at what you want your potential partnerships to accomplish. WRL has developed six reasons for partnering that guide staff in considering partnerships and guide administrators in prioritizing partnering possibilities:

- Reach new library users.
- Reach current library users in a new way.
- Tap into unique community assets and strengths.
- Gain support for library resources and/or programs.
- Gain valuable community feedback.
- Create new resources.

Partnerships established at WRL must successfully achieve at least one of these goals. Some partnerships may achieve more. If a relationship does not meet at least one of these requirements, a partnership should not be established.

In a smaller library, one way to keep partnering efforts manageable is to choose fewer reasons for partnering. Instead of six reasons, perhaps look at one or two. Look at what is currently important to your institution, and build your reasons around a particular need. It may be that the current priority for your library is to reach new library users. If this is the case, then your partnering efforts should primarily focus on looking for relationships that will help you to meet this need. Remember, partnering needs to bring some specific benefit to the library. Too often, libraries are willing to give without expecting any return, but a true partnership must have some reward for the library. Each year, it will be important to look at the current reason or

Williamsburg Health Foundation Partnership

The Williamsburg Health Foundation (WHF) is a local nonprofit organization that supports health-related community programs in the Williamsburg area community through a community grant fund. A partnership with the library was established in 2000 to set up the Funding Research Center, with $15,000 from the WHF. The center contains print and electronic resources for local residents and nonprofit agencies to use in seeking grant opportunities and in developing and administering funding programs. These resources are provided in the library and through the Funding Research Center website, hosted by the library.

In addition to providing funding for building a collection of materials related to fund-raising and grantsmanship, the partnership involves the development of programs for nonprofits in the community, covering such topics as legal issues and technology issues for nonprofits. In 2005, an e-mail discussion list, hosted by the library, was established under the auspices of the partnership to improve communication between local nonprofits. In 2014, more than 100 nonprofit organizations were exchanging information through the list.

By working through a community gatekeeper, this partnership has enabled the library to enhance its collections, improve services, and to build a lasting relationship with an important community organization. Through the partnership, the library has been able to reach a new user group, area nonprofits, and to increase the importance of the library within the community.

reasons for partnering to determine whether they are still valid or whether there is a more pressing need to address.

Issues, Challenges, and Opportunities

Developing a partnering program is a challenge for all libraries. It requires that library staff and administration be willing to take on a new way of thinking about the institution and its mission, which can create a level of discomfort in the initial stages. As smaller libraries embark on building partnerships, they will find that they face some challenges that are particular to their size.

The most common challenge that small libraries will encounter is realistically assessing what they have to offer to a potential partner. The size of your library will place some limits on the assets that are available. There are several areas where these limits may have an effect on partnering efforts:

- **Staff limits:** Typically, a smaller library may have only one or two professional librarians. Although partnership development is by no means limited to those who have a master's degree in library and information science, the library may find it harder to find staff with a library-wide view or project management expertise to become involved in partnering.
- **Facility limits:** Many potential partners will be attracted to collaborative efforts with libraries to gain access to library facilities. In a smaller library, there may be limited meeting room space available to use as a bargaining chip in partnership negotiations.
- **Financial limits:** Although partnerships do not always come with a direct price tag, there can be costs involved in partnerships that may be difficult for smaller libraries to absorb. These could include developing promotional materials and extra staff time.
- **Time limits:** Small institutions will find that becoming active in partnering means that decisions have to be made about the allocation of staff time. Partnering initiatives may cause conflicts with other programs and services that the library is trying to offer.
- **Administrative limits:** It is not uncommon for smaller institutions to have boards of governance that take a more active role in the day-to-day affairs of the institution. This offers both opportunities and challenges to smaller libraries. The governing boards often are well connected in the community and can open doors to potential partnerships. At the same time, there is always the potential that a board member will see partnering as a way to promote pet projects. The library needs to be careful that favoritism does not set aside library priorities for partnership development.

In all these cases, the limits are by no means insurmountable. Addressing them will require careful analysis and work on the part of the library staff and administration. Questions to ask when you are considering partnership development as a strategic tool are, "Is community partnership development a priority for the library?" and "Why is it important?"

In addition to these internal challenges, libraries that serve smaller communities (be they public, academic, or special libraries) will find that the smaller size of their communities presents challenges as well. A smaller and/or rural community will, by its nature, present fewer potential partners. This is particularly the case when looking at partnering with government agencies. Consolidation of services such as motor vehicle departments, post offices, and hospitals into regional centers means that small-town libraries may find it harder to locate strong local partners.

In smaller or more rural communities, obstacles to partnering may arise that are less common in larger settings. The past relationship of community members to the library may play a bigger role in smaller communities than it does elsewhere. Political issues between members of the community may also have a larger impact on small libraries, which may find themselves caught in the middle of disputes.

Despite all of these concerns, partnership development does offer small libraries the same opportunities that it offers to larger institutions. Partnering can be an important tool to make the library relevant in the community. Successful partnerships build support for the library that can be drawn on during funding periods or when difficulties arise. Establishing a formal partnership can result in increased recognition for existing work that the library is already doing. Finally, partnerships make the library valuable to community institutions, not just to individuals. Again, this kind of support can prove invaluable to the library as an institution. Basic promotion of the library and a stronger connection to the community may be the best reasons for smaller libraries to consider partnering.

The Realities of Partnership

There are some realities to keep in mind as you explore the opportunities afforded by developing community partnerships.

- **The library must have something to offer:** Assess your library's assets and strengths to understand what it is that the library can bring to the table in a partnership. It may be physical space, staff skills, collections, unique role in the community, the library name, or other items. But you must to have something to offer. Partnering is a shared relationship.
- **Partnering is not a substitute for sound funding:** While some partnerships have a financial component, particularly grant-funded collaborations, do not count on getting funds

to supplement your current budget through partnerships. It is particularly crucial that your funding agencies understand this, and that they do not penalize the library for developing successful partnerships. Also, it is important that the library recognize that grants which require evidence of collaborative efforts should be sought only if there is a strong need, not simply because they offer a partnering opportunity.

- **Partnering is not going to solve existing problems:** If there are staffing problems or communication issues in your institution, do not look to partnering to put them right. In fact, it is most likely that these sorts of issues will be exacerbated by the time and effort needed to establish a partnering program. Things do not have to be perfect (where are things ever perfect?), but you do need to have strong internal communication and a staff that is willing to work interdepartmentally in order to partner successfully.

The First Steps

Having considered the advantages and disadvantages of establishing a partnering program, and concluded that it is something that your institution wants to implement, these are your next steps:

1. Know where your institution wants to go. Have a clear plan in mind, and use the library's mission, vision, and goals to guide your partnering efforts.
2. Carefully and honestly assess what your library has to offer to a potential partner.
3. Do not be afraid to ask potential partners what they have to offer to you. Remember that partnering is a shared relationship.
4. Think about your community in a broad fashion. Do not limit yourself when considering potential partners. Nonprofits, government agencies, businesses, and other libraries all offer possibilities for collaborative endeavors.
5. Look at what you are already doing collaboratively as a starting point for partnership development. What organizations in the community are you currently working with? Are these relationships meeting the library's priorities? And which of these relationships would benefit from formalization?
6. Know why you are entering into a particular partnership. Be clear about the reasons for each relationship you develop.
7. Remember that partnership development is only a tool, not an end in itself. It should serve the library, not the other way around.

Further Reading

Crowther, Janet L., and Barry Trott. *Partnering with Purpose: A Guide to Strategic Partnership Development for Libraries and Other Organizations.* Westport, CT: Libraries Unlimited, 2004.

Diamant-Cohen, Betsy. *Children's Services: Partnerships for Success.* Chicago: ALA Editions, 2010.

Sagawa, Shirley, and Eli Segal. *Common Interest, Common Good: Creating Value through Business and Social Sector Partnerships.* Boston: Harvard Business School Press, 2000.

Development

Patty Purish O'Neill

Over the past decade, the fund-raising landscape has changed significantly. The introduction of electronic solicitations, online giving, and crowdfunding coupled with donors who expect greater organizational transparency, prefer to give to a specific need, and want to see the tangible impact of philanthropy have forced organizations to think differently about how to successfully secure private funds. This chapter examines traditional modes of fund-raising for libraries and what it takes to implement a comprehensive advancement program for the twenty-first century.

The key elements of a comprehensive advancement program include communications, fund-raising, and stewardship. Library administrators must be prepared to be involved with all aspects of advancement activities in addition to the day-to-day management of the organization. Securing private funds continues to become increasingly important because other streams of library funding are not growing and in many cases have been reduced.

Having a strategic plan for the library helps define fund-raising needs and allows resources to be aligned with priorities. This provides a focused effort on those opportunities that will advance the library, serves as a baseline for fund-raising goals, and encourages buy-in from key stakeholders to view development as everyone's responsibility.

Communications

Libraries need to have a comprehensive communication plan to support the organization's overall fund-raising and external relations efforts. This has traditionally been accomplished by periodic print newsletters, but now it is important to utilize multiple communication channels to more broadly share the library's story. In addition to print media, leveraging the library's website, developing an online newsletter, and incorporating social media into the communication plan result in reaching a larger audience.

Websites communicate operational and general information about the library. They are excellent tools if stories and news are updated frequently. A well-designed and well-maintained website serves as a key resource for prospective and current donors to learn more about the library's services, its leadership and governance, and its mission and goals. A staff member needs to be responsible for managing the website to ensure the information is relevant and timely.

Dedicating a section of the website for development stories helps articulate the library's focus on private support and creates a space for gift- and donor-related stories. Communicating the impact of philanthropy is critical to garner donor confidence and promote transparency as donors want to understand the tangible impact of giving. This is also a good place to include a wish list of needs and the funding amount for each item. Many donors value the convenience of online giving so providing this option on the website encourages contributions. Incorporating the ability for online gifts also allows the library to send electronic solicitations with a link to the online giving site.

Fund-Raising

Annual fund campaigns provide expendable, and often unrestricted, support for organizations. These gifts help supplement the operating budget and fund new initiatives and opportunities that emerge during the year and that may not otherwise have a planned budget. Traditionally, annual funds have been fueled by mail and telephone appeals. These requests typically are designed to (1) acquire new donors to the library, (2) renew donors from the previous years, and (3) secure increased gifts from consistent donors. Annual funds attract a broad base of donors at all levels and build a pipeline of potential major/special gift prospects.

Building the potential pool of annual fund donors starts with the registered patrons of the library. Supplement this group by also including library board members, volunteers, employees, community leaders, local school librarians/media specialists, and library special event participants. Including a guest registry at the library and a vehicle on the library's website to allow individuals to self-identify themselves as interested in learning more about the library and its programs/resources are other opportunities to add to the prospect base.

Effective mail appeals are personalized with an inside address and familiar salutation based on the donor's relationship with the organization. The signatory should be a peer, either a volunteer, board member, or patron, who is passionate about the library and is a donor. It is also important to include a specific ask amount in the letter. For current or previous donors, the ask amount can be calculated based on the last gift amount to encourage an increased gift. A personalized gift ticket, prepopulated with donor name and address, should be sent with the mail appeal and suggest several gift

In 2012, charitable giving in the United States totaled more than $316 billion, an increase of 3.5 percent over the previous year, demonstrating the magnitude of philanthropy's effect on nonprofits in the country. More than $41 billion supported education.

(Indiana University 2012)

levels, including the one that is printed in the letter. Inserting an addressed return envelope provides an important convenience for the donor to return a gift promptly.

With the increased cost of postage, fund-raising appeals sent by mail can be expensive. It is important when planning annual fund strategies that return on investment be considered and tracked from year to year. New donors are the most costly to acquire, so carefully consider the best approach and the most cost-effective strategy to solicit their support to help ensure resources are utilized wisely.

Telemarketing fund-raising often complements mail solicitations, although it is becoming more and more challenging. With the National Do Not Call Registry and the decrease in the number of households maintaining a landline, contact rates on phonathons continue to decline. Many large organizations outsource this service to companies that are equipped to hire, train, and manage a phone center. This is efficient but loses the personal touch with the organization since the paid callers have no affiliation to the organization. Callers can rely only on the script to answer questions or talking points about recent accomplishments. Smaller organizations can easily coordinate a volunteer phonathon to supplement the mail appeal. Scheduling several nights of calling hosted at a central location with volunteers using either office phones or cell phones is a simple way to organize such an effort. The volunteer callers are provided calling sheets for each contact and a script to use for the call. Having a staff member present to coordinate the effort and be available for any questions asked of the volunteer callers is recommended.

More and more, organizations are now making a second ask to benefactors that have already donated during the fiscal year. This practice was once considered taboo but actually is very successful. Developing a comprehensive plan for annual fund appeal activity is critical to ensuring each funding request is timed appropriately and does not become a nuisance to the recipient.

Libraries have successfully launched crowdfunding campaigns to raise money for specific projects. These are short-term campaigns, typically online, to fund a specific project. This type of fund-raising rallies the collective impact of many donors who want to support the designated project, and if done well, it can attract new donors to the library. There are many examples of libraries utilizing this approach to fully fund new projects. Key success factors for a crowdfunding campaign include strategic communication before, during, and after the campaign. Sharing the success of the effort with donors is an opportunity to communicate the immediate and direct impact of these gifts.

Major or special gift fund-raising takes a more personal approach than annual fund solicitations. These gifts are larger than annual gifts and can include a multiyear pledge, and the process engages a variety of library stakeholders. It is most successful when matching a donor's interest with a funding priority identified by the library. Cultivating meaningful relationships with major gift prospects allows library staff to understand the donor's passions and how to leverage for larger support of the library. Major gifts can fund an endowment or a new project. The library's director and other members of the leadership team need to be engaged with major gift prospects. Securing a major gift is a process that involves meeting with the donor in person and developing a gift plan. Through these conversations, the library staff may need to prepare a written proposal that outlines the need for support and the impact a major gift will have on advancing the library. The size of the gift often dictates the time needed to successfully cultivate and finalize a major gift.

Deferred or planned gifts are those commitments that donors make through an estate provision. There are many technical details required to ensure the gift documentation utilizes proper legal language, so it is important for libraries to have this information available for donors. Making donors aware of this gift option can encourage donors to consider a future gift. Stewardship of these donors, even if they are not making current outright gifts, is important, so developing a plan to recognize those who make an estate provision cannot be overlooked.

Many organizations utilize special events as fund-raisers. Auctions, benefit dinners, and golf tournaments are examples of this type of activity. These events are labor intensive and require a lot of attention to detail to execute successfully. Libraries with a small staff need to consider if the investment of time and energy to plan and implement a benefit event will yield the financial return necessary for it to be a success. These events are an opportunity to attract new donors and volunteers while building visibility for the library through public relations efforts promoting the event.

Stewardship

The marketplace for charitable dollars is becoming more competitive, with the number of nonprofit organizations growing by 25 percent over the past decade, making donor stewardship a vital aspect of an advancement operation. Stewardship brings donors back to and fosters trust in the organization. Successfully communicating the impact of gifts and engaging donors in meaningful ways that make them feel genuinely appreciated are expectations of donors. If these are not provided, donors may redirect giving to other organizations.

Stewardship needs to be genuine and supported by a variety of library personnel. The director's leadership team should play a role in addition to development staff. Working together as a team to identify opportunities for donor engagement creates broad support for this important responsibility across the organization. A personal thank-you note for gifts and pledges is the starting point for donor stewardship. Strong development programs create an acknowledgment system based on gift amount and donor type. For example, a first-time donor should receive a thank-you note with a message that welcomes them to the community of supporters for the library.

For donors making larger gifts, several thank-you notes from different individuals at the library are appropriate. Personal phone calls from staff or board members are also an excellent way to immediately acknowledge a patron's support.

Communicating the impact of individual gifts is an important part of stewardship. Creating opportunities for donors to meet beneficiaries or participate in programs funded by private support strengthens the connection between the donor and the organization. Utilize newsletters and websites to profile donors and the initiatives supported. These stories demonstrate appreciation to the donor and can inspire others to consider making similar gifts.

Special events for donors are another way to express appreciation to groups of benefactors. It is important to ensure that events are scaled to the organization and fit with the donor base. Soliciting ideas for stewardship events is an excellent way to engage donors and board members. Consider developing individual stewardship plans for major donors.

In the development cycle, effective stewardship is essentially cultivation for the next gift. It can also be the step that is most easily overlooked, so it is important that libraries have a documented strategy to properly express appreciation to donors at all levels. Be creative with stewardship efforts; the more customized the approach is for the donors, the more likely it will appear genuine and be more meaningful for the donor. Stewardship highly influences decisions about future gifts to the organization.

Conclusion

Building a base of donors and growing private support are a critical aspect of any library operation. Regardless of the size of the organization, the work that feeds into a successful development strategy is the responsibility of many, not just those in the development office. A solid fund-raising plan that is grounded in the library's mission and vision provides a strong framework from which staff and board members can work in concert to advance the aspirations of the library.

Further Reading

American Library Association. *Frontline Fundraising Toolkit*. Chicago: American Library Association, 2011. www.ala.org/advocacy/sites/ ala.org.advocacy/files/content/advleg/advocacyuniversity/frontline _fundraising_toolkit/fft.pdf.

Cottrell, Megan. "Libraries Find Success in Crowdfunding." *American Libraries* (May 12, 2014). www.americanlibrariesmagazine.org/ article/libraries-find-success-crowdfunding.

Moorman, John A., ed. *Running a Small Library: A How-To-Do-It Manual*. New York: Neal-Schuman, 2006.

Oguntoyinbo, Likan. "Demonstrating the Difference." *CASE Currents* (November–December 2012): 16–21.

Simic, Curt, and Laura Simic. "A Matter of Trust: Stewardship Comes Down to Demonstrating Values." *Currents* (November–December 2012): 13–14.

References

Indiana University, Lilly Family School of Philanthropy. 2012. *Giving USA 2012: The Annual Report on Philanthropy for the Year 2011.* 57th Annual Report. Giving USA Foundation. http://givingusareports.org.

Part III

Public Services in the Small Library

Adult Services

Alicia Willson-Metzger

Adult services involves all the help provided to library users on a daily basis. An adult services library professional deals primarily with the over-eighteen crowd, providing services such as circulation and reference services. This chapter offers assistance in the variety of opportunities that are presented to individuals providing services to adults in the small library. Topics include the basic provision of reference service, advising readers on items they may wish to read, how to conduct a reference interview, ideas for successful library displays and their management, outreach to the community outside the library's walls, and how to deal with the many unusual patrons encountered in the course of everyday work.

Reference Work

In the first class meeting of a reference class somewhere in the Midwest, a professor smiled and said, "I can tell you essentially all you need to know about reference work in one sentence: 'The patron is always wrong.'"

Shock! Horror! The professor did not mean that patrons are as a rule either uninformed or not too bright. He meant that (1) people often have a difficult time verbalizing precisely what it is that they need and (2) it can be a long trip from what they say they need to what they actually do need. Since the librarian is their tour guide on that trip, it is up to the librarian to point out what would best serve their needs, and this is done through conducting what is popularly known as the reference interview.

What is the reference interview? The phrase makes the whole process sound decidedly more formal than it needs to be. It is simply the give-and-take discussion between the reference staff member and the patron seeking information. Part of what needs to be determined in the opening moments of a discussion with a patron is what sort of response is required, including the breadth and depth of the answer. Doing this involves knowing the types of questions likely to be asked. There are different terms used for a variety of question types, but, generally, questions can be broken down into two categories: directional and informational.

Directional questions are precisely what they sound like: "Where's the bathroom?" or "Where are the study rooms?" While responses to these questions are generally no-brainers, do keep in mind that you work in your library every day, and the patron probably does not. If you tend to give awkward directions, if it is at all possible, walk the patron over to whatever area he or she is trying to find.

Informational questions will require some effort to answer. These sorts of questions can range from "How do I use your online catalog?" to "I need five book reviews of an extremely obscure work only my professor has heard of." These are the sorts of questions the reference interview will help you to answer.

The Reference Interview

While for many years, the reference interview consisted of either a face-to-face or phone encounter, advanced technologies have ensured that this is no longer the case, no matter whether your library is small or large. As the employee of a small library, you may have the opportunity to engage in other forms of reference contact beyond the traditional, including chat, text, or e-mail reference.

The In-Person Reference Interview

- The reference interview essentially begins before either you or the patron starts to speak. Make eye contact with people who seem to be about to request assistance; look pleasant and attentive. This does not mean that you have to greet someone as though he is your long-lost relative. If you are naturally somewhat reserved, a pleasant "How can I help you?" will get the interview ball rolling.
- Let the patron tell you what he or she needs in his or her own words without your interrupting.
- If you are not sure of precisely what the patron requires, you can rephrase the question, hopefully without sounding like an awkward parrot. ("Do I understand correctly that you need information on the economic history of Baltimore?")
- Use open-ended questions to glean more information from the patron regarding the specific information needed. Open-ended questions involve a response other than "Yes" or "No" and are invaluable in discovering what the patron actually requires. These questions typically seek to discover some of the following bits of information:

    What information format the patron requires. ("Did your professor specify whether you are supposed to use books, articles, or websites?")

The depth/breadth of the information needed (aka "Why do you need this information?"): Although a whole generation of reference librarians seem to have been trained never to ask this one most obvious question, generally because it has been perceived as an invasion of the patron's privacy, if properly and carefully phrased, the question can elicit a response guaranteed to help you answer the patron's inquiry. The information needed for a five-minute how-to speech on analyzing a piece of modern art is markedly different from that needed for a senior thesis on themes in the works of Basquiat.

Where the patron has already looked for information: Doing this can achieve two goals. (1) You will find out where to begin in helping the person, and (2) if the patron is missing the mark in his or her choice of reference tools, you will be able to guide him or her to the right one(s).

When the patron is already having problems in locating information before his or her initial reference inquiry, the difficulties tend to fall into three broad categories:

- The patron is using the wrong information tool for the job. This can be a matter of a mismatch in scope (e.g., using the online catalog to find journal articles or using a database such as Historical New York Times to find articles published yesterday) or, frequently, because the patron is using an unreliable, unvetted source of information, assuming it is a reliable tool (e.g., *Wikipedia*).

- Some aspect of the mechanics of using the resource is unclear; for instance, the patron wants only full-text articles but failed to notice there was a "full-text only" checkbox beneath the search box. In all fairness, this often results from the reference source's not being intuitively designed for a novice user. Particularly if the resource, either print or electronic, does not have an intuitive interface, tell the patron about its major quirks; this will, ultimately, save both of you a good deal of searching time.

- Your patron has developed the tunnel vision of the novice library user. Often, your user will envision only one way to describe and define a topic. Frequently, and which is even more frustrating for the user, it is an entirely viable description; it is not, however, how that topic is indexed by the Library of Congress or your user's favorite reference database. Help the user find synonyms for his or her topic; for instance, doing a keyword online catalog search on "Civil War" would certainly give the patron some items on the American Civil War, but so would searching "War of the Rebellion," "War of Northern Aggression," and "Ulysses S. Grant." Be a human thesaurus for your patron and, even more important, teach him or her how to use "see" and "see also" links, as well as subject heading links in online catalogs and periodicals databases, to find other information on a chosen topic. In addition, the patron may be relying on only one or perhaps a few tried-and-true resources for information. Novice patrons, upon discovering one database/tool that works well at least one time, will continue to use that resource time and again, regardless of whether or not it is the best tool for the job. This behavior frequently takes the form of using a general-interest database (e.g., ProQuest or JSTOR) to locate highly specialized articles on a topic. Steering patrons toward more relevant tools for their myriad reference needs is an important part of creating a self-sufficient library user.

Finally, and this is a *really* important rule in the book of reference "dos," do *teach* the patron how to perform the search for himself or herself. Although it is extremely tempting to simply do it for him or her, particularly if there is a long line of patrons waiting, you will only make more work for both of you in the long run. You will hear any number of reasons why the patron cannot do it for himself or herself—"I'm late for class." "You're so much better at this than I am." "I'm just no good at computers." Do not fall for any of it, because you will see the same person with the same question back at the reference desk over and over again. Be both patient and persistent. A big smile with an accompanying "Let me show you how to do this yourself" or "Remember yesterday when I showed you how to search for a title in World-Cat?" can begin to wean the patron from excessive librarian intervention. While it may take more than one encounter to keep the patron from relying on you exclusively to answer his or her inquiry, keep trying. The reference interview is ultimately one more teaching tool afforded to librarians. Do not waste the opportunity.

As the transaction comes to a close, ask the patron if you have answered his or her question and, even more important, mention that if it turns out that he or she has not found what was needed, to please come back for more help.

How to Blow the Reference Interview, or Problem Patrons in Our Midst

Everybody is different—this is a terribly banal observation, but one that is wholly relevant to reference work. Cultural misunderstandings and sheer human nature can disrupt the reference interview, and it is incumbent upon you, the person doing the helping, to avoid these misunderstandings as much as possible. Remember, one reference librarian's "difficult" patron is another's "quirky" or "interesting" patron. However the patron appears to you, you still have to learn to deal with him or her effectively. What follows is some simple advice for some of the more common distractions in reference work.

Language barriers: Any reference librarian, if he or she has not already, has to develop an ear for accents other than his or her own, and this does not necessarily mean the accents of international students. A former supervisor once remarked that a student she referred to as "the Hickory Hick" (the student was from Hickory, North Carolina) had stopped by to chat with her. The condescending attitude behind her remark was shocking. Because someone has an accent or uses nonstandard English, for whatever reason, does not indicate a lack of knowledge or intelligence on his or her part. It does, though, tell you that you may have to work a little harder to get to what the person needs. Do not be shy about repeating what you think a patron has said, just to make sure you have got it, and if you have to ask the patron to reiterate what was said, do it. While you may feel understandably awkward asking the patron to do this, such awkwardness is nothing compared to how you will feel if you send the person in the utterly wrong direction. Your positive attitude will go a long way toward making a success out of what otherwise could be a tricky transaction.

The "I'm having a bad day" patron: This patron comes to the reference desk with an air of anger and frustration even before either of you has said a word. The questions asked might indeed be laced with an undertone of combativeness, that is, "Well, you probably wouldn't know this . . ." or "I never can find anything in this place anyway, so I don't know why I'm asking . . ." To the best of your ability (this is nearly impossible for me, but I know it is good advice), ignore the extra snarkiness and proceed straight to the question that is hidden under the layers of anger. Stay calm; the anger, in all likelihood, is not directed at you personally, and, even more important, being combative in return gives credence to the person's inappropriate behavior. Getting a rise out of you might make the patron feel better, but it is not going to help you at all, and it will certainly make a bad situation even worse. If the patron's attitude becomes too combative to handle, either (1) politely excuse yourself so you can find someone else to help the person— sometimes a change of face can help—or (2) put the onus of the patron's behavior squarely on his or her shoulders: "What specifically is it that you would like me to do to assist you?" Most people will not be able to answer this question, and it will make them realize that they are being quite difficult, and at that point, you can move the dialogue to a higher level.

The homeless and/or mentally ill patron: The homeless and/or mentally ill patron has long been viewed as a problem within public libraries, although such patrons appear in every type of library; they are from every walk of life. They are grouped together here because many homeless patrons are mentally ill, and vice versa. Here are some basic tips for effectively dealing with them:

- Take their information requests seriously and answer them to the best of your ability. For instance, the patron who consistently requests tomorrow's newspaper or the one who needs rocket fuel for his rocket double-parked in front of the library (each honest-to-goodness questions from public library land) has a genuine concern. Taking the time to simply and seriously respond to the request is often all these patrons really want. No, you can provide neither tomorrow's newspaper nor rocket fuel for an imaginary rocket, but you can be respectful in communicating those facts.

- Although not all homeless and mentally ill patrons have issues with personal cleanliness and hygiene, many do. A trick (learned at the reference desk of a public library within a block of a homeless shelter) is to keep Vicks VapoRub in your desk, and before leaving for reference desk duty, put a very small amount in your nostrils. This is an unobtrusive and inoffensive way to deal with a very real problem that many people feel uncomfortable discussing.

- Compose a security/library behavior policy and have it approved by your library's board, or if you are in a small academic or special library, your administration. Clearly delineate those things you will and will not tolerate, and stick to it. Have your institution's lawyer vet the document to ensure its legality, and then post the policy in prominent places throughout your library, including on your library's website. Refer to it when indicating a patron's noncompliance. Have a good working relationship with your building's security guard (if you have one), and always keep emergency (police, fire, ambulance) numbers close at hand. Do not assume that these patrons will be difficult to the point of requiring a police presence, but do not be naive, either. Have all the resources at hand to deal with a sticky situation, and simply hope you never have to use them.

The "clingy" patron: This patron believes that you, and only you, can provide the reference assistance that he or she has come to count on. The patron is often lonely, horribly needy, and frequently may confuse the good help you have provided at the desk as a sign of friendship. Invariably, this patron shows up when you are not scheduled at the reference desk, when you are eating lunch at your desk, or when you are on your way to an important meeting. The reason this situation is a catch-22 is that, invariably, the patron likes and trusts you because you have provided excellent service in the past and knows you will continue to do so. You have also probably always listened, as librarians are all trained to do, to his or reference queries and (possibly endless) stories with great patience.

Although each of these falls under the category of "good service," you have to learn to draw the line somewhere. Do not be a doormat for this type of patron. If the person is becoming a problem, insist that he or she call before coming to the library to make an appointment to see you, explaining (if necessary) that your schedule is normally quite full, and in order to give the patron sufficient attention, you would like to make an appointment to assist him or her. Framing the issue in terms of how your undivided attention is a plus for the patron can help to stave off any offense that might be taken when you suggest an appointment. If the patron shows up without calling, do not hesitate to "be on your way to a meeting" or to have your colleagues intercept the person before he or she reaches your office. If the patron calls the desk and will not let you go, say you have a patron waiting for help (whether you do or not). Enlist the help of coworkers. Do not refuse to help the patron; after all, chances are the patron is a decent person with interesting questions. There are, however, other fish in the sea (or librarians in the office) who can assist him or her every bit as well as you can. Introduce the patron to one or more of them; make him or her feel special; tell the patron these other librarians will assist him or her with the greatest attention. In short, broaden the patron's narrow viewpoint a bit. Do not offend; just show the patron other people who can help.

Multiple patrons, one you: It is lunchtime and every patron in the library has descended on the reference desk, where you are working by yourself. What do you do?

- Always acknowledge the person or persons waiting in line. A pleasant smile accompanied by "I'll be with you in just a moment" establishes a relationship with the patrons and shows that you recognize their presence and the importance of their questions.

- If you know immediately that the person you are helping has an extremely involved question—say one that is going to take more than five minutes to answer properly—ask if you might quickly respond to any directional inquiries from people waiting in line. That way, they will go away happy and you will be able to focus your full attention on the involved question.

- Depending on the level of technological expertise available in your library, develop either hard-copy or electronic pathfinders for common research questions you receive day in and day out. Pathfinders are simple bibliographies, often with brief annotations, of resources readily available in your library. While not every reference resource lends itself to being placed on a library's website, pathfinders certainly do, providing another means of accessing this information for your patrons. Many libraries of varying sizes now use various content management systems for such guides; for instance, Springshare's LibGuides is an easy-to-use, relatively inexpensive product for producing professional-looking guides to your library's holdings.

- The phone rings, and rings, and rings—and you have still got that pesky patron with the involved question. Every library employee has a different take on this topic, but I personally like to handle the real live person in front of me first, politely asking the phone patron if he or she would be willing to hold for a few moments. If the phone patron does not want to hold, get his or her name and number and call back when your line of patrons is gone. You might also consider voice mail as an alternative to immediately answering the phone, allowing the call to go to a prerecorded message indicating that you are with another patron and will return the person's call as soon as possible. Doing this could prove a little tricky, as your public may think that you do not care to answer the phone, but it can offer an out for you during your busiest moments at the reference desk.

- Offer a service through which you can provide in-depth reference assistance by appointment, away from the reference desk. In my library, we call this a research assistance form and ask the patron to fill out a one-page form with such basic questions as "Where have you looked for information so far?" and "Specifically describe your information need." Once the patron has completed the form, you can make an appointment to meet with him or her, allowing enough time for you to do some preliminary research on the topic. Use this time to identify search terms and synonyms for the topic at hand; make a special effort to point out sources of information that the patron may not have considered, such as using Project MUSE in addition to ProQuest in his or her search. Post the form in a prominent place on your library's website to encourage use and commit to responding to appointment requests within a reasonable amount of time (i.e., within twenty-four hours of receipt). Follow up with the requestor promptly and schedule a time to meet that works well for both parties, and as with any reference query, when the meeting comes to a conclusion, provide the patron with your contact information in case he or she should have any additional questions.

Virtual Reference

Virtual reference is, in essence, a patron's communicating a question or questions to you electronically and your responding to these questions. These interactions may take place in several different ways: by e-mail, text, or chat, for instance. Which (or how many) of these methods of contact you choose to employ depends entirely on the depth of your staffing, the amount of money you wish to spend on the services, and your comfort level with the various modes of virtual contact. Each method is addressed in detail in this section.

E-mail reference: E-mail reference is probably the cheapest and easiest of the virtual reference services to implement. An e-mail address dedicated solely to reference inquiries can be a relatively low-tech, inexpensive way to provide virtual reference service. Consult with your systems administrator or with the person responsible for maintaining your server for the best way to go about this. Post the e-mail address in a prominent place on your website, or if you do not have a web presence, include it on your hard-copy library promotional materials, particularly on your library hours handouts and signs. It is helpful to make the e-mail address something that can be easily remembered (e.g., library@abc.edu). It is essential to have a set time (or times) for accessing this e-mail so you can tell patrons that their requests will be answered within a particular amount of time (to be determined by you). Committing to a twenty-four-hour turnaround time in answering is fairly standard; that way, you can check the e-mail once a day and have plenty of time to either answer the question or refer the patron to someone else who can answer it. If you think that you would not receive enough information from a patron through a free-text e-mail, post an online information request form similar to the research assistance form mentioned earlier to elicit as much information as possible. Clearly indicate that the patron must provide another form of contact information (e.g., phone number or alternate e-mail address) in case you have questions for him or her.

Text reference: Text (SMS) reference involves the text messaging of a question from patron to librarian. Text reference can often be a very inexpensive method of communicating with a patron; in the simplest model, the library can purchase a cell phone with a texting plan, kept at the reference desk, solely for the purpose of text reference. Alternatively, if staffing is more robust, the phone may be placed with a librarian—not necessarily at the reference desk—whose shift is dedicated solely to monitoring the cell phone for text messages. In addition to the dedicated phone line model, many low-cost services exist through which patrons can text their questions to a librarian who is monitoring an account on the computer. These services include LibraryH3lp (libraryh3lp.com), Mosio for Libraries (www.textalibrarian.com), QuestionPoint (www.questionpoint.org), among many others. These services allow easy tracking of numbers/types of questions, in addition to affording the reference librarian the opportunity to multitask by having the chat reference as part of the computer's setup.

Chat reference: Chat reference is the process by which a librarian and patron remotely engage in the reference interview through an Internet connection. The interaction is (for the most part) synchronous. Many companies offer chat interface products that offer libraries customization of their chat services, such as the storage of chat transcripts (good for evaluative purposes), patron FAQs (frequently asked questions), and the ability for both patron and librarian to browse webpages concurrently. Products include Springshare's LibAnswers (www.springshare.com/libanswers) and Altarama's VRLPlus (www.altarama.com/Products/VRLplus). The companies mentioned previously under text reference provide chat reference services as well.

Print versus Online Reference Resources

Great—now you have done the reference interview, but how do you find the answer to the question? A combination of online and print reference resources plus e-mail capability and a telephone can carry you through most reference inquiries. Having access, whether print or electronic, to the following basic reference resources is a must.

An unabridged dictionary: Especially in the public library, word spelling and definition questions are legion. *Webster's* and *American Heritage* are still among the best resources in this category. Online dictionaries, too, are equally helpful; check out *Merriam Webster* Online (www.m-w.com), Dictionary.com (www.dictionary.com), and the comprehensive online reference

Advantages and Disadvantages of Text Reference

Advantages

- Texting is good for simple, direct, ready-reference questions (hours, location information, etc.).
- Texting can be done virtually anywhere and is convenient, particularly for tech-savvy patrons. A trip to the library, which may be inconvenient, becomes unnecessary.
- Texting is anonymous. Shy patrons or those with sensitive questions may find it easier to use an impersonal method of making their inquiries.

Disadvantages

- The limited number of characters available for communication may make complicated reference interactions difficult.
- As with any electronic librarian-patron interaction, including chat, e-mail, or text reference, all visual cues and body language observed in a face-to-face encounter are lost, thereby further limiting what the librarian might be able to learn about the inquiry from an in-person discussion.
- Unless there are absolutely no distractions for either the patron or the librarian, texting can often fail to be a real-time interchange. Patrons, if not receiving immediate answers from the librarian, may disengage and look elsewhere for information. Librarians can feel as if they are sending information into a void unless the patrons respond immediately.

Advantages and Disadvantages of Chat Reference

Advantages

- Chat reference is convenient.
- The synchronous communication provided by chat reference is designed to be a conversation between the librarian and the patron.
- Chat reference avoids the necessary brevity of a texting interaction; therefore, a fuller explanation on the part of both patron and librarian is possible.
- Many chat reference products facilitate co-usage of a webpage or database between patron and librarian, thus giving the interaction a more in-person feel.

Disadvantages

- As with texting, chat reference is quite impersonal. A patron will not be able to identify or necessarily form an ongoing working relationship with a librarian over chat.
- Having to communicate each step and action taken to a patron who cannot see you can become somewhat tiresome. A significant portion of each interaction can be taken up by such written cues as "Please wait a moment while I check ..." simply because the patron does not witness what the librarian is doing.
- Simply put, it takes longer to type out directions than it does to verbally communicate them. This can be frustrating for both patron and librarian.
- It is sometimes difficult for the librarian to tell if the information given has been useful, particularly when the patron abruptly ends the chat.

source Bartleby.com (www.bartleby.com). Bartleby includes access to many standard reference sources (for free!), including the *Columbia Encyclopedia*, Sixth Edition; *World Factbook* (published by the Central Intelligence Agency); *Roget's II: The New Thesaurus*; the *American Heritage Book of English Usage*; the *Columbia World of Quotations*; *Simpson's Contemporary Quotations*; *Bartlett's Familiar Quotations*; *Gray's Anatomy*; and the *Columbia Gazetteer*. A number of literary anthologies are also included.

A general encyclopedia: Unless your library is hopelessly financially strapped, do consider purchasing either a hard-copy or an e-book version of a general encyclopedia. Free online encyclopedias such as *Wikipedia* are distinguished mainly by the wildly differing quality of their content; remember that such resources can be edited by anyone, anytime. The articles included are simply not consistently reliable resources of information and, particularly if you are in a small academic library, will not be considered by your faculty to be an acceptable resource for student research papers. Outstanding encyclopedias include *Encyclopaedia Britannica*, available in online and DVD formats; *The World Book Encyclopedia*, available in print and online formats, and *Encyclopedia Americana*, available online through Grolier Online.

A world almanac: Again, whether it is online or hard copy, a world almanac provides access to statistics, addresses, esoteric facts, and weather-related information. Popular almanacs *The World Almanac and Book of Facts* and *The Farmer's Almanac* are but two of the almanacs currently available on the market. Again, these items are also available, either directly from the publisher or through library jobbers, as e-books.

A world and/or road atlas: Geographical questions are always popular in almost every library. Make sure you have a current world atlas (countries' names and borders change more frequently than you think) and a detailed atlas for the United States. Such atlases include *The Times Atlas of the World* and the deservedly popular *Rand-McNally Road Atlas*. Several free online services provide maps and directions to and from worldwide locations. Among the best are Mapquest (www.mapquest.com), Yahoo Maps (maps.yahoo.com), and Google Maps (maps.google.com).

Phone information: While for many years print phone books were a staple of a basic reference library, local phone companies are beginning to reduce or eliminate hard-copy phone books entirely. However, there are several excellent free phone number/address resources on the Internet, such as AnyWho (www.anywho.com) and the 411.com database (www.411.com). Each of these sites provides name, address, and mapping capabilities as well as a reverse lookup feature that will allow you to discover what name and address are associated with a particular phone number. (Cell phone and unlisted numbers are not available in these resources.) Have these sites bookmarked on your reference computer for easy access.

Subject resources: The specific resources you choose in this area will depend on the focus and scope of your reference work. Subject encyclopedias and dictionaries are available in every discipline; decide which are most important for you and purchase them.

Periodical indexes: Increasingly, these resources are being published in an electronic format and are unfortunately increasingly expensive as a result. Leading publishers of general-interest online periodical databases include ProQuest (www.proquest.com), EBSCO (www.ebsco.com), and JSTOR (www.jstor.org). There are also, however, very good free periodical indexes online, including Google Scholar (scholar.google.com). Another good free resource is the FindArticles website (www.findarticles.com). Each of these databases indicates whether full-text access to the listed articles is free or not. (If there is a charge listed, try ordering the item through your interlibrary loan service, or send the patron to the local public library for interlibrary loan. Frequently, there is no charge incurred for interlibrary loan services.)

Finally, part of the decision regarding whether to have print, online, or mixed reference resources is your and your staff's preference regarding the availability and accessibility of computers on which to access reference resources. The vast majority of reference works, no matter what the format, are expensive. If you do want to develop a basic print reference collection and cannot afford new titles, keep an eye out for large public library book sales, in which entire reference sets, often only one year out of date, are offered to the public for sale at drastically reduced prices. Also investigate consortial agreements with area libraries—the aggregated resources of several small libraries can result in online access to reference databases for far less money than an individual subscription. Always consider your telephone, e-mail, and Internet access extensions of your reference collection, and keep a list of area libraries and librarians who have been helpful in answering reference questions. State libraries, in particular, provide excellent reference assistance for other, smaller libraries and have virtual reference service as well. Take every opportunity to increase the range of your networking activities. Another free option is the Internet Public Library (www.ipl.org), a consortial reference venture hosted by Drexel University. Visitors to the Internet Public Library website may ask reference questions (answered by library school students or librarians of the consortium) and/or access freely available reference sources arranged by subject, user group, and type of information (e.g., "For Kids" or "Newspapers and Magazines").

Readers' Advisory

Readers' advisory is a service provided both formally and informally to patrons of all types of libraries; essentially, it involves the library employee giving patrons advice about books he or she might enjoy reading, particularly given prior reading selections. This service is most often utilized in public libraries, and you, as library employee, can do many things to assist patrons in making appropriate and enjoyable reading choices.

- Read, read, read. While this may seem like an obvious suggestion, many librarians will say that they do not have time to read. Make time, especially if you will be doing readers' advisory work. You cannot advise if you do not *do*.

- Monitor the major best-seller lists in *The New York Times, Publishers Weekly*, and so on. Notice that these publications have both fiction and nonfiction best-seller lists as well as specialty lists, such as "Religion Best Sellers" and "Young Adult Best Sellers." Knowing the titles and authors of popular books will give you a start in recommending good reads for your patrons.

- Take a look at the best-seller lists on Amazon.com and read their customer reviews. The honest opinions of nonlibrarians are often very helpful in deciding whether a patron might enjoy a particular title or series—or not. (My all-time favorite Amazon review: "A drunk walrus, high on Novocain, hung upside down and using only Scrabble letters, would have written a better 'book.'")

- Listen to what books your coworkers, friends, and acquaintances are discussing, anywhere, anytime. Your best friend might have picked up a good beach read to take on vacation; your minister might have just read something by St. Augustine. Stop, look, and listen for reading suggestions everywhere.

- National Public Radio (NPR) has some of the best in-depth book discussions available. Frequently, Terry Gross's NPR staple *Fresh Air* offers hour-long interviews with popular, but not always wildly well-known authors (e.g., a 2014 interview with Edward St. Aubyn, author of *Lost for Words*). A wide variety of authors guarantees you will find someone whom you might not normally have taken the time to read. To find information about books featured on NPR, visit the website (www.npr.org), where you can also click on a link to your local NPR station's website.

- Any number of books, commercial databases, wikis, and websites provide readers' advisory in general as well as genre-oriented information. The following are some of the best:

Book Lust: Recommended Reading for Every Mood, Moment, and Reason (Sasquatch Books, 2003), by Nancy Pearl (the action-figure librarian). Pearl's book is an esoteric, delightful summary of suggested books (fiction and nonfiction) in such categories as "Techno-Thrillers," "Chick-Lit," and "Bicycling." A sequel, *More Book Lust*, was published in 2005; *Book Lust to Go: Recommended Reading for Travelers, Vagabonds and Dreamers* appeared in 2010.

What Do I Read Next? This Gale-Cengage database provides access to reading lists by author, title/series, genre, award winners and librarians' top picks, who/what/where/when, and the particularly useful category "Help Me Find a Book," in which the reader enters the genre, time period, authors, and so on, that he or she likes and the system provides a list of "readalike" titles. Readers may limit searches to fiction, nonfiction, adult, or children's titles or search all these categories at once.

Genreflecting: A Guide to Reading Interests in Genre Fiction (Libraries Unlimited, 2013), edited by Cynthia Orr and Diana Tixier Herald. Now in its seventh edition, this work spawned an entire series of *Genreflecting* titles for the overworked and underappreciated readers' advisory librarian. Chapters devoted to such genres as crime, the western, romance, and adventure are subdivided into types; for instance, the "Adventure" chapter includes survival, military and naval adventure, and political intrigue and terrorism, with titles and main characters listed. Categories are updated with each edition; recent additions include graphic novels and Christian fiction. Additional titles in this series include *Teen Genreflecting, Make Mine a Mystery: A Reader s Guide to Mystery and Detective Fiction* and *Jewish-American Literature: A Guide to Reading Interests.*

A Year of Reading: A Month-by-Month Guide to Classics and Crowd-Pleasers for You and Your Book Group (Sourcebooks, 2002), by Elisabeth Ellington and Jane Freimiller. Five titles in each of the following categories are listed for each month of the year: crowd-pleasers, classics, challenges, memoirs, or potluck options. The book includes bibliographies of related readings and discussion questions, with brief annotations of each work listed.

Goodreads. The Goodreads website (www.goodreads.com) provides a forum through which readers can enter a title already read and find recommendations for further reading on the same topics and genres. It also includes book lists and the ability to search and browse books by subject area.

LibraryThing. LibraryThing (www.librarything.com) encourages users to catalog their own personal libraries, lists of favorite books, and so forth. Billing itself as "the world's largest book club," it is also a networking site for readers. Create a free account and see what other people have said about particular books and authors.

Displays, Exhibits, and Programs

Library Displays and Exhibits

The main goals of any library display or exhibit are to (1) catch the attention of the patron and (2) interest him or her in some aspect of your library, campus, or institution. The ideal library display will result in some benefit for the patron—increased knowledge by reading books associated with a certain topic, learning about a community service, or finding a new hobby, for instance. The library benefits in several ways as well. Well-designed library displays can potentially increase the library's circulation by showcasing certain authors, topics, or collections. The library can become a more integral part of the parent institution by highlighting various activities or topics that are not specifically library related. In addition, a well-designed display will make the library seem more inviting and less institutional, thereby contributing to patron enjoyment of the facilities.

A current library display policy is a must and should be completed and approved by your governing board or administration before you mount any displays. Particularly important issues to address include whether or not community groups may use the library's display areas and whether controversial issues may or will be topics (e.g., a hotly contested community bond issue, gay rights in your community, and so on). Having a well-written, comprehensive policy will save you and your library's administration a great deal of trouble.

The initial stages of designing a display are perhaps the most difficult, beginning with the task of identifying a catchy focus. Use all the resources at your disposal to find a topic, and go beyond the tried-and-true. A resource such as the annual *Chase's Calendar of Events* lists both popular and obscure holidays and celebrations and provides ample starting points for an interesting display. Local celebrations, such as a fall carnival or the community choir concert season, can also be the impetus for a prominent display. If you have enough people on your library staff, form a small committee to discuss possible displays and to rotate responsibility for designing them.

Basic materials for constructing a display need not be expensive. Purchase a few lengths of cloth, even remnants, to use as an attractive backdrop in a display case. Use small boxes or Princeton files as pedestals (to be covered up by that inexpensive cloth you just purchased). Small, clear-plastic book stands serve well to display books. Above all, resist the urge to clutter up the space; the KISS ("Keep it simple, stupid") rule works very well in this venue. Clearly label items that require explanation, but otherwise let the display tell its story through its items. Use library books and videos, CDs, and the like, but also use coworkers as a resource for unique display items. Keeping up with world and local events can also be a great way to generate ideas for a display.

Library Programming

Library programs can run the gamut from book talks to musical performances. Think about the following when planning a program for your library:

- What is your institution all about? Are you running a rural public library or a small branch library of a research university? What topics would be interesting to or informative for your patrons?

Tip

Rotate your displays on a regular basis. There is nothing worse than seeing the same display in the same display case for months on end. If you have run out of ideas, talk to coworkers and patrons, peruse the newspaper, think about authors you would like to know more about, and start displaying. Be as familiar as possible with your library's holdings and use them to generate interesting displays; local history collections can be great resources of display materials, as can new library purchases.

Remember that a library program can be a performance, a lecture, a discussion group, a town hall meeting—you name it; it can happen in your library. If you are at a loss for ideas, sit down and brainstorm ten general subjects for a library program. Do not censor yourself; just let the ink flow. Just as in readers' advisory service, each part of your life and community is a potential resource for a terrific library program. Do not think *cannot*.

- After you brainstorm your program list, consider the resources that you would need to offer the programs. The first and most obvious of these is money. Remember that, even if you are the person doing the program, you will require some form of advertising to boost attendance. The more you advertise, the better. On any given day, your library presentation is competing with any number of other community events. Advertising can be as simple as putting an announcement on your library's or institution's website or placing flyers around your institution. Informally publicizing the program among colleagues is always useful. Find out advertising rates among your local newspapers and consider that free community-based newspapers have an audience that's probably ready-made for your program. Public radio stations are dedicated to serving the community; if your city has a local NPR affiliate, call to ask about its advertising rates. Think carefully about the populations that would enjoy the program, and target those audiences in your advertising. Particularly if you wish to reach a younger demographic, create a Facebook account for your library and use it to highlight library programming, activities, and your library's collections. A Facebook presence not only is free but also has the potential to reach a tremendous number of existing and potential library patrons. In addition, a Twitter account provides the opportunity to communicate brief, pithy information about your library and its activities.
- Start small. If you have never done programming in your library or it has been a while since you have, plan a few well-designed, interesting programs to see how they go. If you arre reading this book, chances are your staff is small, so do only what you can comfortably do.
- Know where to find speakers. If you are in an academic library or in a small public library in a college town, look to the educational institutions in your area for speakers. Every professor has an academic specialty; most, if not all, enjoy sharing their knowledge and would be naturals at leading a book discussion. Local authors love sharing their material; host a creative writing seminar led by an author and/or a book discussion on one of the author's works. Local clubs are rich resources for presentations; ask the president of the club to give a talk or to suggest a speaker from the club's ranks. Use everyone you know as a resource for a presentation.

You may not know everybody in your town or city, but invariably, somebody knows somebody else who would be a fascinating speaker. Step outside your comfort zone to embrace ideas and topics in which you have no particular interest but that you suspect might interest others. You may not know anything at all about, for instance, graphic novels, but chances are that some of your patrons do. Use everything and anything as a mechanism for engagement.

- Also remember that you will need to provide refreshments, which can be as simple as punch and cookies, for the program; in addition, it is good form to offer the speaker a small honorarium or gift for presenting his or her program.

- Construct an evaluation form for the session, and leave a few minutes at the end of the program for attendees to complete it. (You have a much better chance of getting feedback at the event than through an online or snail-mail evaluation after the fact). The form does not have to be fancy; go for basic information such as what the attendee enjoyed most/least about the program, suggestions for improvement, suggestions for future programming, and so on. Always leave a space for comments. The purpose of this evaluation is twofold: (1) to see what works and what does not work and (2) if the evaluations are positive, to use them as ammunition when asking your administration for financial support for your next program.

Outreach

Outreach is another way to interact with the user community. It involves traveling to another location to deliver, or highlight, the services and collections available in the library. Whether it is done by special services, such as a bookmobile or other mobile vehicle, or through individual staff visits to offsite locations, the library is interacting with users in a nonlibrary setting.

Each type of library should seek to find opportunities to reach outside of the library. These efforts can vary from providing awareness of the library's collections and services, to an off-site location for the corporation that the special library serves, to a full-blown bookmobile service that brings 3,000 or more items on a regular basis to stops throughout the community that the library serves. Many community groups are constantly looking for new speakers to help them learn something out of the ordinary. This, too, is outreach and should be pursued.

In the public library setting, Boy and Girl Scout troops are good targets for your expertise. Show them books on activities that could help them earn merit badges, or find out what their "theme of the month" is and focus on that. Develop relationships with your library's patrons and find out the kinds of groups they participate in that might afford opportunities for outreach; for example, a Civil War reenactment group might find interesting a presentation on the library's holdings on a particular battle or perhaps an in-depth look at local history holdings having to do with that same battle. The more creative you can be in developing ideas, the better your program will be. Although you work in a small library and may be the only or one of only a few employees, outreach activities can inspire goodwill among different populations for your library and your institution.

As with any other kind of service, start small, have the audience evaluate it (as discussed in the previous programming section), and find out what works and what does not work. Outreach services are important in even the smallest library and can be a gold mine of good publicity for the library.

Conclusion

If there is a theme for this chapter, it would probably be "Network, network, network." In addition to having a good service orientation and reference knowledge, you should know colleagues, the community, and area libraries. The Internet has provided each of us with an amazing breadth and depth of remote access to colleagues and collections in places far removed, something unheard of only a few years ago. That knowledge, gleaned both locally and beyond the confines of our own communities, will go far in making the library the best that it can be. While it is sometimes daunting being the only adult services employee, or perhaps the only employee, period, of a library, think of this as a positive. There is a unique opportunity to serve a number of different populations through outreach, programming, and the simple good service given every day that will make the library the best it can possibly be.

Further Reading

Anwyll, Rebecca, and Brenda Chawner. "Social Media and Readers' Advisory: A Win-Win Combination?" *Reference and User Services Quarterly* 53 (Fall 2013): 18–22.

Chase's Calendar of Events. Chicago: Contemporary Books, 1995– .

Courtney, Nancy D. *Academic Library Outreach: Beyond the Campus Walls.* Westport, CT: Libraries Unlimited, 2008.

Ellington, Elizabeth, and Jane Freimiller. *A Year of Reading: A Month-by-Month Guide to Classics and Crowd-Pleasers for You and Your Book Group.* Naperville, IL: Sourcebooks, 2002.

Katz, William A. *Introduction to Reference Work.* Boston: McGraw-Hill, 2002.

Luo, Lili. "Text Reference Service: Delivery, Characteristics, and Best Practices." *Reference Services Review* 39, no. 3 (2011): 482–96.

Orr, Cynthia, and Diana Tixier Herald. *Genreflecting: A Guide to Reading Interests in Genre Fiction.* 7th ed. Santa Barbara, CA: Libraries Unlimited, 2013.

Pearl, Nancy. *Book Lust: Recommended Reading for Every Mood, Moment, and Reason.* Seattle, WA: Sasquatch Books, 2003.

Phillips, Susan P. *Great Displays for Your Library Step by Step.* Jefferson, NC: McFarland, 2008.

Ruppel, Margie, and Amy Vecchione. "'It's Research Made Easier!': SMS and Chat Reference Perceptions." *Reference Services Review* 40, no. 3 (2012): 423–48.

Shearer, Kenneth D., and Robert Burgin, eds. *The Reader's Advisor's Companion.* Englewood, CO: Libraries Unlimited, 2001.

Stover, Kaite Mediatore. "Working without a Net: Readers' Advisory in the Small Public Library." *Reference and User Services Quarterly* 45 (Winter 2005): 122–25.

Youth and Young Adult Services

Noreen Bernstein and Jessica McMurray

16

Youth services and young adult services involve all the assistance and resources provided to library users on a daily basis. A youth services staff member deals primarily with those under age thirteen. A young adult staff member works with those aged thirteen to eighteen. Staff members provide a range of services, including reference, programming, outreach, and library-sponsored technology and online resources.

An old Siberian proverb says, "If as a child you don't learn the trees, as an adult you may get lost in the forest. And if, as a child, you don't learn the stories, as an adult you may get lost in life." In essence, youth and young adult librarianship is about making sure that individuals do learn the stories, both fact and fiction, that will keep them from getting lost in life.

Service to youths is one of the most rewarding and challenging aspects of providing service in the small library. The population being served is in the process of growing and maturing in different ways and at different times. What you see in a user's interest varies from day to day. The delight in providing this service is the opportunity to direct individuals to materials, programs, and opportunities that will enrich their lives forever. This chapter provides an introduction to the various aspects of providing library service to youths from birth through roughly eighteen years of age.

Youth Services in Historical Context

Historically, public libraries were established for adults, and the development of children's departments in libraries was literally due to demands of youths themselves. As children and youths flooded into public libraries about 100 years ago, it became clear to librarians that the comfort of adult users was at risk. As these young individuals would not be denied, it seemed prudent to provide a separate area to keep them from disrupting the more serious work of adults.

Research on the importance of early language experiences was basically nonexistent. Illiteracy rates did not overly concern the public in general, and those rates were far lower since early language experiences for children were largely accomplished through communication with stay-at-home mothers. Single-parent families and children relegated to day care were an anomaly. Our economy and growth as a nation were predicated on agrarian and product productivity. Jobs for people with limited literacy skills were more prevalent. In essence, almost no one was concerned.

Nineteenth-century literature for youths and young adults was largely comprised of cautionary tales that helped to teach individuals appropriate models of behavior, morality, and Judeo-Christian values. The original versions of works by the Brothers Grimm, Hans Christian Andersen, and Charles Perrault constituted a body of literature filled with dark morality tales that are a far cry from modern versions, such as the Disney adaptations that fill library shelves today. Today's students of children's, young adult, and teen literature may find humor in the tales of Hilaire Belloc, such as *Melinda Who Told Lies and Was Burned to Death*, but their original purpose was to teach and mold behavior. Story times were socialization experiences promoting good behavior by contemporary standards.

Moving forward, Betty Smith's *A Tree Grows in Brooklyn* (1998; originally published in 1943) provides an interesting snapshot of children's and youth library services as librarianship moved into the twentieth century:

> The library was a little old shabby place. Francie thought it was beautiful . . . She stood at the desk a long time before the librarian deigned to attend to her. . . . "Could you recommend a good book for a girl?" "How old?" "She is eleven." Each week Francie made the same request and each week the librarian asked the same question. A name on a card meant nothing to her and since she never looked up into the child's face, she never did get to know the little girl who took a book out every day and two on Sunday. A smile would have meant a lot to Francie and a friendly comment would have made her so happy. She loved the library and was anxious to worship the lady in charge. (20–22)

Librarianship for youths and young adults has come a long way. Librarians have a unique opportunity to enrich the lives of youths and young adults through providing information and books for pleasure reading and by fostering a love of reading and literature. They also now have current research that provides a scientific basis validating their role.

Readers' Advisory and Reference Services

The best collections in the world are useless unless they are appropriately placed in the hands of readers. Readers' advisory services can help to promote emergent literacy and to shape an individual's future love of reading by providing the most appropriate and best books. Books that rhyme, teach

For Further Information

To learn more about the importance of fairy tales, see *The Uses of Enchantment: The Meaning and Importance of Fairy Tales*, by Bruno Bettelheim (Vintage, 2010).

concepts, and provide a rich experience literarily and visually are crucial to reading readiness. Therefore, it is critical for the young adult services librarian to know the collection and to understand how to connect a child, a parent, and/or a caregiver with the book that best meets a current need.

While most young adult services librarians bring a certain level of knowledge of children's literature to the job, this can be somewhat cursory, focusing on fiction, mostly the classics and award winners. The ability to mine the depth of a collection takes on-the-job work. One way to start is by perusing all new books as they are added to the collection and reading as much new fiction as possible. Browsing nonfiction shelves is also a must, and browsing shelves with standard sources, such as titles listed in this chapter's Further Reading and References sections, makes the task easier. You will find new picture books for story times and new recommendations for older readers. Reading older fiction also gives you advance knowledge of any potential problems a book might present. In some cases, the maturity of content or the language may suggest a recataloging of the book to a teen collection. With nonfiction, checking tables of contents and scanning the books will provide a quick snapshot of the information included. Even the most sophisticated cataloging system cannot substitute for personal knowledge of the contents of your collection.

The other essential tool for both reference and readers' advisory is an appropriate, effective reference interview. Most people using a library do not clearly articulate their need. A good youth services librarian knows how to probe gently to determine what the user really wants or needs. With readers' advisory, a librarian generally needs to know the age and general reading ability of the child, subjects of interest, and other books that he or she has enjoyed. With reference, the need to isolate just what information is required and what types of sources are usable for the assignment, if it is a school assignment, are foremost. Many new librarians tend to start off with search engines and other electronic sources. However, young adults need to learn that research is more than searching Google.com. They need to gain analytical skills to determine which sources are the best. Books, although they can contain errors, do have some accountability; they have an author and publisher who have presumably done their jobs. Many Internet sources do not. Starting with printed material helps young adults to gain these skills.

For Further Information

While learning a collection, another tool to help with readers' advisory is *A to Zoo: Subject Access to Children's Books*, a subject guide to picture books (Thomas and Lima 2014).

Collection Development

Learning the collection is a start, but library collections are living things that must be both developed and maintained. Collection development includes adding newly published items as well as finding collection areas in need of expansion or updating. Weeding outdated items, books in poor condition, or shelf sitters on a regular basis is a must. In the twenty-first century, it is embarrassing to find books that speculate about potential space travel on library shelves!

Acquisitions

Libraries manage collection development in several ways. Some libraries have centralized acquisitions with specific staff responsible for selecting new materials for all collections. While this can be efficient, often these staff members have little interaction with the public, which can result in their overlooking items that may appeal to specific populations. Youth and teen services librarians working within this type of structure need to take action to keep their collections as strong as possible.

The basis of collection development is a materials selection policy. This policy needs to be broad enough to allow the inclusion of a wide range of materials that meet the different sensibilities and needs of a community but also specific enough to provide a rationale for any items that might be challenged. While developing and maintaining a collection, librarians need to keep the scope of the materials selection policy in mind. The *Core Collections* (formerly *H. W. Wilson Standard Catalogs*), available from EBSCO*host* (www.ebscohost.com), assist librarians in developing a basic collection. Titles in the series include *Children's Core Collection*, *Middle and Junior High Core Collection*, *Senior High Core Collection*, and *Graphic Novels Core Collection*, all of which provide valuable assistance in developing a collection.

When moving beyond the basic collection in development efforts, librarians need to be aware of what is being published by staying current with selection tools. They also need to work with selectors to fill gaps and to request those items that are appropriate for their particular populations. In some libraries, particularly smaller systems, frontline librarians make their own selections using tools such as *School Library Journal*, *Booklist*, and *Kirkus Reviews*. Each review journal is structured differently. *Kirkus* uses paid reviewers and publishes both good and bad reviews. *Booklist* also uses paid reviewers but primarily publishes only reviews of books it recommends for inclusion in medium and large libraries. Any caveats for inclusion in the collection are included in the reviews. *School Library Journal* uses the skills of frontline librarians who volunteer to perform reviews. They attempt to review everything published by mainstream publishers, and the reviews vary with the sensibilities of the reviewers. *The Horn Book Magazine* is another trusted review source, but it reviews far fewer books than other journals and its publication schedule often makes its reviews the last to become available.

While there are many print sources to assist with materials acquisition for the collection, a few others available online are worth mentioning. The *School Library Journal* website (www.slj.com) offers a variety of reviews, searchable by grade level, including reviews of graphic novels, audiobooks, and adult books for teens. The *Publishers Weekly* website (www.publishers weekly.com) also includes a review section with features that include the best children's books of the year and sneak previews at the next season's debuts. *Kirkus* has a very user-friendly website (www.kirkusreviews.com) that lists an array of reviews that can be limited to children and teens. Another idea for keeping up-to-date with publishers' activities is to join

Tip

While not always timely, *The Horn Book Magazine* is an excellent tool for making sure that quality titles have not been missed. Use it as a cleanup tool for collection development.

e-mail discussion lists or sign up to receive e-mail updates on upcoming book publications.

The *Voice of Youth Advocates* (*VOYA*), online (www.voyamagazine.com) and print magazine, is also useful for those dealing with teen collections. The reviews include a rating for excellence of content and writing plus a second rating for teen appeal. By balancing the two ratings, a librarian can find excellent choices for a teen fiction collection.

Generally, using these sources together will result in making intelligent choices for your collection. However, information about materials from nonmainstream publishers and Christian presses is much harder to find. Librarians can contact them directly, using *Literary Market Place* to find addresses and request catalogs. If a library serves a large number of homeschooled children from the community, staff can check on the periodic Home School Book Fairs that are held. Attending them provides an opportunity to observe personally many of the materials that are not found in reviews.

Previewing is another selection tool with pluses and minuses. Librarians actually get to look at items before purchasing, which is a plus. Previewing can be done through plans from publishers that send periodic boxes of new books from which librarians can choose and then return those which are not desirable for the collection. Salespeople from publishers will happily visit and preview new titles. Previewing provides the advantage of actually seeing what is being purchased, but it is time intensive and will not provide access to everything available.

Subscriptions can be purchased for series items and periodicals. These make sense for necessary basic sets about countries, states, presidents, and various other topics. Subscribing to these sources saves time and ensures ultimately getting the entire set. It is necessary to examine the sets from various publishers and decide which ones best meet local needs. Popular paperback series can also be done through subscriptions.

In selecting and purchasing a collection, librarians must be vigilant about including items that express multiple viewpoints on sensitive topics, such as gun control, animal rights, and a multitude of others. Collections need to include materials that satisfy the needs of all users. This is equally true of fiction. One way to avoid many book challenges is to have a wide variety of choices for readers. There are numerous Christian presses that produce youth and teen fiction that will fit the sensibilities of many parents. By offering these choices, staff can comfortably give parents a wide selection of materials from which to choose, allowing parents to select those which they find most appropriate for their children.

Collections must reflect the needs of users. More and more materials are becoming available in multiple languages. As populations change, decisions about multiple-language collections need to be made, not only for youth and teen materials, but also for the entire collection. These decisions will be based on local and administrative dictates, available space, and budgetary allotments. Youth and teen services librarians also have to be aware

Tip

Many publishers offer series on presidents, countries, and other curriculum-related topics. Oddly, these series are usually updated at approximately the same time. This is one time when previewing is extremely helpful. Try to arrange sales representative visits to examine new series and decide which are most suited to your users.

of a special collection responsibility. It is now well-known that in order to attain language and future reading skills, all babies need early language experiences, and those experiences are primarily provided by parents or child-care providers. Unless librarians make available materials in the languages spoken by parents and child-care providers, those early language experiences will not happen. Therefore, small collections of board books and picture books in whatever languages are prevalent in your community are important. These collections are an investment in the future.

Collection development is also controlled by what is made available by the publishing industry. Librarians need to be aware that changes in youth and teen publishing will have an increasingly powerful impact on collections. The number of publishers is diminishing, and most of the publishing houses are now part of large conglomerates. This has led to significant changes in what is published and what remains in print. Marketing and licensing are often driving the bus. For example, the Curious George books have been part of children's collections for years, and Curious George is still with us, but in a different way. Just log on to Amazon.com to see the Curious George sheets, pajamas, lunch boxes, cereal bowls, blankets, stuffed toys, and whatever. A child today can eat, sleep, and play with Curious George without ever reading or even knowing that the books exist. Youth and teen publishing is a multimillion-dollar industry, but most of that money comes from the licensing and marketing of realia rather than books. The popularity of the American Girl stores in New York and Chicago are another example. The books are a minuscule piece of what is sold and bought. School book fairs contain at least as many nonbook items as they do books. And just look at the series of books inspired by the *Blue's Clues*, *Care Bears*, and *Barbie* cartoon series and toys.

Inclusion of these publications in a collection is a personal choice dictated by the materials selection policy, space, and budget. If you believe that it is important for early language experiences to include excellence in language and demand the best that is available, consider passing on books that are created solely to merchandise or capitalize on other items. If you believe in always providing customers with what they want, and space and budget are not a problem, selection should include those series which are good sellers in bookstores. But it is important to be aware that if this publishing trend, supported by licensing and marketing potential, continues, what will be available for collections may ultimately lack the depth of diversity and richness that can be found today.

Weeding

As noted at the start of this section, weeding outdated items, books in poor condition, or shelf sitters must be done on a regular basis. How and what to weed is often obvious, but the industry standard is usually *CREW: A Weeding Manual for Modern Libraries* (Larson 2008).

The introduction and consistent improvement of software programs to facilitate collection development have proved invaluable for staff worldwide.

> Youth and teen services librarians need to know that one of the major forces determining what is published today is not library sales or even chain bookstore sales, but materials that can be easily marketed by retail giants like Walmart, Kmart, and Target.

Most libraries use some type of software program to aid their weeding process. The software interfaces can vary, but at the most basic level, they should be able to provide a way to sort through collections based on number of uses, last use, age of material, and so on. Training of some sort should be provided for staff so everyone is able to use the software successfully. Generally speaking, the software can account for a large part of the assistance staff members require in deciding what to weed. However, it cannot determine the condition of items, so it is very important to go through the stacks periodically looking for items that need to be mended, reordered, or, if no longer relevant, weeded.

Reference and Readers' Advisory

In addition to normal resources, there are many tools available online that can help staff when providing readers' advisory. If your library subscribes to an advisory type database like NoveList, staff can easily show patrons read-alikes based on their interest and age. An added benefit of having these databases is the easy access from any computer using a library card. Patrons are able to search for themselves using a resource provided by the library and thereby not impact staff time. Another option is perusing the read-a-alike lists other libraries have created by using an online search engine. These are great because they list materials staff may not have thought of and they can be printed for patrons to take home. Many libraries feature book blogs that are updated several times a week, if not daily. Blog posts are often searchable by genre, collection type, and audience level. These are good for both librarians and patrons because they offer easy-to-build collection knowledge and provide a digital space for users to connect with the library while obtaining readers' advisory assistance.

> A good youth and teen services librarian acts in two ways to ensure a minimum of book challenges: the library's selection policy contains a statement that parents are the final arbiters on what is appropriate for their children to read, and there is a timely process in place for reviewing challenged items.

Challenges to Items in the Collection

The final piece of collection development is handling any book challenges that might arise. Every library needs a procedure for handling these challenges. Librarians need to know this procedure and need to be prepared to handle these challenges quickly and carefully. Philosophically, the parents who challenge a book are those parents who are doing exactly what librarians ask parents to do. They are paying attention to what their children are reading. Your job, as a librarian, is to acknowledge that, to listen carefully to their concerns, and to help them to understand that you respect and applaud their interest in what their children read. The hard part is helping them to understand that they can and should be making these decisions for *their* children, but not necessarily for *all* children. Many challenges can end with an honest and tactful discussion; those that do not need to be handled quickly, tactfully, and according to library procedure. It is important to keep in mind that with older fiction and some nonfiction, a book that is equally appropriate in a teen collection can be recataloged and moved, which can often solve the problem. While the library culture certainly includes a strong intellectual-freedom component, it is sometimes more beneficial to retain a title without a public quarrel.

Programming

This is the area of library service to youths and teens that provides the widest latitude for creativity and imagination. It is also the part of library services that is changing as more and more information about emergent literacy and reading development becomes available. The basic and most traditional piece of library programming is story time. Originally, story times were primarily aimed at preschool children aged three and older. Children, with or without their parents, gathered together to enjoy stories shared by enthusiastic librarians. Librarians felt secure in the knowledge that they were building future reading skills as they shared the treasures from their collections with young children. As more and more research about emergent literacy became available, librarians adapted by creating and offering age and developmentally appropriate story times. "Lapsits for Babies," "Time for Twos," and "Toddler Times" were added to library schedules in the 1980s. In the late 1990s, things changed again. First, as families became busier and busier, the trend was to come to whatever story time was convenient with whatever children one had, regardless of age. The solution here is to offer specific story times but to allow whoever is present to participate. It is appropriate to advertise the story time for whatever age group it is intended for, but no child will be hurt by attending a story time developed for younger children.

When advertising story times, in communities with varied cultural and religious groups, it helps to advertise that holiday stories at Christmas, Halloween, Valentine's Day, and Easter may be included. While in many ways these holidays have become very secular, some families may prefer not to expose their children to holiday story times with religious content with which they do not identify. Be inclusive; include Hanukkah, Passover, Kwanzaa, and any other holidays celebrated in your area. Be sure to advertise this also. Just a general statement that holiday stories may be used during a particular month allows parents for whom this might be a concern to inquire about a specific story time and then make a personal decision to attend or not.

In recent years, scientific research on how emergent literacy develops and how children become ready to read has exploded. It is now believed that the literacy value of a group story time is relatively small, although the socialization value of being part of a group is significant. Research also shows that one early language experience a week is not sufficient. Librarians need to shift their focus slightly but not necessarily change what they do, except in minor ways. The real value of library story times is modeling how to use books with young children for parents and caregivers who spend much more time with these children than a librarian can. The first step is opening up all

Tip

If you want to provide a good modeling experience for parents, include comments during the story time that explain your choice of materials, for example, "I chose this book because of the rhyming language" or "I chose these books so the children could count the items on each page."

story times to the adults accompanying the children. Many librarians prefer not to do this for many reasons, including space and the potential for adults to be disruptive through talking during the story time. However, providing the modeling of how to use books is vital, and in our litigious society, it just makes sense for librarians to include adults in all programs for young children. The second step is a simple amplification of any story time. When a story is finished, asking one or two questions of the adults will help them to see what the particular book is accomplishing. For example, explaining that this book was chosen because it uses rhyme and repetitive language that help a child's brain to develop the synaptic connections needed for reading readiness is a valuable clue for parents when selecting books to use at home.

Research also tells us that movement and music provide the cross-lateral brain action needed for reading readiness. Finger plays and musical ditties with movement should be a part of every story time. It does not matter if you cannot sing. Get that CD player out and go from there. The inclusion of crafts is another issue. Current research says that including the kinds of crafts most libraries use with very young children is actually counterproductive to artistic development. Using precut pieces and coloring sheets that result in a presentable product actually retards artistic development, particularly in very young children. The dilemma here is that parents love these crafts. Thankfully, just as a once-a-week literacy experience is not sufficient, a once-a-week craft experience is not detrimental. However, if librarians are modeling for parents, they should not model behavior that will be repeated but will not be productive. Rather than a carefully prepared craft, give children a large piece of paper and a crayon or marker and let them draw whatever they want.

Currently, more and more libraries are offering or participating in family literacy programs. These include Motheread (www.motheread.org), Mother Goose Programs offered by the Vermont Center for the Book (http://bernan .com/MGP/aboutVCB.aspx), Prime Time (www.primetimefamily.org), Family Place Libraries (http://familyplacelibraries.org), and Every Child Ready to Read @ your library (http://everychildreadytoread.org), among others. Each library needs to assess its needs and resources when deciding to purchase materials for and/or train staff in a particular program. The costs vary widely; some are proprietary, while others are not. Prepackaged programs can save time and often include scripts that can be used, which are helpful to librarians for whom this may be a new direction. When choosing a program, be sure it is based on research. This will afford better opportunities to seek and receive grant funding.

Successful family literacy programs are usually done in collaboration or partnership with schools, Head Start programs, human service departments, or other agencies that work with children. Before starting a program, find out what is already available in your community and make connections with the people and agencies involved. Many of them may have funding or other resources available that will help your library get started and continue the program, and many of them may not have considered the library as a potential resource and partner.

Tip

If you choose to do a family literacy program, select one based on the cost of training, whether every staff member must be trained, and the cost of supporting materials. It is also important to consider when you will offer the program. Evenings work for many families, but you usually need to provide both dinner and child care. A Saturday morning or Sunday afternoon may be a better choice.

The second, sacred part of library programming is summer reading programs. Traditionally, a summer reading program was almost a contest. Children competed with one another or with themselves to see how many books they could read, and the library awarded small prizes for achievements and a certificate of completion at the end of the program. In addition, special programs, such as puppet shows, and other entertainment were offered to attract children to the library. In recent history, state libraries and other local consortia have banded together to produce summer reading program themes and materials. This certainly has made it easier for children's librarians and resulted in better graphics, which are often done by children's book illustrators. In the 1990s, the philosophy behind the summer reading program started changing. Consistency in both reading and library visits was considered more important than the quantity read. Libraries refashioned programs to stress weekly library visits and daily reading.

Programs for teens often have a different theme and incentives. Using teen volunteers during the summer can help you by providing extra laborers and also help to promote teens' participation in the program.

Since modeling for young children is an important part of emergent literacy, having a reading program for adults makes sense. Children seeing parents reading and enjoying it can be a powerful literacy tool.

Summer reading programs may be undergoing more changes in the near future. Research on summer reading programs indicates the value of these programs for children in the early grades. Various research studies are available through the National Summer Learning Association (www .summerlearning.org). The results of that research may shape future summer reading programs.

Library programming throughout the year serves multiple purposes. It attracts new people to the library; it highlights collections, people, and organizations in your community; and it affords additional opportunities to promote emergent literacy. Programming includes paid performers such as puppeteers, storytellers, musical groups, and children's theater groups. These performers come in all price ranges and quality levels, and this is one situation in which libraries do not necessarily get what they pay for. Many groups, storytellers, and entertainers are just getting started and provide charming programs at reasonable prices. Librarians need to check with other libraries and schools to ferret them out. The best way to decide if a performer meets a library's needs is to preview a performance at another library or a performers' showcase. If that is not possible, then ask for and check references. When hiring a performer or group, be sure to check space and technical needs.

Local museums can be an excellent source of programs. Many have educational departments that create and offer programs to the community. Local colleges and universities often have faculty that are happy to do programs in their areas of expertise. Local police and fire departments are usually happy to provide programs. And do not forget the business community. Many small businesses and professional offices are willing to

Tip

Almost every community has people willing to share their expertise or hobbies. Chess clubs, gardening groups, dancing schools, college professors, and local businesses may be excellent sources of programs. Ask around and be creative.

collaborate with the public library. A series of story times featuring community helpers is always popular. So check with local veterinarians, bakeries, dancing schools, karate instructors, newspaper writers, weather forecasters, construction workers (ask them to bring trucks), artists, and musicians. Your job is to find an appropriate story for the volunteer or a staff member to read and then have the volunteer talk about a typical day in his or her life.

Author visits are another wonderful programming event. However, these are a lot of work and often very expensive. Author honoraria range from a few hundred to several thousand dollars a day. And all authors are not created equal when it comes to speaking with children. Some of the best include Claudia Mills, Mary Downing Hahn, Katharine Patterson, Steven Kellogg, Eric Kimmel, Tedd Arnold, George Ella Lyon, Amy Hest, Diane Stanley, Judith Caseley, Megan McDonald, Peter Catalanotto, Bernard Most, R. L. Stine, Phyllis Haislip, Marc Brown, and Vicki Cobb. Two sources for information about author visits are Authors for Libraries (www.authorsfor libraries.org) and Invite an Author through Scholastic Books for Children and Young Adults (http://teacher.scholastic.com/products/tradebooks/ inviteanauthor.htm). Author visits can also be arranged through publishers. Keep in mind that local authors may well have as good a program to offer as the more well-known authors. When hosting an author, be sure to understand all of your responsibilities. Libraries will be paying not only an honorarium but also expenses. Many authors require a hotel rather than staying in someone's home. Some have dietary requirements. Others will or will not autograph books. These are all reasonable questions to ask up front. Most authors do three presentations a day for their basic honorarium. Programs can be offered to schools or shared with schools and/or other closely located libraries to help defray costs.

Sharing programs leads to the last piece of complete youth and teen services—outreach. Librarians have long known that many of the youths who need library services the most do not have easy access to library buildings or bookmobiles. Busier schedules, more children in day care, and increased Internet access at home have changed the face of who comes to the library. Simultaneously, increased school accountability has left less time for inclusion of literature in the classroom.

Librarians need to find ways to go to where youths are or to arrange library visits by schools and day-care centers. This includes not only the school year but the summer as well. A carefully devised outreach program includes bringing story times to day-care centers and preschool programs such as Head Start. It includes finding ways to read to school-aged youths at before- and after-school programs as well as in the classroom. When planned collaboratively, these programs allow libraries to reach more youths, and they also help to share expertise in youth and teen literature and how to effectively use it with youths with those educators and day-care providers who spend much more time with youths than any librarian can. This is definitely a win-win situation. Such collaboration also helps to make a library visible in all parts of the community.

Tip

Authors are available through publishers. Most large publishing companies have staff that arranges such visits. Balkin Buddies (balkinbuddies.com) has a good selection of authors and illustrators. The company offers excellent guidelines on doing a first author visit and will provide books for purchase at a discount if you want to include a book sale to offset costs.

The incorporation of technology in youth programming over the past few years has increased at an enormous rate, and for good reason. Current technology provides a plethora of resources that were not available to public libraries in years past. These resources are incredibly valuable and can enrich programming experiences. Adding technology can mean as little as purchasing an MP3 player or iPod and downloading songs for playing music during story times through a compatible speaker system. It can include projecting a tablet or laptop to create a program featuring TumbleBooks (tumblebooks.com). For younger users with developmental disabilities, the inclusion in programming of specialized apps that help enable learning can be a tremendous asset. The elusive teen user also benefits from technology in programming. All around the country, libraries are hosting programs like Minecraft meetups, digital design, digital photography, video gaming, coding, and robotics. Some now even feature makerspaces that allow for activities like 3-D printing. The limiting factors in regards to technology in youth programming are similar to those in general for small libraries: staff time and available financial resources. However, the best thing about technology today is its somewhat progressive affordability. Each year sees price decreases in gaming systems, televisions, DVD players, cameras, and so on. While still not cheap, the lower prices have certainly made technology more attractive for those on a tight budget. Staff time, unfortunately, is not always as promising. Many public libraries today have fewer staff members than in the past, and they often cover the same number of duties, if not more. But on the positive side, many technology-centered programs can be self-sustaining and do not require constant supervision. A video-gaming session or online code academy program can be set up in advance while teens use the consoles or computers independently. The trick is to find out what forms of technology and kinds of programming are the best fit for your library's individual needs and abilities. It is worth noting that collaborating with a nearby nonprofit organization could also be of use. The organization's additional resources, whether they be material or staff based, could be a perfect supplement to what your library is capable of providing.

Conclusion

A good youth and teen services librarian has an excellent working knowledge of the collection, which he or she maintains rigorously, provides opportunities to model the use of books with adults who have frequent access to youths and teenagers, and offers a variety of programs, both in the library and on an outreach basis. A youth and teen services librarian does everything possible to be sure that the youths who live in his or her community learn those stories that will keep them from becoming lost in life.

Further Reading

Alessio, Amy J., and Kimberly A. Patton. *A Year of Programs for Teens 2.* Chicago: ALA Editions, 2011.

Bettelheim, Bruno. *The Uses of Enchantment: The Meaning and Importance of Fairy Tales.* New York: Vintage, 2010.

Booth, Heather, and Karen Jensen. *The Whole Library Handbook: Teen Services.* Chicago: ALA Editions, 2014.

Cart, Michael. *Cart's Top 200 Adult Books for Young Adults: Two Decades in Review.* Chicago: ALA Editions, 2013.

———. *Young Adult Literature: From Romance to Realism.* Chicago: ALA Editions, 2010.

Carter, Betty, and Pam Spencer Holley. *What Do Children and Adults Read Next.* Farmington Hills, MI: Gale Cengage, 2012.

Ernst, Linda L. *The Essential Lapsit Guide: A Multimedia How-To-Do-It Manual and Programming Guide for Stimulating Literacy Development from 12 to 24 Months.* Chicago: ALA Neal-Schuman, 2015.

Feinberg, Sandra, Barbara Jordan, Kathleen Deerr, and Michelle Langa. *Including Families of Children with Special Needs: A How-To-Do-It Manual for Librarians.* Rev. ed. Revised by Carrie Scott Banks. Chicago: ALA Neal-Schuman, 2014.

Gillespie, John T., and Catherine Barr. *Best Books for Children.* 9th ed. Santa Barbara, CA: Libraries Unlimited, 2010. Supplement to 9th ed., 2013.

———. *Best Books for Middle School and Junior High Readers.* 3rd ed. Santa Barbara, CA: Libraries Unlimited, 2013.

H. W. Wilson. *Core Collections* (formerly *H. W. Wilson Standard Catalogs*). Available online at www.ebscohost.com. Print versions available through Grey House Publishing at www.hwwilsoninprint.com.

Robb, Laura. *Literacy Links.* New York: Heinemann, 2003.

Roginski, Dawn R. *A Year in the Story Room: Ready-to-Use Programs for Children.* Chicago: ALA Editions, 2014.

References

Larson, Jeanette. 2008. *CREW: A Weeding Manual for Modern Libraries.* Austin, TX: Texas State Library and Archives Commission. www.tsl.texas.gov/sites/default/files/public/tslac/ld/pubs/crew/crewmethod08.pdf.

Smith, Betty. 1998. *A Tree Grows in Brooklyn.* New York: HarperCollins Perennial Classics.

Thomas, Rebecca L., and Carolyn W. Lima. 2014. *A to Zoo: Subject Access to Children's Books.* Santa Barbara, CA: Libraries Unlimited.

Digital Services

Barry Trott

As research continues to show, library users most commonly associate the library with objects that they can check out. In December 2013, the Pew Research Center released the report *How Americans Value Public Libraries in Their Communities* (Zickuhr et al. 2013). The study on which the report was based found that over 80 percent of those surveyed indicated that books and media were either "very important" (54 percent) or "somewhat important" (27 percent) library services. Items to read, view, and listen to continue to be the brand of the public library. It is important to keep in mind, though, that some library users are interested in accessing those items in digital form as well as in print form. In fact, a second Pew Research Center study indicated that "there is a strong tie between technology [use] and library use" (Zickuhr, Purcell, and Rainie 2014, 17). With this in mind, public libraries of all sizes need to look at how best to provide digital collections, programs, and services to their users.

There are a variety of reasons why digital services are an essential tool for libraries. First, these services allow the library to provide expanded access to collections, programs, and services of interest to current users. Current users provide the foundation of support for the library, and as indicated earlier, the Pew Research Center report *From Distant Admirers to Library Lovers—and Beyond* posits a connection between heavy library use and interest in technology (Zickuhr, Purcell, and Rainie 2014). So it makes sense to increase the connection that these technologically savvy users have with the library by offering digital resources that are of interest to them.

At the same time, it is also increasingly clear that many people are faced with barriers to accessing library collections, programs, and services. These barriers could be related to time; users who work two jobs or have family commitments may not be able to get to the library when it is open. They can also relate to transportation; not all libraries are easily accessible by public transportation, limiting user access, and elderly users who live in assisted living or retirement communities may no longer have the ability to get out to the library. For all of these users, a library's digital collections may be the only way to access library resources. This is not a matter of convenience.

Rather, for these users, using the digital collections of the library, available outside normal operating hours, may be the only way to take advantage of the library.

By providing library collections, programs, and services outside the walls of the library and outside the normal operating hours, the library can expand its brand, reach existing users in new ways, and reach new users at their points of interest. For all of these reasons, it is essential for libraries to look at opportunities to expand their digital presence. Even a small public library can create a "virtual branch" by bringing together its digital offerings and presenting them to its users in an easily accessible way.

It is important to make clear that this chapter's discussion of digital services in the library does not include information technology (IT) services. While there are obvious overlaps in the areas covered here, and in a small library they may be handled by the same person, they are not the same. IT services deal with the networks and technology infrastructure that allow digital services to be offered, but they are generally behind the scenes, not engaging directly with library users. Digital services, on the other hand, revolve around the intersection of users and technology. These are the library areas where our users are accessing library collections, programs, and services in digital formats or where the library is using technology to extend its reach into its community. The provision of digital services in the public library relies on a robust network and reliable hardware, provided by IT staff. Without this sort of firm foundation, library users will quickly become frustrated as they try to access the library's digital resources. Librarians working in digital services need to be technologically adept, but it is even more important that they be skilled at connecting users with technology and explaining how to use the library's digital resources.

For purposes of this chapter's discussion, digital services include library collections (e-books, digital audiobooks, database resources, etc.), programs offered online, and online library services (chat reference, etc.). Also included in the discussion are library websites and catalogs and social media. Each of these topics is covered in more detail in the following sections.

Digital Collections

Libraries now have the opportunity to provide digital analogs to all of their physical collections. E-books, downloadable audiobooks, downloadable music, downloadable magazines, and streaming video are all available to libraries. One issue with all of these collections that is especially challenging for small libraries is price. The current world of digital publishing is one of constant change, and publishers are responding to these changes by making much of their digital content quite expensive. Fortunately, many products are priced by service population, which can help to ease the cost for smaller libraries. There are also other ways to make these collections more affordable. Smaller libraries should explore the opportunities offered through working in a consortium with other libraries to provide digital content. State libraries are sometimes another source for digital collection access for small libraries by providing starter collections for no cost or at reduced prices through negotiated discounts. Keeping in touch with the state library staff working on digital issues will be crucial to building an affordable digital collection.

E-books

There are a number of vendors providing e-book content to libraries, including Baker & Taylor, EBSCO, Library Ideas (Freading), OverDrive, and Recorded Books (OneClick). These vendors offer a variety of lending models and pricing structures that you will need to keep in mind, and these models and structures can vary, not only from vendor to vendor, but also within a single vendor's content from publisher to publisher. For instance, at the time of writing, only OverDrive was offering e-book titles in Amazon's Kindle format as well as in ePub and its proprietary Read format. All of the other vendors offer titles only in ePub or PDF format. On the publisher side, currently several publishers have set fairly strict use limits on e-book titles from their collections. Titles from Penguin can be lent for one year and then must be relicensed. HarperCollins limits libraries to twenty-six e-book circulations and then the title must be relicensed.

Regardless of the vendor or publisher restrictions specific to the e-book product that you are working with, there are some general things that you need to keep in mind when developing an e-book collection. Most important is that e-book content accessed through a vendor is not being purchased; rather, it is being licensed to the library under whatever licensing terms are stipulated in the contract. This has some implications, as lending policies and other factors are no longer controlled solely by the library. In addition, the library cannot simply turn over e-books to the Friends of the Library book sale when they are no longer needed in the collection.

Another consideration in developing an e-book collection is the need to develop staff skills with digital devices so that they can assist users who might have questions. One very useful option here is to acquire at least a small number of digital devices for staff to work with that can also be used when working one-on-one with users who have questions. Although there is an upfront cost in doing this, that cost will be more than recouped as staff familiarity with the devices leads to improved service to users. When considering what devices to get, be sure to check with public service staff to see what devices users are bringing to the library and seeking help with. Also, be sure to provide time for staff training prior to implementing any new digital collection. If staff are not comfortable with using the collection, they will neither sell the collection to your users nor be able to assist with questions.

Downloadable Audiobooks

Like e-books, there are several vendors offering libraries access to digital audiobooks. At this writing, these included Midwest Tape (Hoopla), Over-Drive, and Recorded Books (OneClick). As discussed earlier, the library lending and licensing models differ from vendor to vendor, and it is important to choose a model that you feel will best fit the needs of your users while also being sustainable for your library. Subscription models (e.g., Recorded Books' OneClick digital program) allow libraries access to a large collection of simultaneous-use titles, with new items added to the subscription each month. An advantage here is that you are freed from the necessity of making regular selections of materials because Recorded Books builds the collection. This can be an issue, though, if your users are looking for titles that are not included in the subscription package.

Again, purchasing some devices, both iOS and MP3 players, will assist staff in becoming comfortable with whatever service you choose to use and ultimately result in an increased ability to help your users get connected. With the multiplicity of devices that users have to listen to audio files, it is essential that staff become comfortable with the process of downloading and playing audiobook files. So do not stint on the training. Often there is a staff member who is an avid user of the technology, and bringing that person into the process to help train other staff can be a great tool.

Downloadable Music, Magazines, and Streaming Video

Libraries are finding increasing opportunities to provide access to digital music, digital magazines, and streaming video for their users. All of the caveats stated previously apply to these formats as well. In fact, the models here are perhaps even more varied than with e-books and audiobooks. They range from allowing users to download and keep individual song files (Library Ideas' Freegal) to checking out albums for a set period (Hoopla or OverDrive) to streaming music (Freegal). Digital magazines are available from services such as Recorded Books' collaboration with Zinio or EBSCO's Flipster, and, again, you will want to look for the service that offers the titles that your users are interested in as well as the one that seems to offer the most seamless access for users. In the area of video, OverDrive, Freegal, and Hoopla, all offer options that you should consider in terms of both access and content.

These newer additions to the library's digital holdings often are initially of appeal to a small set of users. It is important to reach out to users to let them know that you have these new offerings and to offer training on how to use them, as they are not always the most straightforward items to access. At the same time, adding collections like these to your overall library collections can help to reach new users who may have previously felt that the library did not have materials of interest to them.

Databases

Most libraries, even smaller ones, have had database collections for quite a while now. Often aimed at students, these tools provide access to magazine and journal articles, encyclopedias, and critical scholarly commentary. While it is still important to include these sorts of student-focused tools in your digital collections, it is also worth taking a look at database resources that are aimed at adults with a variety of interests. More and more users are expecting to find information online, and the library can stay relevant in their minds by providing resources that allow them to easily locate useful and accurate information that they need. Some examples of these topics are car and small engine repair, genealogy, language learning, investing information, consumer information, business information, crafting and hobbies, health and medicine, and books and reading. There are database resources out there for all of these topics and more from vendors like EBSCO, Gale, and ProQuest. It is essential to talk to your users to see what topics might be of interest to them as you consider adding new tools to your database collections. Also, it is essential that you monitor use of your collections, as you would with the print collections, to see what resources are being used and which ones could be dropped. It is not a bad thing to discontinue a subscription to an underperforming database after giving it a couple of years.

Digital Programs

Most libraries, large and small, offer a wide range of programming. From story times, author visits, and book talks to concerts, gaming, and beyond, libraries bring programs to their communities to engage users, highlight collections, build literacy, and start conversations. With the ease of recording digital video, there is an opportunity for libraries to bring some of these programs, or at least parts of them, to users in the online world, again expanding the reach of the library in its community.

While it may be beyond the budgetary capacity of a small library to produce a more complex video, involving lots of editing and costly software, you can use an iPhone or iPad to capture short video clips that can be posted on the library website, YouTube, or Facebook. These videos could be something like a one-minute book talk from a staff member talking up a favorite title or a short clip of a story time that gets across the excitement of being there. These short clips of programs can be used both to promote upcoming events and to create a buzz about an event that has already occurred.

If your local funding body (city or county) has a public access channel, you might want to contact them about working together to create content that promotes the library. Often, the communications staff are looking for filler content and would be willing to do the filming and any editing. Then, you can use the final product on the library's YouTube channel. In Virginia, Williamsburg Regional Library has successfully worked with James

For Further Information

While the idea of digital programming can seem a bit overwhelming and can be challenging in reality, it is worth considering what options you might have to offer at least some programs from the library in digital form. David Lee King, with the Topeka & Shawnee County Public Library, often has some interesting, and provocative, ideas about digital programming on his blog. For a discussion of online library programming, see www.davidleeking .com/2014/05/22/developing-an -online-first-mentality-part-two-in -the-library/#.U4tY-i96HWo.

City County communications staff to create a popular series of book talks called *Checking in at the Library*. These run on the local cable channel but are also on the county and library YouTube channels (see http://youtu.be/ D7uBgMvgQqQ for a sample program).

Online Library Services

Like library programming, it is worth taking some time to consider how to bring library services into the digital world. Many things that libraries do for users can translate into the online realm fairly easily. Again, staffing and budgetary concerns have to be taken into consideration when planning how to reach users online, but as more of your users expect to find your library online, you need to consider how to connect with them where they are, rather than where you hope they will be.

One way to start offering digital services is to make sure that it is easy for your users to ask you questions online. Your library's website should have an easily findable "Ask Us" link that goes either to a webform or directly to an e-mail option, allowing users to ask questions about library collections, programs, and so on. It is also essential to respond to these questions in a timely fashion. Users expect to get the same quick response from the library that they would when texting their friends; you need to create processes that allow you to live up to that expectation. It can be very helpful to have "Ask Us" questions go to more than one library staff person, so that if someone is out of the office for any reason, the question does not languish until that person returns. Keeping a file of boilerplate responses to common questions can be a useful tool for speeding up response times. If you get a lot of questions about how to place a hold, use your e-book collection, or other things of that nature, create a prepackaged response that can be customized for the individual user.

If you already have an "Ask Us" service on your website, the next thing to consider is offering live chat help during library hours. You will need to consider how you will staff a service of this sort to ensure quick response time to user queries. It is extremely important in text and chat services to respond quickly, letting the user know that he or she has connected with someone who can help. The American Library Association vendor fact sheet noted in the sidebar has some useful links for libraries interested in getting started with virtual reference services.

In addition to directly answering questions online, you may want to consider what other library services can be duplicated in the online world. David Lee King (2014) suggests that "everything your library does [should be] represented online." While this may not always be possible, it is certainly a good exercise to sit down with staff to review your services and talk about opportunities to offer online users access to these services. Things like readers' advisory services (book displays, book discussion groups, read-alike lists, reading suggestions), technology training, assistance with digital collections, and other similar services could all have a digital counterpart that you might consider offering. By doing so, you will connect with your users in new ways as well as reaching new users.

Library Website and Catalog

Library Websites

There are numerous articles and books on building websites as well as a host of classes on website design that can be found online from the ALA and other sources. If you are redesigning your site or building a library website from scratch, you will want to do some reading in this area before you get started, and you should also spend some time looking at examples of websites that you think are well-designed. Be sure to involve staff in the process, asking for suggestions of good websites, testing out designs on staff, and getting their feedback where appropriate.

If your website is hosted by your funding body, it can be more of a challenge to develop and make changes in a timely fashion. Working through a municipal or county IT department to update the website can slow things down. In these cases, it is worth the effort to get to know the IT staff and to see how much autonomy they are willing to give to the library's website person. Building this relationship can be slow, but it will yield good results.

There are some things to consider when developing a library website. First, many users think of the library's online catalog as the website. If you ask them what they like or dislike about the library website, you will find most of the comments relate to the ease of use of the catalog. So, if you have staff or budgetary limitations, it may be more effective to look at ways to enrich your catalog records than to spend a great deal of time and effort on the library website (see next section on the library catalog for ideas). That being said, the website still has a role in connecting the library to its users.

It is most important to keep the website simple. Think about what basic information your users are going to want—library hours, contact information, a way to ask a question, event information—all of these should be easily discoverable on your website. Make sure that there is a link to the library catalog from the front of your website or, even better, put a catalog search box on every page of the website. Then, think about what other content will be valuable for your users. Talk to staff about what they need to be able to access and also about what they are hearing from users, and then use that information to develop the website. It is always a challenge to divvy up the front page real estate on a website. Everyone wants to make sure that their information is easily accessible in the fewest number of clicks. This is why it is valuable to be able to gather statistical data on your website so that you know what areas of the website are being used. Google Analytics (www .google.com/analytics) offers a fairly easy way to get detailed data on your website, and you should consider setting up an account and using the information that you gather to make thoughtful decisions about website changes.

For Further Information

There are many tools out there that allow libraries to set up services for chat, instant messaging (IM), and short message service (SMS) for little or no money. The ALA has put together a useful list of vendors for virtual reference tools at www.ala.org/tools/libfactsheets/ alalibraryfactsheet19#Vendors.

The library website should be considered an evolving project, where changes are made based on user and staff comments and analysis of use patterns. Resist the temptation to create or update a website and then let it go unattended. Keep an eye on how things look, think about ways to improve access to the website, and, above all, be responsive to user comments about the website.

Library Catalogs

As mentioned earlier, for many users, the library's online catalog is the library website. The catalog is the one place where almost every library user goes, even if they visit the physical building only to pick up their holds. With this in mind, it makes sense for us to look for ways to make the experience of using the catalog as rich as possible. Small libraries may face staff time and budget limitations with respect to catalog enrichment, but time spent on this piece of the website will make a real difference to your users.

There are two aspects of building a richer catalog to consider. First, you should be thinking about what sort of records to include in your online catalog beyond those for the physical materials that you have in your library. Most database vendors provide libraries with MARC records for databases and electronic reference books. By including these items in your catalog, with the appropriate subject headings, you make it possible for your users to locate databases that might otherwise never be found. For instance, if you have an online language learning tool such as Mango Languages, you can add a catalog record with subject headings such as "French language—Self-instruction—Interactive multimedia." Then, when a user searches the catalog for French language materials, he or she will find the database as well.

As well as considering cataloging database resources, you should also look into adding records for e-books or downloadable audiobooks to the catalog. Again, most vendors of digital products provide MARC records, either for free or at a minimal cost, that can be used with little or no modification. Taking this step will increase the discoverability of your digital content as well as alerting uninformed users that the library has e-book and other digital content. Depending on your catalog system, it may be possible to enable users to directly check out digital materials from the catalog, so talk to your ILS (integrated library system) provider to see what options exist here to save the time of the user.

Another way to make the catalog a richer tool for users is to consider cataloging web content. Does your library collect and catalog local government documents? Many government bodies are no longer producing printed agendas and minutes of meetings, so you may want to consider how to provide users access to those resources. If you already have a catalog record for the print collection of meeting agendas and minutes, add a MARC 856 field (location and access information to electronic resources) to the record that gives the URL for the digital versions of these items. Other libraries are creating curated collections of digital content that might be of interest to their users. Things like TED Talks or other content of that sort might be worth considering adding to the catalog if your users would find it of value.

Yet another way to make library catalog records richer is to add content to existing records. There are a number of fee-based options that do this sort of enrichment. LibraryThing for Libraries (www.librarything.com/for libraries) and NoveList Select (www.ebscohost.com/novelist/our-products/ novelist-select) both offer interesting options to enrich item records. These include reading recommendations, series information, book reviews, tags, similar books, and awards. Providing this information directly in the catalog enhances the reader's experience and also increases the library's value to the reader.

If fee-based services are not an option, there are still ways that you can make your catalog richer using locally produced content. Adding series information to records, using the notes field to indicate items of local interest, and, as mentioned earlier, adding links to records for local government resources that are now found only online are all possibilities. It may also be worth considering how you can take advantage of any locally produced content for readers, such as read-alike lists or genre reading suggestion lists. If you have these lists in digital form, you can again use the MARC 856 field to link to them. For instance, if you have a David Baldacci read-alike list on your website, you can put a link to that list in all the David Baldacci records in the catalog. Give it a catchy name and your readers will be able to find other titles to check out even if they never come to the desk to ask for readers' advisory help.

Social Media

It is increasingly expected that organizations will have a presence on social media. In terms of libraries, this is another place where librarians can meet users where they are rather than waiting for them to come to the library. When considering how to get started with social media, you should always begin from the library's strategic plan. This should be the guiding document for all new directions in the library, as it lays out the library's vision and mission and the strategic directions that will be used to achieve them. The second part of getting started in social media, or really any digital service, is to develop a plan for what you want to achieve and how you are going to measure success.

It is essential to remember that social media are not simply about promoting library collections, programs, and services. In fact, if that is all you do on your Facebook page or Twitter account, you will find that there is minimal user engagement. Rather, social media are about telling stories and having conversations. So, look at the variety of social media platforms available to the library (Facebook, Twitter, Instagram, Pinterest, YouTube, Vine, Tumblr, Google+—the list goes on and on) and decide which tools make the most

---

For Further Information

If you are interested in further exploring options for using the library catalog as a tool to engage users, check out *The Library Catalogue as Social Space*, by Laurel Tarulli (Libraries Unlimited, 2012). Tarulli does an excellent job of presenting possibilities for integrating the catalog more closely into all library work, breaking down silos between technical services and public services.

sense for your library. Do not feel that you have to have a presence on every social media platform. As Ben Bizzle, of Craighead County Jonesboro (AR) Public Library notes, trying to be everywhere "dilutes our brand and message. . . . Successful libraries will determine what platforms most effectively reach their target audience and aggressively build sustainable presences there"(ALA 2013, 41). So, start small and build from there.

Social media are all about conversations and connections. In a useful article on social media, Nancy Dowd (2013) points out, "If your library is posting and not getting any interactivity, then you are probably posting the wrong things." Dowd also reiterates the need to develop a plan for using social media. In the same article, she also gives several examples of successful, and sometimes unsuccessful, library social media efforts. All of the libraries profiled indicate that having a plan for what you want to achieve in social media increases the likelihood of success.

Social media tools do allow libraries to bring some of their services online in new ways, and you might want to consider some of these possibilities as you look at your social media plan. For instance, if readers' advisory services are popular among your users, consider offering reading suggestions through your Facebook or Twitter account. Users can post a title that they enjoy, and library staff can offer reading suggestions. If you schedule this sort of service on a regular basis (say, every Friday afternoon from 1:00 to 3:00 p.m.—Get reading suggestions for the weekend!), you can begin to develop a core following and build an ongoing conversation with your users as they respond to suggestions or comment on ones that staff make. You could post a short (140 characters) book review on Twitter every morning, complete with a link to the catalog record for the book, or as discussed earlier, you could use YouTube to post short videos from the library. The possibilities are pretty broad here, and almost any library can find opportunities to engage users through social media that will fit their staffing, budget, and strategic directions.

Conclusion

While the concept of the library as a physical space continues to be important to communities, library participation in digital space offers opportunities to librarians to bring library collections, programs, and services to their current users in new ways and to reach new users who might not come into the library buildings. Developing a plan for incorporating an online component, where possible, for all aspects of the library will help to keep libraries of all sizes relevant to and valued by their communities.

References

ALA (American Library Association). 2013. *The State of America's Libraries 2013*. www.ala.org/news/sites/ala.org.news/files/content/2013-State -of-Americas-Libraries-Report.pdf.

Dowd, Nancy. 2013. "Social Media: Libraries Are Posting, but Is Anyone Listening?" *Library Journal*, May 7. http://lj.libraryjournal .com/2013/05/marketing/social-media-libraries-are-posting-but-is -anyone-listening/.

King, David Lee. 2014. "Developing an Online First Mentality, Part Three: Everything Online." *DavidLeeKing.com* (blog), May 29. www .davidleeking.com/2014/05/29/developing-an-online-first-mentality -part-three-everything-online/.

Zickuhr, Kathryn, Kristen Purcell, and Lee Rainie. 2014. *From Distant Admirers to Library Lovers—and Beyond: A Typology of Public Library Engagement in America*. Pew Research Center. Released March 13. http://libraries.pewinternet.org/2014/03/13/typology.

Zickuhr, Kathryn, Lee Rainie, Kristen Purcell, and Maeve Duggan. 2013. *How Americans Value Public Libraries in Their Communities*. Pew Research Center. Released December 11. http://libraries.pewinternet .org/2013/12/11/libraries-in-communities.

Part IV

Collection Development in the Small Library

Selection

Barbara Riebe

Selection is the process of choosing library materials in various formats for the library collection. The goal of selecting library materials is to have a balanced collection that encompasses and reflects all viewpoints and interests. As stated in the Williamsburg Regional Library's *Selection of Library Materials* "given the wide range of community tastes and interests, items selected for the collection will not necessarily appeal to all users." Items may not necessarily appeal to the materials selector either. Nevertheless, it is the responsibility of the selector to omit personal bias so as to accommodate the tastes and needs of the library user and the community the library serves. This chapter addresses collection development in the small library. Beginning with initial questions to consider, the chapter then covers the major areas of collection development and presents resources to aid library staff as they purchase materials, deal with user concerns, and provide a collection that meets the needs of the community served.

Questions Before Beginning

One of the first questions that must be answered is who specifically will have the responsibility of making materials selection. Is the selection process centralized or are a number of people involved? Do librarians or acquisition staff make the decisions on what to acquire for the collection? At the Williamsburg Regional Library, the collection development librarian makes final decisions on whether or not to purchase most items. All librarians, however, share in the selection process by maintaining assigned collection areas, suggesting items to order from professional journals and catalogs, reviewing online resources, and drawing on their own knowledge and expertise in recommending library materials. Patron requests are also given great weight, as the patrons are the very users the library is accommodating.

Decisions on the scope of your collection must also be made with the pros and cons of various formats being considered. These formats include

Library Bill of Rights

The American Library Association affirms that all libraries are forums for information and ideas, and that the following basic policies should guide their services.

i. Books and other library resources should be provided for the interest, information, and enlightenment of all people of the community the library serves. Materials should not be excluded because of the origin, background, or views of those contributing to their creation.

ii. Libraries should provide materials and information presenting all points of view on current and historical issues. Materials should not be proscribed or removed because of partisan or doctrinal disapproval.

iii. Libraries should challenge censorship in the fulfillment of their responsibility to provide information and enlightenment.

iv. Libraries should cooperate with all persons and groups concerned with resisting abridgment of free expression and free access to ideas.

v. A person's right to use a library should not be denied or abridged because of origin, age, background, or views.

vi. Libraries which make exhibit spaces and meeting rooms available to the public they serve should make such facilities available on an equitable basis, regardless of the beliefs or affiliations of individuals or groups requesting their use.

Adopted June 19, 1939.
Amended October 14, 1944; June 18, 1948; February 2 , 1961; June 27, 1967; and January 23, 1980; inclusion of "age" reaffirmed January 23, 1996, by the ALA Council.

paper (both hardbacks and paperbacks), music CDs, feature and nonfeature DVDs, microforms, e-books, audiobooks (tapes or CDs), and electronic databases. Can the library afford all formats or only a select few? Do you want the same title in more than one format? How many copies of an item should be purchased? These are all important questions about your collection that must be answered.

You must also decide whether purchases will be made title by title or through standing order plans. Standing order plans allow automatic ordering of such items as annual updates of travel guides, specified numbers of copies for popular authors, audiobooks, and large-print books. Though more labor intensive, title-by-title selection permits greater flexibility and freedom in choosing titles, number of copies, when to purchase, and from which vendors to purchase.

Will you stock erotica? R-rated movies? How will you respond to an objection about a particular item? The American Library Association's "Library Bill of Rights," shown in the sidebar and found on the ALA website (www.ala.org/advocacy/intfreedom/librarybill), may serve as a guide in answering these questions.

Considerations When Making a Selection

A number of criteria must be considered before making a specific purchase. If the item is not electronic, the physical qualities are important if the item is to have a long shelf life. Examine the accuracy and timeliness of the information being presented, particularly for legal and consumer health collections. Reviews and reputation of the author and/or publisher will be most useful in making these determinations.

How will an item fit in with the rest of the collection? Do you need more or fewer titles on the subject matter? If you have enough information on the topic, consider interlibrary loan (ILL) if the patron wants a specific title. ILL is also very useful if a requested item is too expensive, outdated, or outside the scope of your collection.

What is the expected use of an item? The subject matter of a potential acquisition should satisfy your intended audience. If yours is a public library, will your patrons use items published for academia? Will they want to read scientific journals or more popular health periodicals? If yours is an academic or a special library, will your patrons also want more popular items, such as the latest fiction best seller?

Handling "Objectionable" Material

Any material purchased for the library may be objectionable to one or more patrons or even to the selector. How will you handle such objections? It is advisable to have a plan of action already in place.

Often, a patron merely wishes to express his or her opinion. Knowing someone has attentively listened to his or her concerns usually proves sufficient to address them. The key here is to listen. If that is not enough, ask the patron if he or she would like to speak to someone who has more authority in the library. If this is still not acceptable to the patron, then suggest that the patron might want to make a formal complaint about something he or she has found objectionable in the library's collection. On such occasions, you will need an official formal complaint form. Figure 18.1 presents one such form used by the Williamsburg Regional Library in Virginia.

To address the patron's concerns, a number of steps are helpful. Go over your collection policy. Does the item in question comply with it? Find out how many times it has been checked out and if other complaints have been made. What kind of reviews has the item received? Do other libraries own it and, if so, how many? Answers to all of these questions will help you decide whether or not the item does in fact belong in the library. If you decide in favor of retaining the item, the answers will also aid in formulating a defense for keeping the item in the collection when you contact the patron who registered the complaint. Once again, remember that you represent all library patrons, so be sure your own biases do not affect your decision.

Another issue that might arise is the veracity of items being added to the collection. While you want to ensure that nonfiction materials are unbiased and factual, this is not always as simple as it sounds. With science, law, history, and medical materials, you can, and should, check the credentials of the authors. But what about materials related to religious beliefs? Which are "true" and which are not? Obviously, you want to stock items on the three major belief systems of Christianity, Judaism, and Islam. Will you also stock items about witchcraft and Santeria? Then there are extraterrestrials, the occult, and ghosts. All of these topics need to be represented in your collection if your collection is to be balanced and all, not just the majority, of your patrons' interests and needs met.

How should you handle adding something that you honestly believe should not be part of the library's collection? Balancing the collection along with a little creativity may be the answer. For instance, many of the patrons in a library where I once worked began requesting a book they had heard about on a television infomercial. This was one of the very few patron requests I initially refused to buy because the TV personality pedaling the book was under investigation for fraud by the Federal Communications Commission (FCC). However, so many requests for the book came in, including ILL requests for the book, that I finally had to go ahead and purchase it. To ease my concerns about adding something I thought was flagrantly factually false, I decided to add to the collection a notebook

For Further Information

For assistance on handling a formal objection to library materials, you may refer to "Challenged Resources: An Interpretation of the Library Bill of Rights" on the ALA website (www.ala.org/advocacy/intfreedom/librarybill/interpretations/challenged-resources).

FIGURE 18.1

Collection Reconsideration Form

Collection Reconsideration Policy

The library collects materials that appeal to a wide spectrum of community interests and tastes. Consequently, not all materials in the collection will appeal to all individuals. This principle may be especially noticeable in the Youth Services collection, where items meet the needs of children ranging from infants to teenagers. The library encourages parents and guardians to review its materials and use the ones they deem appropriate for their families.

Users may discuss concerns about library materials with staff at the Youth or Adult Reference desk. If these discussions do not prove satisfactory, concerns about Youth Services materials are referred to the Youth Services Director and objections to Adult Services materials are referred to the Adult Services Director. If, after talking with these directors, the matter is still not resolved, the user may complete a written "Request for Reconsideration of Library Materials." The appropriate director responds to the completed form within seven days of its receipt, examining the work in question, checking for reviews, and continuing the negotiation process. If the director's response does not prove satisfactory, the next appeal is to the Library Director. Such appeals receive the Director's written response within fourteen days of receipt.

Final appeals may be made to the Library's Board of Trustees. Once a final appeal is received, the Board conducts a hearing at its next regularly scheduled meeting. The Board may consider the matter until the following regularly scheduled meeting. The Board will issue a written response to the appeal within ten days after this second, regularly scheduled meeting.

Request for Reconsideration of Library Materials

Author: _____

Title: _____

Publisher: _____

Request initiated by: _____

Telephone: _____

Address: _____

Individual represents: Self _____ Organization _____

1. To what do you object? (Please be specific.)
2. What do you believe might be the result of reading, listening to, or viewing this material?
3. For what age group would you recommend this material?
4. Did you read, listen to, or view this material in its entirety? If not, what part(s)?

with information on the FCC's investigation of the author. I also made sure both items would appear as results from any catalog search on either the title of the book or its author. If a patron chose not to read about the FCC investigation, that was the patron's decision, but at least the information was readily available.

Finally, do not automatically assume an item does not belong in the collection because of its subject matter. Do not try to discern the reasons specific information or something by a specific author or singer-songwriter is wanted. It is your role to provide for the recreational and informational needs of your patrons regardless of their reasons for wanting it.

Selection Resources

The following is an annotated list of resources that are useful in the selection process.

Print Materials

- Professional journals, such as *Publishers Weekly, Booklist, Library Journal, The Horn Book, VOYA (Voice of Youth Advocates)*, and *School Library Journal*, provide reviews, upcoming titles, and articles on specific subjects.
- Local newspapers, as well as the *New York Times* and the *Wall Street Journal*, are good sources of book reviews that have a wide audience.
- Magazines, such as *People* and *Entertainment Weekly*, are sources of popular book, music, and film reviews.
- *Smithsonian* and *Discovery* magazines review titles that are scientific or historical in nature.
- Barnes & Noble online and Amazon.com are excellent sources for checking on the availability of items, finding reviews, and doing subject searches.
- Title Source and Ingram are wholesale jobbers that provide reviews and information on availability.
- *ForeWord Magazine*, available online and in print, reviews works from small publishers and self-publishing houses.
- *Booklist*, a book review source published by the ALA, is available online and in print.
- Consult Fantastic Fiction (www.fantasticfiction.co.uk) to find a complete list of an author's works and to decipher the order of titles in a series. This web resource also provides information on new and forthcoming titles.
- For graphic novel reviews, consult *Booklist, School Library Journal, VOYA*, and the websites for Comic Book Resources (www.comicbookresources.com/) and IGN Comics (www.ign.com/

comics). The Diamond Comic Distributors' PREVIEWSworld website (www.previewsworld.com) and the *New York Times* best-selling graphic novels list provide information on new and forthcoming titles.

- Your state library and state library association may provide reviews of titles of local interest.
- When a review is unavailable, check the OCLC database to see if other libraries own a title.
- Best-seller lists and Internet searches for "best books of . . ." are also good ways to find popular materials or lists of titles on specific topics.

Nonprint Materials

- Amazon.com, Midwest Tape (www.midwesttapes.com/home) and *AudioFile* (www.audiofilemagazine.com) focus on reviews and the availability of music CDs, audiobooks, and DVDs.
- AllMusic.com features reviews and complete discographies.
- CDHotList.com recommends new releases for libraries.
- Playbill.com lists new music releases pertaining to theatre, and Metacritic.com summarizes film and music reviews from other websites.
- PBS (www.pbs.org) is an excellent resource for nonfeature DVDs and the ever-popular BBC series.
- For e-books, consult EBSCO, OverDrive, Recorded Books, and Midwest Tape.

Miscellaneous Resources

- Patron requests provide insight on library materials wanted by the community your library serves.
- Award lists, including, but certainly not limited to, the Pulitzer Prizes, Grammy Awards, Academy Awards, Newbery Medals, Caldecott Medals, Nebula Awards, and Hugo Awards, are useful across genres and formats.
- Ask for trial subscriptions to databases or preview copies from publishers if you want to look before you buy.

Funding the Collection

Besides your annual materials budget, you can tap into other resources. Get as creative as you want in finding sources for funds or materials.

- Donations from library patrons can be in the form of cash donations, in-memoriam donations, perpetual book funds, or gift subscriptions to periodicals.

- Grants from your Friends of the Library group may fund upgrades of specific collection areas or provide seed money for a new collection.
- Book donations from local authors provide access to materials published by authors in the community.
- Cash or materials donations from local groups or national groups include, among others, bird watching and gardening clubs, native plant societies, sports and hobby groups, and mental health associations.

Conclusion

Selection of material for the library's collection is a collaborative effort. For a well-rounded collection, the selector should seek input from as many resources as possible, including other librarians and staff members, patrons, and print and online resources.

Selection is also a balancing act. The informational and recreational needs and wants of library patrons are the point of the whole selection process, but these must be offset by the funds available to you.

Finally, selection of library collection materials requires a basic knowledge in many subject areas or a willingness to seek out such information, an understanding of the interests of the library's patrons and the community, and sometimes a "gut feeling." It is not an exact science but a combination of knowledge, resources, experience, and intuition.

Further Reading

American Library Association. "Collection Development." www.ala.org/tools/atoz/Collection%20Development/collectiondevelopment.

Bogart, Doug, ed. *Library and Book Trade Almanac.* 58th ed. Medford, NJ: Information Today, 2013.

Johnson, Peggy. *Fundamentals of Collection Development and Management.* 2nd ed. Chicago: American Library Association, 2009.

Ordering

Laura Morales

19

Ordering is the process by which items that are selected for addition to the library collection are purchased from a supplier for addition to the library collection. This chapter covers the steps required to buy an item from a vendor and get it ready to be turned over to the catalogers for additional processing. Ordering is a fairly straightforward process, but it has a lot of moving parts, so attention to detail is important, as is a strong sense of the needs of your users and the priorities of your library. This will allow you to make the decision between the vendor with the best price and the one with the fastest fulfillment. For the purposes of this chapter, no assumptions have been made concerning whether or not an acquisitions module is being used or even whether or not your library has an integrated library system (ILS).

Determining the Nature of the Material

Once you are aware of a material that you need to purchase, you have to gather certain pertinent information concerning that item. If it is a book, you need to know the title, author, publisher, print type, and type of binding. If it is an audiovisual resource, you will need information such as what format, who recorded it, and who is releasing it. For digital items, the format and platform for access are important in addition to title and author. All this information will not only help you identify the correct item for purchase but often also dictate from which vendor you will be able to purchase the item.

Deciding on a Vendor

Once you have gathered full information on the material you intend to purchase, you will have to decide where to buy it. Items that are currently in print are usually available through wholesalers, publishers, or local bookstores and music stores. Rare or out-of-print items can be purchased through

Ordering Resources

- Amazon: **www.amazon.com**
- American Book Company:
  www.americanbookcompany.com
- Baker & Taylor: **www.btol.com**
- Blackstone Audio:
  www.blackstonelibrary.com
- Brilliance Audio:
  library.brillianceaudio.com
- Brodart: **www.brodartbooks.com**
- Center Point Large Print:
  www.centerpointlargeprint.com
- EBSCO: **www.ebsco.com**
- Ingram: **www.ingramlibrary.com**
- Midwest: **www.midwesttapes.com**
- Tantor: **www.tantorlibrary.com**
- Thorndike Press:
  thorndike.gale.com
- W. T. Cox: **www.wtcox.com**

overstock/remainder sellers, out-of-print dealers, or other online sources.

Wholesalers carry a large variety of titles from many different publishers and focus their business model on selling to bookstores and libraries. They have a large stock of items, most of which have been recently published. Examples of wholesalers include Baker & Taylor, Ingram, Midwest Tape, and Brodart. As these are robust businesses that move a lot of merchandise, they are often able to offer the best discounts on popular items. They also usually offer to libraries electronic ordering and a searchable database that allows the individual who is ordering to verify that the desired item is in stock or available for back order before an order is sent in.

The publisher is the business that actually produces the item. Although much of what the larger publishers produce is also available through wholesalers, titles produced by smaller publishers or works that are less popular but still in print are usually best acquired directly from the source. Publishers do not offer the same steep discounts as wholesalers, but they can be more assured of having the item in stock.

Local bookstores and music stores, though disappearing rapidly, are also options when purchasing items. Although they are the least likely to offer significant discounts, they do allow you to have an item in hand that same day, as long as you have access to a credit card or cash to make the purchase. They will also not offer as much depth of selection as a wholesaler or publisher, but if you need an item immediately and they have it in stock, they should still be considered.

Some libraries are members of a regional or national group that develops and negotiates contracts with vendors for library materials. Because these alliances represent the large buying power of all their respective members combined, they are often able to lock in higher discounts than the members would have been able to get individually. If you are not already a part of one of these groups, conduct some research about what is available to you locally. The savings can be significant over the course of a year.

For some items, you will be limited to only one vendor. This is especially the case with electronic items, such as e-books or downloadable audiobooks. If this is the case, the ordering process is very straightforward, although the vendor is not likely to offer any discounts, mainly due to exclusive agreements that publishers signed with different vendors when they took the jump from physical products to digital ones. Hopefully, as the formats mature somewhat, these kinds of contracts will not be as prevalent and libraries will have a wider selection of vendors in the future as well as more library-friendly pricing schemes.

Selecting the Method of Payment

Most vendors accept payment in several ways. Depending on the flexibility of your finance department, one or all of the following can be used to pay for materials.

The first method is payment through a purchase order; the vendor fulfills your order, sends you an invoice, and accepts payment after you receive the items. Setting up a purchase order account with a vendor is usually done before you submit your first order, so that you and the vendor establish a relationship. This can include, if applicable, sending the vendor your tax exemption information as well as name and contact information so that the vendor can contact you if there are any issues with your account.

Some libraries use prepaid accounts. As the name implies, these work by sending the vendor a set amount of money that the vendor then debits for the appropriate amount each time the vendor fulfills an order. For some libraries that use only one main vendor for their orders, this reduces the amount of paperwork that they need to fill out, but it does require them to keep thorough records of discounts and items received to ensure the charges are being properly deducted.

Another method of payment is through a business credit card account. This is certainly the most flexible method, as it allows the acquisitions staff to purchase from almost any online vendor as well as local stores.

Selecting Add-Ons

Many vendors will also process an item before sending it to you. This can be either a full treatment, including bar code, security tagging, wrapping the dust jacket, and adding spine labels, and so forth, or an à la carte selection that suits your library's needs. While this does add a cost to each item processed, smaller institutions that have relatively few employees might find it well worth their money due to the amount of staff time saved. More and more vendors are also offering full catalog records for the items they sell. While these records are of varying quality, depending on which vendor is providing them, they can be a necessity for both small and large libraries that can accept quality as a tradeoff for getting their items out to their users more quickly.

Creating and Submitting Your Order

Whether you are purchasing one item or thousands at a time, gather up only the relevant information that is required for the selected vendor to identify the exact item or items you are trying to purchase. This usually includes the title and author/performer. Standardized numbers, such as ISBN (International Standard Book Number) or UPC (Universal Product Code), are often the most vital to differentiate between various editions or bindings of the same work, and many vendors require this information to ensure they can correctly match the order with the stock in their database. Once you have gathered this information for each item on your order, submit the order to the vendor using the payment method selected earlier.

Tracking Your Budget

Small libraries usually have pretty tight budgets, so the only thing worse than overspending your budget is having funds left over that were desperately needed. Libraries purchase thousands of items each year, and keeping track of what has been spent can be tricky. If you have an ILS with a robust acquisitions module, this job is a lot easier, but if not, something as simple as an Excel workbook can be used. The key is to make sure that every item and every purchase is entered correctly, and if the final price is less than anticipated, alter the entry to reflect the price paid.

Handling Cancelled and Back-Ordered Items

Even with the best care taken by the person placing the order, items that a vendor indicates are in stock might not actually be so or an item with a projected publication date can get cancelled. When this occurs, your vendor will hopefully notify you about the changed status of an item, whether it is completely cancelled or just put on back order. Sometimes this communication gets missed, so it is important to check regularly on the status of items that have not yet been received. If an item is no longer available through the seller you initially selected, you can then decide to reorder from another vendor. Make sure to update your budget tracking with the new information so that you are able to have the most complete picture of the status of your budget.

Receiving Items

The last part of the process is to receive the item. This involves checking to make sure the item received is the correct one and matches both what is printed on the invoice and what was actually ordered. The items must also be checked to make sure there is no physical damage. If everything is correct and in good shape, the item can be marked in your system as having been received, and the invoice sent for payment if the item is from a purchase order. Also, be sure to mark the item as being paid in your budget tracking. At this point, the item itself can be turned over to your catalogers, who will begin the process described in the next chapter.

Conclusion

Libraries offer a wide variety of materials on various formats, and this requires an expansive knowledge of different vendors and pricing schemes. The person who processes orders for your library has to go through the steps outlined in this chapter for each and every item that your library purchases. Although on the surface the process may seem complex, the steps quickly become second nature to staff who order with regularity. These employees are crucial in helping your library fulfill its mission by procuring the materials that are required by your users, while balancing the various stresses on the budget. Although ordering can be difficult, you will feel enormous satisfaction when a particularly challenging item is tracked down or a budget is spent within pennies at the end of the fiscal year.

Further Reading

Breeding, Marshall. "Coping with Complex Collections: Managing Print and Digital." *Computers in Libraries* 32, no. 7 (2012): 23.

Chapman, Liz. *Managing Acquisitions in Library and Information Services.* 3rd rev. ed. New York: Neal-Schuman, 2004.

Holden, Jesse. *Acquisitions in the New Information Universe.* New York: Neal-Schuman, 2010.

Laskowski, Mary S. *Guide to Video Acquisitions in Libraries: Issues and Best Practices.* New York: Neal-Schuman, 2011.

Cataloging

Laura Morales

Cataloging in libraries is a process of creating a record using both descriptive cataloging and subject cataloging to describe an item so that it can be organized in an appropriate place within the library and discovered by the library's users. This chapter provides an introduction to basic cataloging procedures and services, including descriptive cataloging, subject cataloging, cataloging systems, authority control, and the development of local collection schemes.

Descriptive Cataloging

The first thing a cataloger does is to create a description of the item that is being added to the collection. This requires the cataloger to identify the item using descriptive elements such as title, author, publisher, performer, format, and so on. This process acts to separate, for example, a hardcover version of Shakespeare's *Hamlet* from an audiobook version or a first edition from an eighteenth edition. As with all parts of cataloging, this procedure is done with the users in mind, so that they know before they go to pull an item off the shelf whether it is what they are seeking.

Subject Cataloging

The second thing a cataloger embarks upon is assigning subject headings. Subject headings usually come from a designated thesaurus, such as the Library of Congress Subject Headings (LCSH) or the Sears List of Subject Headings. A cataloger will often assign multiple subject headings to a record in order to fully describe an item. In most online library catalogs, subject headings are indexed, searchable, and linked so that a user can click on the subject heading in a particular item and pull up a list of all other cataloging

Cataloging Resources

- Library of Congress Authorities:
  http://authorities.loc.gov
- Library of Congress Cataloging
  and Acquisitions Home:
  www.loc.gov/aba/
- 025.431: The Dewey Blog:
  http://ddc.typepad.com
- NISO Z39.50 Resources Page:
  **www.niso.org/standards/
  resources/Z39.50_Resources**
- OCLC Dewey Discussion Papers:
  **www.oclc.org/dewey/discussion
  .en.html**

entries that have been assigned the same subject heading. This helps the user browse the collection to find related, relevant material.

Authority Control

As defined by the Library of Congress (2011), "Authority records enable librarians to provide uniform access to materials in library catalogs and to provide clear identification of authors and subject headings. For example, works about 'movies,' 'motion pictures,' 'cinema,' and 'films' are all entered under the established subject heading 'Motion pictures.'" Authority records use "See" and "See Also" to cross-reference and show relationships between headings. Authority control allows the cataloger to apply structured and consistent access points to the item record that allow for efficient use of the library catalog by users.

Assigning a Classification Number

Most libraries use one of two major classification schemes: Dewey Decimal or Library of Congress.

Dewey Decimal System

The Dewey system breaks down subjects into ten main classes and then down again further, with each number in the sequence representing a specific subject under the umbrella of the number to its left. For some works, decimal places are used to further place the item within the hierarchy of the subject. These are the main classes:

000	Computer science, information & general works
100	Philosophy & psychology
200	Religion
300	Social sciences
400	Language
500	Science
600	Technology
700	Arts & recreation
800	Literature
900	History & geography

Further breakdown of the 500 class would look like this:

500	Science
510	Mathematics
520	Astronomy

530 Physics
540 Chemistry
550 Earth sciences & geology
560 Fossils & prehistoric life
570 Life sciences; biology
580 Plants (Botany)
590 Animals (Zoology)

Library of Congress Classification

Originally developed in the late nineteenth century to organize the collection of the Library of Congress, the Library of Congress Classification (LCC) system has since been adopted by many academic libraries. LCC breaks down subjects into twenty-one main classes using letters and then breaks them down again using a second letter to designate a subclass. Topics associated with this subclass are designated by a number, from one to four digits in length. Subtopics can also be assigned using a combination of letters and numbers. This approach can create a potentially long call number, but one that is flexible and less hierarchical than those used in the Dewey system. These are the main classes:

A   General Works
B   Philosophy. Psychology. Religion
C   Auxiliary Sciences of History
D   World History and History of Europe, Asia, Africa, Australia, New Zealand, etc.
E   History of the Americas
F   History of the Americas
G   Geography. Anthropology. Recreation
H   Social Sciences
J   Political Science
K   Law
L   Education
M   Music and Books on Music
N   Fine Arts
P   Language and Literature
Q   Science
R   Medicine
S   Agriculture
T   Technology
U   Military Science
V   Naval Science
Z   Bibliography. Library Science. Information Resources (General)

> **Example**
>
> A book on bats would be cataloged using the Dewey Decimal System in the 599.4 section.

Further breakdown of main class Q into subclasses would look like this:

Q   Science (General)
QA   Mathematics
QB   Astronomy
QC   Physics
QD   Chemistry
QE   Geology
QH   Natural History—Biology
QK   Botany
QL   Zoology
QM   Human anatomy
QP   Physiology
QR   Microbiology

Applying a Local Collection Scheme

The final step in cataloging is to assign an item to a local collection scheme, if applicable. Many libraries find that just using Dewey or LCC to catalog an item does not serve the needs of their users without a little tweaking. This portion of cataloging is where libraries have the ability to organize their collection in a way that best suits the needs of their users. After all, the purpose of every library is to connect its users with the collection. Each library has the ability to further organize its overall collection into smaller collections. Creation of these collections can be driven by subject, reading level, format, or circulation policy.

An item that the library does not desire to make available for circulation might be housed in a separate collection in the reference department. To designate that an item belongs in this collection, the cataloger might add either "R" or "REF" to the beginning of the call number. The library could own several copies of a particular item and want one copy permanently available in the reference collection, while allowing the others to circulate.

Many public and school libraries separate the bulk of their fiction collection from their nonfiction. Instead of using the appropriate Dewey 800s number, the books are grouped alphabetically based on an author's last name. This is preceded on the spine label by either an "F" or "Fic" to designate the work as fiction. This collection can, depending on the needs of the library and its users, be even further broken down into "M" or "Mys" for mysteries, "Fan" for Fantasy, "SF" for Science Fiction, and so on. These subcollections can either stay interfiled with the rest of the fiction or be housed separately. Those libraries which separate out the genres do so because it gives them a more easily browsed, concentrated collection for people who are interested in only a specific kind of book, such as romances or mysteries. The downsides are that many books are not easily placed into only one genre and some users might have preconceptions about certain genres. People

Example

In the Library of Congress system, the same book on bats would be cataloged as QL737.C5.

Example

Circulating copies of the *World Almanac and Book of Facts* might have the call number 317.3 WOR 2014, while the reference copy would have R 317.3 WOR 2014.

who do not think they would like science fiction will potentially miss out on good books if they never enter the SF stacks.

Public and school libraries also often place items that are aimed at children or a teen audience into a separate collection. Because reading level is often as important as, if not more important than, subject for those users, arranging these items by reading level is a better way to serve the users of the library. Libraries that shelve these items separately might also consider creating local subject headings that designate the items as being juvenile to increase the browsability of the collection for younger readers.

Academic and special libraries, along with some public libraries, have a unique collection of items that do not circulate. These special collections can be rare books, archives, local history, government documents, genealogy collections, or any other kind of special collection that a library wants to protect from loss or damage. These items would also be given a special designation to label them as being part of that collection.

Conclusion

Because many libraries share the same titles, descriptive and subject cataloging may have already been done by another institution. The resulting bibliographic records are shared so that the work does not need to be redone by your internal cataloger. Millions of these records are available to be downloaded. Some record databases, such as OCLC, require membership and payment, but others, such as the Library of Congress, do not. Downloading these records and then adding relevant local classification schemes do still require the cataloger to check the quality of the records and the correctness of their entries but, in the end, save a lot of time. This is referred to as copy cataloging because it involves copying a record and importing it into your database.

Cataloging may appear to be a confusing process, but it is important to focus on the needs of your users when developing cataloging procedures. Users need materials to be described accurately and organized in an accessible manner. All the rules that surround descriptive cataloging, subject cataloging, authority control, and classification schemes, both local and global, have been created with this aim in mind. Good cataloging will allow your users not only to find an item but also to browse and discover additional relevant items in the collection through the linked authorities, thus increasing your circulation numbers as well as accomplishing the goal of connecting users with items that fulfill their informational or recreational needs.

Example

A copy of *Harry Potter and the Chamber of Secrets* by J. K. Rowling has the LCC subject headings *Wizards, Magic, Schools,* and *England.* When it is cataloged locally for a youth audience, those subject headings can be altered to become *Wizards–Juvenile Fiction, Magic–Juvenile Fiction,* and so on.

Further Reading

Broughton, Vanda. *Essential Library of Congress Subject Headings.* New York: Neal-Schuman, 2011.

Hider, Philip. *Information Resource Description: Creating and Managing Metadata.* Chicago: American Library Association, 2013.

Jones, Ed. *RDA and Serials Cataloging.* Chicago: American Library Association, 2013.

Maxwell, Robert L. *Maxwell's Guide to Authority Work.* Chicago: American Library Association, 2002.

Weber, Mary Beth, and Fay Angela Austin. *Describing Electronic, Digital, and Other Media Using AACR2 and RDA: A How-To-Do-It Manual and CD-ROM for Librarians.* New York: Neal-Schuman, 2010.

Welsh, Anne, and Sue Batley. *Practical Cataloguing: AACR2, RDA and MARC21.* New York: Neal-Schuman, 2012.

References

Library of Congress. 2011. "Frequently Asked Questions: What Is an Authority Record?" Library of Congress Authorities. Last updated October 4. http://authorities.loc.gov/help/auth-faq.htm.

Circulation

John A. Moorman

Circulation is the process by which items in the collection are taken out of the library by a user and then returned to the library. While the circulation of materials is a straightforward operation, several factors must be considered in developing policies and procedures for this operation:

- To whom does the library circulate materials?
- For what time periods does the library circulate materials?
- How does the library handle materials when they become overdue?
- How does the library get materials back on the shelves?

The answer to each of these questions will vary according to individual libraries and the communities in which they operate. This chapter examines each of these main factors in the circulation process.

Circulation Audience

The question of to whom the library circulates materials is more nuanced than it might appear at first glance because circulation decisions must take into account the nature of the library and its specific setting and circumstances.

School library questions include these:

- Does the library allow circulation of materials beyond the faculty, staff, and students of the school in which the library is housed?
- Does the library allow faculty, staff, and students from other schools in the district to check out materials?
- Does the library allow the public to have access to the collection? Is the collection available through interlibrary loan?

Each of these questions will have a different answer depending upon the local setting and the relationships that the library has with other libraries in the community.

Special library questions include these:

- Does the library allow circulation of materials beyond the facility in which the library is housed?
- By whom within the agency are materials permitted to be accessed and used? (Some businesses will have categories of users depending upon security clearances and other factors.)
- What level of access, if any, does the general public have to the collections, either in person or through interlibrary loan?

Unlike other types of libraries, special libraries have wide variations in their organizational support, from entities that are totally governmentally funded, such as libraries within federal and state agencies; to entities that are nonprofit, such as historical and museum libraries; to entities that are a part of a for-profit company. Each of these operational situations will bring different answers to the questions mentioned earlier.

Academic library questions include these:

- Does the library circulate only to students, faculty, and staff?
- Does the library treat staff differently from faculty?
- Does the library allow individuals from the community access to its collections? If so, is their use of the collection limited to in-house use or may they use materials away from the library?
- What level of access does the library allow through interlibrary loan?

Public library questions include these:

- Does the library permit individuals from outside the local jurisdiction to obtain materials from the collection? If so, is it free access, or does the library charge a fee for this use?
- What evidence of residence does the library require before the individual can obtain a library card?
- What information does the library keep on each library user and how is that material shared with other entities? (Most states have privacy laws that restrict access to patron records.)
- Does the library require the presentation of a user card when circulating materials or can library staff look up the patron's card number?
- What requirements does outside funding such as state aid bring to the question of library access?

- If the library is in a community with a large tourist presence, how does the library accommodate tourists' desire to use the facilities while in the community?

All of these questions are essential to the process of determining how the collection will be accessed and used. Much thought needs to be given to the answers, as the process of determining the answers will involve not only library staff but also administrative and corporate personnel as well as members of the institution's governing body. In this process, no answer should ever be considered final because changes and circumstances can dictate a new look at operating procedures.

Circulation Time Periods

The question of how long materials circulate can have as many right answers as there are libraries. Circulation of library materials should be driven by the needs of the users rather than the needs of the institution. This concept often is difficult to get across to staff and governing officials. The library exists to serve the needs of its clientele for information necessary for education, leisure, and work. While some libraries, particularly special libraries, can have security requirements that affect use, most libraries should place the needs and desires of their users foremost in the setting of time and access limits for collection use.

Academic library loan periods are driven by the educational function of the institution. Loan periods for students can vary according to time periods of semesters or quarters as well as the number of students needing the material. Graduate students might get more extended loan periods than undergraduate students. Faculty and staff might get loans varying from one semester to indefinite in length. A question to consider when determining loan periods is the ability to recall an item when another user requests it. Does the recall ability depend on the status of the individual making the request, and what recourse does the library have in getting material back from users when a request has been made? With faculty members, this can be a difficult and very touchy proposition.

Public library loan periods are always a point of controversy. No matter what loan periods are set up for materials, there will always be a vocal minority of users who are displeased with them. One of the goals of the loan period policy should be to keep these users to a minority, and a small minority at that. Questions to consider include these:

- Does the library have different loan periods for different formats of materials?
- Does the library give new and popular materials a shorter loan period than other materials?

> Circulation of library materials should be driven by the needs of the users rather than the needs of the institution.

- If it is a new book but over a certain length, does the library still lend it out for a shorter period?

In making these decisions, look at what other public libraries in the area are doing with their loan periods, particularly those with whom you library has a close user interaction. Examine how loan periods might affect staff workload. If the building is crowded from a shelving standpoint, a longer loan period might ease problems in this area.

Overdue Materials

The problem of overdue materials is one of the banes of library existence. Librarians deal with human beings, not robots, and human beings, besides having good characteristics, are forgetful and irresponsible. This leads to the inevitable confrontation between a library staff member and a user in which the user claims that he or she did in fact return the material in question and the library has lost it somewhere. How libraries deal with that situation is discussed later.

One of the first issues to be considered when developing policies and procedures for the collection of overdue materials is fines. Does the library charge or not charge individuals when they return library materials past the due date? Most libraries have some sort of monetary charge in this situation, one which is based on the presumption that for extra time and the inconvenience that it causes staff and other users, the person should pay a fee. Also, if there is no fee attached to late return of materials, there is little penalty for nonreturn other than no further use of the library or a blemish on the user's credit rating. A few libraries charge no fines and have had a good experience with this. In any case, libraries should realize that fine money seldom pays for the expense of staff time in preparing notices or the cost of mailing notices and the other responsibilities associated with this process.

Other factors in the overdue process include what procedures the library has in place for checking shelves and reading shelves to see that materials are in proper order. How well have staff responsible for checking in and shelving materials been trained? How well are they performing their tasks? Nobody is perfect and mistakes will be made. Users will also put material back on the shelves to get around late fees.

Decisions also must be made in regard to the timing and handling of overdue notices:

- How long do you wait until the library sends out a first overdue notice?
- How many notices does the library send out before it sends a bill?
- Does the library use a collection agency for overdue material and uncollected fines? If so, when does the library send items to the agency?

- Does the library have a good working arrangement with the city or county attorney's office where they are willing to assist in the return of late material?

These are all factors to consider as the library develops procedures in this area. Again, talk to other libraries in the area to see what their procedures are before deciding on your own.

How does the library handle that mad user who swears up and down that he or she has returned the material in question? The library staff have checked all possible locations and not come up with the material. What next? Always try to keep the situation calm and out of the public view, although this is difficult in the small library. Questions to ask here are these: Is this individual a chronic abuser of library materials? What is the situation in this instance? Who the individual is and his or her position in the community should not play a role in the final decision but will affect how staff handle the situation. At this stage, staff can buy time by requesting that a more thorough search be made of the user's home, car, workspace, and belongings before a final determination is made. However, if it is beyond that stage, there are really only two choices: waive the fine and count the material as lost, or be firm and let the individual know that he or she will be held accountable for the material in question. This is not one of the enjoyable tasks of librarianship, but it is necessary if policies and procedures are to be effective in the long run. If the material does turn up later, a heartfelt apology should be issued. However, very seldom, if ever, will this be necessary if the proper steps are followed by library staff.

> Know your community. What works best in one community might be a disaster in another community.

Return of Materials

How does the library get materials back on the shelves? The simple answer is to shelve them. However, it is more complicated than that.

- Are materials brought back to the desk from which they were checked out?
- Does the library have an automated return system to assist in getting materials back to public use?
- Does the library have inside materials return drops that go either to a central room or to a cart under the circulation desk?
- Does the library have outside materials return drops that are either walk-up or drive-through?
- Does the library have remote-site materials return locations either inside or outside of a building?

Any type of library can use each of these possibilities. However, most special, academic, and school libraries do not have return facilities outside of their buildings.

In any consideration of remote-site materials return, several issues need to be examined. How secure is the site and how open to vandalism is it? Many good remote return sites are in stores such as grocery stores or malls where security is high. The second question is the availability of staff or volunteers to check the sites on a regular basis. Such locations tend to be popular and will fill up with materials more rapidly than anticipated. In some areas, it is necessary to have seven-days-a-week pickup.

One factor to consider when developing an outside materials return drop or any interior drop that empties into a room is the need for extra fire suppression for this space. Material drops are places where flammable material may be inserted, and some libraries have been destroyed through such actions.

The second aspect of materials return is the checking in of the materials and the returning of them to the shelves. Generally, shelvers perform this task, although in small libraries this can be one of the duties of anyone from the library director to the custodian. With an automated return system, much of this process is accomplished without human assistance. However it is accomplished, this part of the process is one of the most important in the whole library operation. If materials are improperly checked in or not checked in at all, the library will have a problem with the last person of record, who will be justly irritated at the lack of competence of library staff. If the materials are not properly shelved, they are for all intents and purposes unavailable to the public. Take your time to do it right the first time.

One concept to aid the small library with the reshelving issue is to have a section of shelving where returned books may be placed in the public area before being returned to the stacks. Users will appreciate this, as they like to see what is of interest to others. The library staff will appreciate it, too, as there will be fewer books to shelve when others take them to be checked out again.

Technology in the Circulation Process

Technology is playing a more important role in material circulation in even the smallest library. While technology can be of great assistance to library staff and users, it can also place undue burdens on the circulation process.

Questions to ask when considering automation for circulation functions, an upgrade to the current system, or a new system include these:

- How flexible is the system?
- Can the system allow for individual privacy as well as the desire of some to have a long-term record of library use?
- Is it easy for the most inexperienced staff to perform all circulation functions?

- What information needs to be collected on library users to not only enable library use but also assist in the return function when necessary?
- Does the system integrate easily with other library functions and allow for financial transactions, if desired?
- If the system is part of a consortium that the library belongs to, does it adequately address circulation situations unique to the library?
- How can technology be used to more efficiently handle the hold/reserve function?
- How does self-check and self-return affect the materials handling flow?

These are but some of the questions that must be considered if automation of the circulation function(s) is to provide both the staff and the public with as seamless a library experience as possible.

Conclusion

Circulation is the most visible library function and the function in which there is the most direct user contact. It is important to have good policies and procedures developed for this area. Also, it is vital that all staff working in this area have a thorough understanding of these policies and procedures. It also helps if staff possess tact and common sense, for these are necessary ingredients for successful public service.

Further Reading

Chamara, Theresa. *Privacy and Confidentiality Issues: A Guide for Libraries and Their Lawyers*. Chicago: ALA Editions, 2008.

Huber, John J. *Lean Library Management: Eleven Strategies for Reducing Costs and Improving Services*. New York: Neal-Schuman, 2011.

Rubin, Rhea Joyce. *Defusing the Angry Patron: A How-To-Do-It Manual for Librarians*. 2nd ed. New York: Neal-Schuman, 2011.

Smallwood, Carol (ed.). *Library Management Tips That Work*. Chicago: ALA Editions, 2011.

Weeding

Barbara Riebe

Weeding is the process of removing items from the library's collection. This chapter examines the various reasons for weeding, discusses weeding procedures and the benefits of weeding, and offers suggestions on how to dispose of weeded items.

Reasons for Weeding

Weeding is an essential component of collection maintenance. Many reasons exist for weeding items from the library collection, not the least of which is space. If you purchase new items for the collection, you must make room for them. As you cannot keep adding rooms and shelves to a building, the only way to make room for new items is to remove other items from the shelves.

The most obvious items to weed are duplicate copies of former best sellers and superseded editions of items published on a regular schedule. The latter include directories, travel guides, and earlier editions of medical or consumer law books. Though other considerations must be taken into account when deciding whether or not to remove duplicate copies or superseded editions, this is certainly a good starting point in the weeding process.

All items with out-of-date or erroneous information should be removed from the collection, unless there is an overriding reason to keep them, such as for historical purposes. This is particularly important for the medical and legal collections, *regardless of their use*. In these cases, it is preferable to have no information rather than incorrect information. At least with no information, patrons would know to look elsewhere for what they need.

Items that are in poor condition, damaged, or no longer used may be weeded. Similarly, books that are no longer appealing because of newer, similar titles in the collection might also be removed, thus providing more shelf space.

Tip

Do not take a job about which you have doubts. Focus your weeding efforts on duplicate copies, outdated materials, and damaged items.

Weeding Procedures

Retention patterns for many items, particularly serials such as magazines, financial periodicals, or travel guides, can be established in your catalog. That way, as new editions arrive, the superseded items are weeded automatically.

If your library uses an online catalog, as most do, the bibliographic record should compile data on how often a specific item is used and when it was last used. That record can also show how often the title, as opposed to a specific item in the bibliographic record, has been used since the record was first added to the catalog. Printable reports utilizing this information make a valuable starting point when making weeding decisions.

Beyond consideration of a resource's use or condition, decisions need to be made on whether to replace weeded items with newer editions or similar titles. Observing what else is on the shelf in the subject area will help you make these decisions. Is this the last title on a topic or is the area overflowing with other titles on the same subject? Is this item a classic? And if the item is of historical value in your community, you may decide not to weed it at all.

Additional Benefits of Weeding

Providing hands-on knowledge of the collection is one of the most important, but least obvious, benefits of weeding. One must physically go to the shelves to weed a book. Doing so allows librarians access to other items in the collection of which they may not have been aware. Being in the stacks may also draw attention to items needing to be replaced that do not appear on any reports printed from data in a bibliographic record.

Weeding can also highlight weak spots in the collection. Conversely, it can let you know that new items might not be needed in a specific collection area, allowing you to spend your money elsewhere.

Weeding also makes the collection physically more attractive. Removing damaged or older items means patrons will more likely be drawn to the newer additions to the collection.

Tip

Use weeding as an opportunity to get to know your collection.

What to Do with Weeded Items

The most obvious task to perform when weeding an item is to remove it from the catalog. The item's bar code should also be crossed out and the item stamped as withdrawn. If there is a bookplate or notation indicating that the item was a gift from an individual or organization, for purposes of goodwill, this should be removed. All items may then be given to your library's Friends organization to be sold, offered to another library or organization, or discarded.

Conclusion

Though patrons often do not understand why libraries weed items from their collections, it is absolutely necessary. It is also a never-ending process. In order to have space in the stacks for newer items and to maintain an up-to-date and physically attractive collection that appeals to all patrons, periodic weeding of a library's collection is an essential part of collection development and maintenance.

Further Reading

American Library Association. "Weeding Library Collections: A Selected Annotated Bibliography for Library Collection Evaluation." Last modified November 2012. www.ala.org/tools/libfactsheets/alalibraryfactsheet15.

Part V

Computers and Automation

Personal Computers and In-House Networks

Karen C. Knox

Computers are as integral to libraries today as heat and electricity. The first thing many librarians do when they arrive at work for the day is turn on their computers, check their e-mail, look at the day's online calendar, and become familiar with any important messages from the staff intranet. Similarly, the first thing many patrons do when they come into the library is look for the computers, whether it is to search the online catalog for an item, spend some time accessing Internet resources, or use software like Microsoft Word to work on a project.

Thus, it goes without saying that your library will need to provide and maintain computer technology for both your patrons and staff to use. You will need either staff members who are knowledgeable enough to maintain your technology or a reliable outside consultant who is available to assist when needed or on a regular basis. In addition, technology is an area where libraries can help each other, in that you may find knowledge and support from your library cooperative or other colleagues, as basic technology services are similar among libraries.

Providing computers in the library is an essential service, and this chapter will help you understand how to manage your computer resources and plan for future technology needs.

Technology Plan

To effectively manage the technology in your library, you will need a technology plan. Similar to other plans that you might have for your library, such as a strategic plan or a marketing plan, the technology plan outlines the current status of the technology in the library, all the projects associated with the technology in the library, and plans for the future of the technology in the library. Without a technology plan, it becomes increasingly difficult to manage the library's technology resources.

Technology Plan Outline

- Library Mission
- Technology Goals
  - Goals for Public Service
  - Goals for Collection Development
  - Goals for Community Relations
  - Goals for Staff Development and Training
  - Goals for Facilities and Equipment
- Current Status and Equipment Inventory
- Staffing and Training
- Budget Requirements and Projections
- Evaluation

"Technically, a computer is a programmable machine. This means it can execute a programmed list of instructions and respond to new instructions that it is given. Today, however, the term is most often used to refer to the desktop and laptop computers that most people use. When referring to a desktop model, the term 'computer' technically only refers to the computer itself—not the monitor, keyboard, and mouse. Still, it is acceptable to refer to everything together as the computer. If you want to be really technical, the box that holds the computer is called the 'system unit.'"

(www.techterms.com/definition/computer)

If you have never prepared a technology plan before, you can access this author's sample plan online at www.karencknox.com/documents/Sample%20Technology%20Plan.pdf (for a quick overview, see the sidebar). As you will see in that sample, the technology plan should align with the library's mission and goals. After all, the library's technology is a support system for the library's services and resources. Therefore, it is critical that the technology in the library provides a way to support the goals of the library and meet the needs of the community. Therefore, the first section of the technology plan is the library's mission statement and a description of how the library's technology will support the library's mission.

The next major section of the technology plan should outline the library's technology goals. These should support the library's goals, perhaps as defined by a strategic plan, if your library has one. For example, many libraries will have goals for public service. Therefore, you will want to define technology goals that support the library's goals for public service. How will the technology support the ways that the public accesses the library's resources? This might include the actual public computers available as well as the library's online catalog and other online resources. It might also include the library's website or technology training classes. You will want to define technology goals for each area of the library's goals, as the technology will be key to the library's ability to achieve its goals.

You will also want to include an inventory of current equipment in your building. Creating this inventory will help you understand what you have available, both in terms of the network infrastructure as well as the actual server and computer equipment. You will want to note how many of each type of equipment you have as well as how old the equipment is. Keeping your equipment up-to-date will help enable your library to continue to meet the needs of your community. However, due to the expense involved with maintaining equipment, this is something you will want to include in your plan so you can allocate funds appropriately as needed. You will also want to include in your inventory a list of the software that is available for use in the library by both staff and patrons. In addition, consider all the equipment, including printers, copiers, and telephones, as these are just as important as your computers.

As you likely know, it is impossible to maintain your information technology (IT) without properly trained staff. Therefore, you will want to include information in your plan on how you will invest in the people resources needed to support your library's technology. All library staff will need to stay up-to-date on how to use the hardware and software. If you are able to have dedicated IT staff, they will likely need additional training to keep the technology running smoothly.

Of course, all these technology resources will cost money. It is very important to include a budget in your technology plan. After all, it may be reasonable to plan projects to keep your technology updated, but you will also need the financial resources to implement the necessary projects. It is a good idea to include a multiyear budget in your technology plan, to cover all the years of the plan, even if future years are estimates or projections. It is likely that you already include information for technology in the overall library budget, but the budget in your technology plan can specify in more detail what the technology projects will include and the financial resources necessary to complete them.

Finally, the last section of your technology plan should be an evaluation. As with most projects, you will want to evaluate how well you are meeting the goals that you specify in the plan. This will help you continue the things that are working well and make necessary changes to improve the things that are less successful. Whoever is ultimately responsible for implementation of the technology plan (whether the library director, an IT staff member, or someone else) should review the plan regularly to ensure that that library is meeting its goals. If circumstances change, as they tend to do, the plan should be revised to address new projects or goals.

Your technology plan can be an extremely helpful road map to finding success with the technology resources in your library. After all, it is increasingly important that libraries maintain technology that supports their overall goals. Computers and Internet access are staples for libraries today, and new technology that can help libraries reach their goals is evolving daily. Creating and maintaining a good technology plan will help ensure your library will stay relevant and important in your community.

Staff Technology Infrastructure

In order for your technology to support the needs of your staff and your patrons, you will need an infrastructure that can support a network of computers. You will need sufficient power outlets and network cabling for all the equipment in your library, both staff and public equipment.

Many different types of equipment will be working together to support the computer infrastructure. Much of the equipment will require access to the Internet. Therefore, all the computers must be on a network, and the library must have an Internet service provider (ISP) to connect the library to the Internet. In many cases, the local cable provider might have an option for a business to connect to the Internet. Alternatively, check with your library cooperative or even your municipality to find out how to best manage your Internet connection.

Some small libraries might have a server, or even a few servers, in their buildings. This depends on how many computers you have and how you might be connected to the Internet. A server can be used for a variety of things, including storing important documents in a central location, managing the computers and/or printers, and sometimes even hosting important software.

Certainly, you will need computers for your staff to use. Staff computers will need access to your integrated library system (ILS), which is the main system you use for cataloging and circulation (the next chapter discusses

"When you have two or more computers connected to each other, you have a network. The purpose of a network is to enable the sharing of files and information between multiple systems. The Internet could be described as a global network of networks. Computer networks can be connected through cables, such as Ethernet cables or phone lines, or wirelessly, using wireless networking cards that send and receive data through the air."

(www.techterms.com/definition/network)

the ILS in detail). In addition, your staff will likely need access to office software, such as the Microsoft Office suite containing programs like Word, Excel, Outlook, and PowerPoint. Internet Explorer or similar web browser software will be needed to access the web.

Your staff will need access to e-mail. This is another service that you can talk with your consortium, ISP, or municipality about if it is not something for which you already have a solution. Your staff will use e-mail daily to keep in touch with one another as well as with patrons. In addition, your ILS may use e-mail to send notices to your patrons. E-mail is a standard form of communication, and all libraries should have a solution in place to provide it.

Your library will need a telephone system, which may be fairly simple depending on how many telephone handsets you have in the library and how much business is conducted on the telephone. Keep in mind that some patrons will rely solely on the telephone to access information about the library, so the system will need to be robust and dependable.

Copy machines and/or printers for both staff and patrons to access will also be necessary. You may also want to have equipment for scanning and/or faxing documents. Often, a copy machine can be used to print, copy, fax, and scan.

The staff equipment infrastructure is the foundation on which any technology services will be built. Libraries, even small ones, need a strong technology foundation, as so many of today's library services depend on technology. The next section looks at some of the key technology services that your small library should support.

Key Technology Services

Just as you have computers for your staff to use, all libraries (regardless of size) should have computers available for the public to use. These computers should also be connected to the Internet and have software available to support patron needs. Office software is a staple on public computers, as is web browser software. The web browser is important to help point patrons to the library's website and online resources. Some libraries also offer additional productivity software, photo-editing software, and other options depending on the needs of their patrons. Remember that some of your patrons may not have access to the Internet at home, so they will rely on the library's computers for their Internet connectivity.

In addition, some patrons will have their own equipment, such as laptops and tablet computers, but will want to use the library to connect their own equipment to the Internet. For this reason, it is important that libraries offer free wireless access to their patrons as well. The wireless equipment is actually part of your technology infrastructure, but it needs to be installed and configured with your users in mind. In other words, your wireless service should be easy to connect to and provide a strong enough connection for patrons to use anywhere in the library.

Many libraries offer self-checkout technology, which enables patrons to check out their own materials instead of relying on a staff member to do it for them. Much like in a grocery store, self-checkout is typically provided as an option, as some patrons will still need or prefer to have a staff member help them. To offer self-checkout, you would need to work with a third-party vendor to ensure that the security system on your materials can be deactivated and that the self-checkout system works with your ILS. Adding self-checkout technology can provide a great service, but it is a large project that requires proper planning and investment.

Finally, it is important that all libraries think about the basic services they provide using technology. For example, all libraries should have a website. The library website should provide information to your community about your library's resources, services, and events. In addition, the library website will be the place where patrons can get access to any online resources that the library might provide, such as online databases. Even if your individual library cannot afford to provide access to online databases, it is possible that your consortium has some available or even your state library might provide some resources. Use your library's website to promote these online resources. You will also use your library website to provide access to your online catalog, where your patrons will go to find materials in your library. If you are part of a shared ILS or if you offer interlibrary loan, your website will be the place for patrons to search these other databases to find and request materials online.

In addition to your library's website, you will want to consider having a social media presence for your library. For example, does your library have a Facebook page or a Twitter account? With so many people relying on social media for information, it becomes important for your library to be able to communicate with your patrons using social media. Your Facebook page and/or Twitter account, in addition to your website, will be important marketing tools and further ways for your library to connect with the patrons in your community. After all, that is what technology really is—a tool to help us achieve our goals.

New Technology Services

As technology continues to evolve, libraries are challenged to support new technologies as part of their services. For example, some libraries are providing tablet computers, such as iPads, for their patrons to borrow, both in the library and at home for a short period of time. Some libraries are providing a similar service for e-readers, such as Kindles and Nooks. Providing access to this newer technology enables patrons who cannot afford to purchase their own equipment an opportunity to learn about the equipment.

In some communities, there is a trend in libraries to create makerspaces, which are spaces where patrons can come and create a variety of things. Some makerspaces contain 3-D printers, and some contain software and hardware for creating and editing photos, audio files, and/or videos. There is a new trend in society for people to use technology to create things, but the technology itself can be very expensive for individuals to purchase. The idea behind these makerspaces is that if libraries are able to provide the technology and share it with the community, this will open the door for many people to learn and create.

New technologies are always under development, so it is important for libraries to keep an eye out for new ways to provide technology services to their patrons.

Technology Security and Support

All this technology sounds great, but what is the reality behind providing and supporting all of this? Libraries are in a unique situation because they not only have resources available for their staff but also open their doors to the public every day. Thus, they need to ensure security of the library's assets while maintaining access for the public users.

First, this means that libraries should create policies that govern the use of their technology, both for the public as well as for their staff. Technology remains stable and robust if it is treated well and handled correctly, so it is a good idea to define rules around what users can and cannot do with the library's technology resources. In addition, a library will need access to technology staff who can help support the equipment. If technology is set up properly, it can run on its own fairly smoothly. However, the trick with technology is that people interact with it every day, which can interrupt the way the technology is intended to work.

Therefore, it is important that you set up the technology infrastructure with tools to control security on your network, such as firewall and antivirus software. It is important that your technology staff take advantage of other tools as well, such as software like Deep Freeze on public computers, which will restore a computer back to its original settings when it is rebooted. In addition, there are software systems available to help manage public computers and printers in libraries. These systems help enforce any time limits on public computers and fees associated with using your computers or printers.

It is always a good idea to make backups of important servers and/or computers in your library as well. For example, if you have an ILS server, you will definitely want to back up the data on that server every night. Your ILS vendor can probably help you set that up. If you save important data on other computers or servers, you will want to back those up as well. Backups are important in case something drastic happens with your equipment because they provide you with a way to restore the data quickly. Equipment will fail. Mistakes will happen. Anything you can put in place to help minimize the damage will be most helpful.

Conclusion

Technology resources have become a vital part of today's libraries. Creating a technology plan and keeping it up-to-date are key to successfully providing technology resources. The actual technology equipment will continue to evolve, but technology as a whole will remain a critical part of every library. Staying current on trends in library technology will keep your library relevant in your community. Plan to invest the necessary resources in technology for your library, and you will be on the road to success.

Integrated Library Systems

Karen C. Knox

The core system in your library is going to be your integrated library system (ILS). It is the heartbeat that keeps your library running, from a system standpoint, and therefore is critical to understand and maintain. The ILS provides a system for managing the acquisition, cataloging, circulation, and public catalog for your library. Everything you need to do to manage your collection and patrons at your library can be done with your ILS. Therefore, it is important that it is reliable and dependable, and that you and your staff are comfortable with both the software and the company supporting the software. As technology continues to evolve, the future of the ILS systems will continue to redefine how these systems help libraries do their work. This chapter takes a look at the important features to have in an ILS, discusses how to integrate the ILS with third-party products, examines the relationship between the library and its ILS, and concludes with a consideration of the ILS's future.

Important Features of an ILS

The ILS will provide functionality to manage the patrons who use your library and how they use your library's resources. Starting from the time your library acquires a new item, the ILS's acquisition function will enable your staff to track the new items from order through delivery and payment of invoice. For each item in the collection, the ILS's cataloging function will enable your staff to create a record of all the identifying information you need for that item as well as the rules that govern how that item can be used by library patrons. For each patron, the ILS's circulation function will enable your staff to create a record of all the contact information you need about that patron as well as a history of the items that patron has used. Finally, the ILS's provision of an interface for the public catalog for your library patrons will enable patrons to search for and locate items within your library collection through an easy-to-use web interface.

An integrated library system (ILS) is "an integrated set of applications designed to perform the business and technical functions of a library, including acquisitions, cataloging, circulation, and the provision of public access. In alphabetical order, the leading vendors of library management software are: Auto-Graphics, EOS International, Ex Libris, Follett, Innovative Interfaces, Polaris Library Systems, SirsiDynix, TLC, and VTLS."

(www.abc-clio.com/ODLIS/odlis_l.aspx#libms)

The features of the ILS should enhance your library staff workflow. Notice how it begins with acquiring a new item. An order is entered into the ILS, either directly or imported from a third-party tool, such as Baker & Taylor's Title Source product. At the time you order a new item, you will specify which collection it will go into, how you will pay for the item, and how many copies you want. You might even specify the call number for the item or other descriptive information if the person who will eventually catalog the item is different from the person who orders the item. The ILS will enable you to store and share this information in one place.

Typically, the next step in your workflow is to receive the item once it is delivered. This is also done through the acquisitions module in the ILS, which can even assist with tracking items that have not been received and making claims to vendors for missing items. Once an item is received, you will receive an invoice for the item that will need to be paid. Although the ILS will not actually expend actual funds or print checks, it will enable you to track your budget funds. You can approve to pay an invoice out of a specific fund, and the ILS will debit the fund by the appropriate amount. An invoice approved for payment will then need to go to the finance staff to actually pay the bill.

While administrative staff handles the invoice payment, other staff will begin to process the item. New items are added to the catalog with identifying information, such as collection, call number, and subject headings. Often catalog records can be imported into the ILS as well, such as records purchased from OCLC or obtained from a Z39.50 search of other libraries' catalog records. These catalog records are bibliographic records in MARC format and item records. For each item, staff will assign the appropriate circulation rules in the ILS, such as loan periods and fine codes. In this way, the ILS will contain all the information needed to find and circulate an item.

The other major part of the ILS is the public interface for the catalog, which is through a mobile and/or web interface. Library patrons will access the catalog in order to search for items and locate them within the library. If an item is unavailable, patrons will use the public interface to place a hold on an item so they can check out the item once it becomes available. Patrons will also use the public interface to view their library account, check due dates, renew items, and possibly even pay fines and fees. The public catalog is perhaps one of the most important parts of your ILS, as it is your library's connection to your patrons, and it can make or break your patron relationships.

Integration of the ILS with Third-Party Products

Third-Party Product Integration to the Patron Data

First and foremost, libraries exist to serve their patrons. Some libraries limit services to only students or residents. The ILS enables third-party products to use the patron library card number (or other data) as a limiting factor in providing services. In other words, libraries can require patrons to enter their library card number and PIN (personal identification number) before gaining access to online databases or library computers or even self-checkout. When this functionality is used, there is a check against the patron database to determine if that patron is eligible for the service. The ILS is the master database. Technologies like SIP (session initiation protocol) and NCIP (NISO circulation interface protocol) enable the communication between third-party software and the ILS.

For example, a library can require that patrons keep their fines below a certain dollar amount in order to check out items. This is very easy for staff to manage at a checkout desk, but it is also possible to manage this at self-checkout. First, the patron is prompted to enter his or her library card number and PIN. The self-checkout software can then verify the library card and PIN against the ILS patron database and also search the patron record for the amount of fines due. If the amount of fines due is larger than the threshold allowed, the patron will see a message that describes the problem and further checkouts will not be allowed. Using the same example, it is also possible for the patron to be prompted to use his or her credit card to pay off the outstanding fines right there; the ILS fines-due amount would then be updated and the patron would be allowed to continue with his or her checkouts. All of this can be handled without staff intervention due to the communication between the ILS and the third-party self-checkout software.

Third-Party Product Integration to the Catalog Data

In much the same way, third-party products can also communicate with the item records in the catalog to enhance the information provided in the public catalog. Some of this functionality has been available for a while, such as Syndetics, which provides book covers, summaries, and other details that will help a patron learn about an item. Most patrons want all databases to look and function like Amazon.com. They want images and details and ways to click to related information. Library catalogs are starting to communicate with more software in order to provide this enriched content.

One example of this is NoveList Select by EBSCO. NoveList Select enhances your ILS public catalog by adding information so that patrons can find similar items, see recommendations, view series information, and even see reviews from other readers (using another third-party program called Goodreads). Patrons do not have to search another website for additional information because this information is available right on the same pages as the library information about the item. The ILS is able to pull data into its online catalog that is applicable to items viewed in the catalog.

Another example that has provided more challenges to ILS vendors is e-books. Library patrons want to be able to check out e-books from the library's collection. However, using a separate website confuses the situation. Although initially e-books could not be integrated with the ILS database and circulated through the ILS, now ILS vendors have made this possible through a much-needed collaboration with e-book providers. Polaris Library Systems first partnered with the 3M Cloud Library e-book lending services in 2013. Others have followed suit, and now e-books can be circulated as part of the ILS. This is a great way to import items in electronic format directly to the ILS.

ILS Vendors and Your Library

The landscape of the ILS market continues to evolve. In fact, at the time of this writing, there were some additional new acquisitions in the industry. Some of the larger commercial ILS vendors include Auto-Graphics, Ex Libris, Innovative Interfaces, The Library Corporation, SirsiDynix, and VTLS (Visionary Technology in Library Solutions). In addition to the commercial vendors, open-source ILSs continue to play a big role in the ILS world, particularly Evergreen and Koha.

Your library may have its own ILS, containing only your library's patrons and items, but small libraries often join together to participate in a shared system. Many library cooperatives will be the central host for a shared system in which libraries share their patron and item data, putting everything into one large database. In this configuration, the libraries work together and often allow patrons to visit any of the libraries in the shared database, offering reciprocal borrowing between them. This is a good way for smaller libraries to share resources and offer more to their patrons. Even if you choose to have your own ILS, some of the ILS vendors offer an option to host the system for the library. This means that your library would not have to maintain the server for the system at your library, but that the ILS vendor would maintain the server in a building that it manages. This provides another alternative for smaller libraries that wish to have their own system but cannot maintain the physical server in their buildings.

However, whether you have your own ILS or you are part of a shared system, it will be important for your library to have a good working relationship with your ILS vendor. Often in a shared system, the cooperative or consortium identifies key staff members to work directly with the vendor, while individual libraries will work with those identified staff members. Nonetheless, having a good relationship with the ILS vendor will go a long way toward positive support when needed. Things can and will go wrong, no matter how great the ILS is. Your library will need help with your system. After all, your library depends on the system every day. Therefore, start early and create a good relationship with your vendor. Get to know the key staff members at the company so you will be able to get help from the best people when needed.

The Future of the ILS

As a library director, pay attention to what is happening with the ILS vendors. One great source for this information is Marshall Breeding, an independent consultant in the library world. Each year, in *American Libraries*, he presents a "Library Systems Report" that gives readers a current view of ILS products and vendors. This report updates industry changes and discusses what the future holds. Be sure to check out this annual report.

The structure of ILS products is also evolving. One recent buzzword is *library services platform*, technology that provides a unified platform to manage and access print, electronic, and digital items. Developed prior to that were *discovery services*, which provide a single interface with integrated access to all the databases to which the library has subscribed, including catalogs, e-books, and databases. At this time, ILS vendors are working toward web-based client software that will allow library staff to access the ILS from any computer. An example of this is Polaris Leap, from Innovative Interfaces (originally from Polaris Library Systems).

Much like all technology, the ILS will continue to evolve and improve. However, it seems likely that libraries' dependence on a system like the ILS will remain. Libraries will need a way to manage their patrons and their collections, in a variety of formats. The demands on libraries to support more types of information will likely increase, and the ILS will be challenged to meet those demands.

Conclusion

Your library's ILS is the most important system in your library. You will depend on it to communicate with all your patrons and to keep track of all your library's materials. If you are able to choose your own system, choose wisely. If you are part of a larger shared system, get to know the system as well as you can. Today's ILSs are very powerful and feature rich. With all the third-party products that can tie into your ILS, your library can use the ILS to meet your patrons' needs in many new ways. Encourage your staff to learn all they can, as they will likely uncover new ways to make their jobs easier as well. Stay current with your ILS, doing upgrades as they become available, to take advantage of new features. Most of all, create and maintain a good relationship with your ILS vendor so that you can work together to provide the best library services to your community.

Tip

If your library's ILS has a "Users Group," as many of them do, become involved with the group. You will get to know others who use the same system and create important contacts in your network of colleagues. These are the people who are having similar experiences to your own, and you can help each other get through issues together.

APPENDIX

Running a Small Library Sourcebook

Source A

List of State Library Agencies

Alabama Public Library Service, 6030 Monticello Drive, Montgomery, AL 36130; 334-213-3900; http://webmini.apls.state.al.us

Alaska State Library, Archives and Museums, 333 Willoughby Avenue, State Office Building, 8th Floor, PO Box 110571, Juneau, AK 99811-0571; 907-465-2910; http://library.alaska.gov

Arizona State Library, Archives and Public Records, 1700 West Washington Street, Suite 200, Phoenix, AZ 85007; 602-926-4035; www.azlibrary.gov

Arkansas State Library, 900 West Capitol Avenue, Suite 100, Little Rock, AR 72201; 501-682-2053; www.library.arkansas.gov

California State Library, 900 N Street, Suite 300, PO Box 942837, Sacramento, CA 94237-0001; 916-323-9759; http://library.ca.gov

Colorado State Library, Colorado Department of Education, 201 East Colfax Avenue, Room 309, Denver, CO 80203-1799; 303-866-6900; www.cde.state.co.us

Connecticut State Library, 231 Capitol Avenue, Hartford, CT 06106; 860-757-6500; http://ctstatelibrary.org

Delaware Division of Libraries, 121 Martin Luther King Jr. Boulevard, North Dover, DE 19901; 302-739-4748; http://libraries.delaware.gov

Florida Department of State, Division of Library and Information Services, R. A. Gray Building, 500 South Bronough Street, Tallahassee, FL 32399-0250; 850-245-6600; http://dos.myflorida.com/library-archives

Georgia Public Library Service, 1800 Century Place, Suite 150, Atlanta, GA 30345-4304; 404-235-7200; http://georgialibraries.org

Hawaii State Public Library System, 465 South King Street, Honolulu, HI 96813; 808-586-3350; http://librarieshawaii.org

Idaho Commission for Libraries, 325 West State Street, Boise, ID 83702-6072; 208-334-2150; http://lili.org

Illinois State Library, 300 South Second Street, Springfield, IL 62701-1976; 217-785-5600; www.cyberdriveillinois.com/departments/library

Indiana State Library, 315 West Ohio Street, Indianapolis, IN 46204; 317-232-3675; http://in.gov/library

Iowa Library Services/State Library, East 12th and Grand Avenue, Des Moines, IA 50319; 515-281-4015; www.statelibraryofiowa.org

Kansas State Library, State Capitol Building, 300 SW 10th Avenue, Room 312-N, Topeka, KS 66612-1593; 785-296-3296; http://kslib.info/

Kentucky Department for Libraries and Archives, 300 Coffee Tree Road, PO Box 537, Frankfort, KY 40602-0537; 502-564-8300; http://kdla.ky.gov

Louisiana, State Library of, 701 North 4th Street, PO Box 131, Baton Rouge, LA 70802; 225-342-4913; www.state.lib.la.us

Maine State Library, 64 State House Station, Augusta, ME 04333-0064; 207-287-5600; www.state.me.us/msl

Maryland State Library Resource Center, Enoch Pratt Free Library, 400 Cathedral Street, Baltimore, MD 21201; 410-767-0440; www.slrc.info/

Massachusetts Board of Library Commissioners, 98 North Washington Street, Suite 401, Boston, MA 02214; 617-725-1680; http://mblc.state .ma.us

Michigan, Library of, 702 West Kalamazoo Street, PO Box 30007, Lansing, MI 48909; 517-373-1300; http://michigan.gov/libraryofmichigan

Minnesota Department of Education, State Library Services, 1500 Highway 36 West, Roseville, MN 55113; 651-582-8791; http://education .state.mn.us/MDE/StuSuc/Lib/StateLibServ

Mississippi Library Commission, 3381 Eastwood Drive, Jackson, MS 39211; 601-961-4111; www.mlc.lib.ms.us

Missouri State Library, 600 West Main Street, Jefferson City, MO 65101; 573-751-4936; http://sos.mo.gov/library

Montana State Library, 1515 East Sixth Avenue, PO Box 201800, Helena, MT 59620-1800; 406-444-3115; http://home.msl.mt.gov

Nebraska Library Commission, The Atrium, 1200 North Street, Suite 120, Lincoln, NE 68508-2023; 402-471-2045; http://nlc.nebraska.gov

Nevada State Library and Archives, 100 North Stewart Street, Carson City, NV 89701-4285; 775-684-3360; http://nsla.nv.gov

New Hampshire State Library, 20 Park Street, Concord, NH 03301-6314; 603-271-2149; www.nh.gov/nhsl

New Jersey State Library, 185 West State Street, PO Box 520, Trenton, NJ 08625-0520; 609-278-2640; www.njstatelib.org

New Mexico State Library, 1209 Camino Carlos Rey, Santa Fe, NM 87507-5166; 505-476-9783; http://nmstatelibrary.org

New York State Library, Cultural Education Center, 222 Madison Avenue, Albany, NY 12230; 518-474-5355; www.nysl.nysed.gov

North Carolina, State Library of, 109 East Jones Street, 4641 Mail Service Center, Raleigh, NC 27699-4640; 919-807-7450; http://statelibrary .ncdcr.gov

North Dakota State Library, 604 East Boulevard Avenue, Bismarck, ND 58505-0800; 701-328-4622; library.nd.gov

Ohio, State Library of, 247 East 1st Avenue, Suite 100, Columbus, OH 43201-3692; 614-644-7061; https://library.ohio.gov

Oklahoma Department of Libraries, 200 NE 18th Street, Oklahoma City, OK 73105; 405-521-2502; www.odl.state.ok.us

Oregon State Library, 250 Winter Street NE, Salem, OR 97301-3950; 503-378-4243; www.oregon.gov/osl

Pennsylvania, Bureau of State Library, Forum Building, 607 South Drive, Harrisburg, PA 17120-0600; 717-783-5950; www.portal.state.pa.us/ portal/server.pt/community/bureau_of_state_library/8811

Rhode Island State Library, State House, 2nd Floor, Providence, RI 02903; 401-222-2743; http://sos.ri.gov/library

South Carolina State Library, 1500 Senate Street, PO Box 11469, Columbia, SC 29211; 803-734-8666; http://statelibrary.sc.gov

South Dakota State Library, 800 Governors Drive, Pierre, SD 57501-2294; 605-773-3131; http://library.sd.gov

Tennessee State Library and Archives, 403 7th Avenue North, Nashville, TN 37243; 615-741-2764; http://tennessee.gov/tsla

Texas State Library and Archives Commission, 1201 Brazos Street, PO Box 12927, Austin, TX 78711-2927; 512-463-5455; www.tsl.texas.gov

Utah State Library Division, 250 North, 1950 West, Suite A, Salt Lake City, UT 84116-7901; 801-715-6777; http://heritage.utah.gov/library

Vermont Department of Libraries, 109 State Street, Montpelier, VT 05609-0601; 802-828-3261; http://libraries.vermont.gov

Virginia, Library of, 800 East Broad Street, Richmond, VA 23219-8000; 804-692-3500; www.lva.virginia.gov

Washington State Library, Point Plaza East, 6880 Capitol Boulevard SE, Tumwater, WA and PO Box 42460, Olympia, WA 98504-2460; 360-704-5200; www.sos.wa.gov/library

West Virginia Library Commission, 1900 Kanawha Boulevard East, Culture Center, Building 8, Charleston, WV 25305; 304-588-2041; http://librarycommission.wv.gov

Wisconsin Department of Public Instruction, Division for Libraries and Technology, 125 South Webster Street, PO Box 7841, Madison, WI 53707-7841; 608-266-2205; http://dlt.dpi.wi.gov

Wyoming State Library, 2800 Central Avenue, Cheyenne, WY 82002; 307-777-6333; www-wsl.state.wy.us

Source B

List of Book and Periodical Vendors

AIMS International Books, 7709 Hamilton Avenue, Cincinnati, OH 45231; 800-733-2067; http://aimsbooks.com

Amazon.com: Books; www.amazon.com/books-used-books-textbooks/b?node=283155

Ambassador Education Solutions, 445 Broad Hollow Road, Suite 208, Melville, NY 11747; 800-431-8913; www.ambassadored.com

Baker & Taylor, 2550 West Tyvola Road, Suite 300, Charlotte, NC 28217; 800-775-1800; http://btol.com

Barnes & Noble, 76 Ninth Avenue, New York, NY 10011; www.barnesandnoble.com

Bernan: Government publications, PO Box 191, Blue Ridge Summit, PA 17214; 800-865-3457; http://bernan.com

Blackwell Mail Order, 60 Broad Street, Oxford, England OX1 2ET; 44 (0) 1865-333690; http://bookshop.blackwell.co.uk

Book Depot, 67 Front Street North, Thorold, Ontario, Canada L2V 1X3; 800-801-7193, x229; www.bookdepot.com

Book House, 208 West Chicago Street, Jonesville, MI 49250; 800-248-1146; http://thebookhouse.com

Bound to Stay Bound Books, 1880 West Morton Road, Jacksonville, IL 62650; 800-637-6586; www.btsb.com

Brodart Books and Library Services, 500 Arch Street, Williamsport, PA 17705; 800-474-9816; www.brodartbooks.com

Continental Book Company, 6425 Washington Street, #7, Denver, CO 80229; 800-364-0350; http://continentalbook.com

Eastern Book Company, 55 Bradley Drive, Westbrook, ME 04092; 800-937-0331; http://ebc.com

EBSCO Information Services, Periodical Sales Division, 5724 Highway 280 East, Birmingham, AL 35242-6818; 205-991-1369; www.ebsco.com

Emery-Pratt, 1966 West M 21, Owosso, MI 48867; 800-248-3887; http://emerypratt.com

ERIC Document Reproduction Services, 7420 Fullerton Road, Suite 110, Springfield, VA 22153; 800-538-3742; http://eric.ed.gov

Follett, 3 Westbrook Corporate Center, Suite 200, Westchester, IL 60154; http://follett.com

Infobase Learning, 132 West 31st Street, 17th Floor, New York, NY 10001; 800-322-8755; http://infobasepublishing.com

Ingram Content Group, 1 Ingram Boulevard, La Vergne, TN 37086; 615-793-5000; http://ingramcontent.com

Midwest Library Service, 11443 St. Charles Rock River, Bridgeton, MO 63044; 800-325-8833; http://midwestls.com

Multicultural Books & Videos, 30007 John R Road, Madison Heights, MI 48071; 248-556-7960; http://multiculturalbooksandvideos.com

Periodicals Service Company, 351 Fairview Avenue, Suite 300, Hudson, NY 12534; 518-822-9300; http://periodicals.com

Perma-Bound, 617 East Vandalia Road, Jacksonville, IL 62650; 800-637-6581; www.perma-bound.com

Puvill Libros, Dror Faust, 1 East Park Drive, Paterson, NJ 07504; 973-279-9054; www.puvill.com

Regent Book Company, 37 Liberty Corner, Lodi, NJ 07606 and PO Box 750, Lodi, NJ 07938; 800-999-9554; http://regentbook.com

United States Book Exchange, 2969 West 25th Street, Cleveland, OH 44113; 216-241-6960; http://usbe.com

Wolper Information Services, 360 Northampton Street, Easton, PA 18042; 601-559-9550; www.wolper.com

WT Cox Information Services, 201 Village Road, Shallotte, NC 28470; 800-571-9554; www.wtcox.com

YBP Library Services, 999 Maple Street, Contoocook, NH 03229-3374; 800-258-3774; www.ybp.com

Source C

List of Library Furniture and Supply Vendors

Agati Furniture, 1219 West Lake Street, Chicago, IL 60607; 312-829-1977; www.agati.com

American Seating, American Seating Center, Grand Rapids, MI 49504; 800-748-0268; www.americanseating.com

Blanton and Moore, PO Box 70, Highway 21 South, Barium Springs, NC 28010; 704-528-4506; www.blantonandmoore.com

Bretford Manufacturing, 11000 Seymour Avenue, Franklin Park, IL 60131; 800-521-9614; http://bretford.com

Brodart, 500 Arch Street, Williamsport, PA 17701; Supplies: 888-820-4377; Furniture: 888-521-1884, x360; www.brodart.com

Buckstaff, PO Box 2506, Oshkosh, WI 54903; 800-755-5890; www.buckstaff.com

Community Furniture, 225 Clay Street, PO Box 231, Jasper, IN 47547; 800-622-5661; http://communityfurniture.com

DEMCO, PO Box 7488, Madison, WI 53707; 800-356-1200; www.demco.com

Display Fixtures, 1501 Westinghouse Boulevard, PO Box 410073; Charlotte, NC 28241; 800-737-0880; www.displayfixtures.com

ENEM Systems by Harrier Interior Products Corporation, 319 Colfax Street, Palatine, IL 60067; 847-934-1310; www.openfos.com/supply/2391813-HARRIER-INTERIOR-PRODUCTS-in-Palatine-IL

Fetzer Architectural Woodwork, 6223 West Double Eagle Circle, Salt Lake City, UT 84115; 801-484-6103; www.fetzerwood.com

Fleetwood Group, PO Box 1259, Holland, MI 49424; 800-257-6390; www.fleetwoodgroup.com

Gaylord Archival, PO Box 4901; Syracuse, NY 13221; 800-448-6160; www.gaylord.com

Gressco, 328 Moravian Valley Road, PO Box 339, Waunakee, WI 53597; 800-345-3480; www.gresscoltd.com

Herman Miller, 855 East Main Avenue, PO Box 302, Zeeland, MI 49464; 888-443-435; www.hermanmiller.com

International Library Furniture, 1945 Techny Road, Northbrook, IL 60062; 847-564-9497; www.libraryfurnitureinternational.com

Kapco Library Products, 1000 Cherry Street, Kent, OH 44240; 800-791-8965; www.kapcolibrary.com

The Library Store, 112 East South Street, PO Box 964, Tremont, IL 61568; 800-548-7204; www.thelibrarystore.com

MJ Industries, 4 Carleton Drive, PO Box 259, Georgetown, MA 01833; 978-352-6190; www.mjshelving.com

Moduform Library Bureau, 172 Industrial Road, Fitchburg, MA 01420; 800-221-6638; www.moduform.com

Mohawk Library Furniture; 847-570-0448; www.mohawkfurniture.us

Montel Aetnastak, 1170 Highway AlA, Satellite, FL 32937; 800-772-7562; www.montel.com

Palmieri Library Furniture, 1230 Reid Street, Richmond Hill, Ontario, Canada L4B 1C4; 800-413-4440; http://palmierifurniture.com

Sauder Manufacturing, 930 West Barre Road, Archbold, OH 43502; 800-537-1530; www.saudermfg.com

Spacesaver, 1450 Janesville Avenue, Fort Atkinson, WI 52358; 920-563-63162; www.spacesaver.com

Steelcase, 901 44th Street SE, Grand Rapids, MI 49508; 616-247-2710; www.steelcase.com

Thos. Moser Cabinetmakers, 72 Wright's Landing, Auburn, ME 04210-8307; 800-708-9710; www.thosmoser.com

TMC Furniture, 119 East Ann Street, Ann Arbor, MI 48104; 734-622-0080; www.tmcfurniture.com

Universal Air Lift, 28010 Northwest 142nd Avenue, High Springs, FL 32643; 866-526-3688; www.universalairlift.com

University Products, 517 Main Street, Holyoke, MA 01040; 800-628-1912; www.unversityproducts.com

Vernon Library Supplies, 2851 Cole Court, Norcross, GA 30071; 800-878-0253; www.vernonlibrarysupplies.com

Versteel, 2332 Cathy Lane, Jasper, IN 47546; 800-876-2120; www.versteel.com

Worden, 199 East 17th Street, Holland, MI 49423; 800-748-0561; www.wordencompany.com

Source D

List of Automation Vendors

Auto-Graphics, 430 North Vineyard Avenue, Ontario, CA 91764; 800-776-6939; www4.auto-graphics.com

Biblionix, 401 Congress Avenue, Suite 1540, Austin, TX 78701; 877-800-5625, x1; www.biblionix.com

Book Systems, 4901 University Square, Suite 3, Huntsville, AL 35816; 800-219-6571; http://booksys.com

COMPanion, 1831 Fort Union Boulevard, Salt Lake City, UT 84121; 800-347-6439; http://companioncorp.com

Cuadra Associates, 3415 South Sepulveda Boulevard, Suite 210, Los Angeles, CA 90034; 800-366-1390; cuadra.com

Equinox Software, PO Box 69, Norcross, GA 30091; 877-673-6457; http://esilibrary.com

Evergreen; http://evergreen-ils.org

Ex Libris, 1350 East Touhy Avenue, Suite 200 E, Des Plaines, IL 60018; 800-762-6300; http://exlibrisgroup.com

Follett School Solutions, 1340 Ridgeview Drive, McHenry, IL 60050; 800-621-4272; http://follettlearning.com

Inmagic, 600 Unicorn Park Drive, Woburn, MA 01801; 800-229-8398; www.inmagic.com

Innovative Interfaces, 5850 Shellmound Way, Emeryville, CA 94608; 510-655-6200; http://iii.com

Jaywil Software Development, 100 Crimea Street, Unit 87, Guelph, Ontario, Canada N1H 2Y6; 800-815-8370; www.resourcemate.com

Keystone Systems, 8016 Glenwood Avenue, Suite 200, Raleigh, NC 27612; 800-222-9711; http://klas.com

LibLime, 11501 Huff Court, North Bethesda, MD 20895; 301-654-8808, x127; www.liblime.com

The Library Corporation, 1 Research Park, Inwood, WV 25428; 800-325-7759; www.tlcdelivers.com

Library Resource Management Systems, PO Box 727, Sedona, AZ 86339; 877-700-5767; http://lrms.com

Library World, 560 South Winchester Boulevard, Suite 500, San José, CA 95128; 800-852-2777; http://libraryworld.com

Lucidea, Suite 5139, 13562 Maycrest Way, Richmond, British Columbia, Canada V6V 2J7; 604-278-9161; http://lucidea.com

Mandarin Library Automation, PO Box 272308, Boca Raton, FL 33427; 800-426-7477; www.mlasolutions.com

Media Flex, PO Box 1107, Champlain, NY 12919; 877-331-1022; http://mediaflex.net

OCLC, 6565 Kilgour Place, Dublin, OH 43017; 800-848-58789; www.oclc.org

SirsiDynix, 3300 North Ashton Boulevard, Suite 500, Lehi, UT 84043; 800-288-8020; www.sirsidynix.com

Softlink, 720 Third Avenue, Suite 2220, Seattle, WA 98104; 206-774-6798; www.softlinkamerica.com

Soutron Global, 1042 North El Camino Real, Suite B-215, Encinitas, CA 92024; 760-870-4243; http://soutronglobal.com

Surpass Software, 517 Oothcalooga Street, Suite C, Calhoun, GA 30701; 877-625-2657; http://surpasssoftware.com

Source E
Professional Organizations

Many professional organizations are able to provide assistance to librarians. These include international library organizations, state library organizations, and type-of-library organizations. This source provides location information about major library professional organizations and guidance in which organization to approach for library informational needs.

Professional organizations may be divided into general national organizations, such as the American Library Association, Australian Library and Information Association, Canadian Library Association, Library and Information Association of New Zealand (LIANZA), and the Chartered Institute of Library and Informational Professionals (Great Britain); type-of-library organizations, such as the Association of College and Research Libraries, Public Library Association, and Special Library Association; and special-interest library organizations, such as United for Libraries. There are also state, provincial, or other subnational unit library associations, such as the British Columbia Library Association and the Texas Library Association. Each of these organizations will provide information and services to the smallest library.

Which organization should be approached with an information request? If it is a public library question, one of the best first stops would be the library development office of the state library. Source A provides the locations of these agencies. Otherwise, it would be good to approach the relevant type-of-library organization at either the state or national level. Many state library associations will have type-of-library divisions. These are good sources for initial enquiries.

National library associations and type-of-library associations are good sources for general materials, including books, audiovisual materials, fact sheets, webinars, and so forth, on all aspects of librarianship and for statements of professional values. They also provide guidance and assistance with questions relating to areas such as censorship issues.

The following sections provide information on some professional organizations.

National Organizations

American Library Association, 50 East Huron Street, Chicago, IL 60611-2795; 800-545-2433; www.ala.org

Australian Library and Information Association, PO Box 6335, Kingston 2604 Australia; Street address: ALIA House, 9–11 Napier Close, Deakin 2600, Australia; +61-2-6215-8222; alia.org.au

Canadian Library Association, 1150 Morrison Drive, Suite 400, Ottawa, Ontario, Canada K2H 8S9; 613-232-9625; www.cla.ca

Chartered Institute of Library and Information Professionals (Great Britain), 7 Ridgemount Street, London, England WC1E 7AE; 020-7255-0500; cilip.org.uk

Library and Information Association of New Zealand (LIANZA), PO Box 12212, Thorndon, Wellington 6144, New Zealand; +64-4-801-5542; www.lianza.org.nz

Type-of-Library Organizations

American Association of School Librarians, 50 East Huron Street, Chicago, IL 60611-2795; 800-545-2433, x4382; www.ala.org/aasl

Association of College and Research Libraries, 50 East Huron Street, Chicago, IL 60611-2795; 800-545-2433, x2523; www.ala.org/acrl

Medical Library Association, 65 East Wacker Place, Suite 1900, Chicago, IL 60601-7246; 312-419-9094; www.mlanet.org

Public Library Association, 50 East Huron Street, Chicago, IL 60611; 800-545-2433, x5028; www.pla.org

Special Libraries Association, 331 South Patrick Street, Alexandria, VA 22314-3501; 703-647-4900; www.sla.org

Young Adult Library Services Association, 50 East Huron Street, Chicago, IL 60611; 800-545-2433, x4390; www.ala.org/yalsa

The Canadian Library Association has networks that can be located through its website (www.cla.ca):

Canadian Association for School Libraries

Canadian Association of College and University Libraries

Canadian Association of Public Libraries

Canadian Association of Special Libraries and Information Services

Canadian Library Trustees Association

Special-Interest Library Organizations

United for Libraries, 109 South 13th Street, Suite 117B, Philadelphia, PA 19107; 800-545-2433, x2161; www.ala.org/united

State Library Chapters

Information on all fifty state library chapters may be found at www.ala.org under Offices, Chapter Relations Office; in the annual *American Library Directory*, published by Information Today (www.americanlibrarydirectory.com/); and through the Special Library Association website at www.sla.org.

Source F
Professional Statements

At the core of librarianship, regardless of type of library, are fundamental statements outlining the principles behind the provision of library services in a democracy. These are the main statements:

"Code of Ethics of the American Library Association"

"The Freedom to Read"

"Libraries: An American Value"

"Library Bill of Rights" and its many interpretations

There are many other statements dealing with access to materials, economic barriers to information access, and guidelines for the development and implementation of policies and regulations.

The best source for these documents is the Office of Intellectual Freedom's *Intellectual Freedom Manual*, Eighth Edition (Chicago: ALA Editions, 2010). The website ifmanual.org makes the source documents available in electronic form.

About the Editor and Contributors

John A. Moorman is owner and principal consultant at Dominion Library Associates, Williamsburg, Virginia. From 1975–2013, he served as director of public libraries and multitype library systems in North Carolina, Texas, Illinois, and Virginia. He is active in state and national library associations, has served on the ALA Executive Board, and is a past president of the Virginia Library Association. Professional interests include library buildings, combined school/public libraries, strategic planning, and organizational operations and theory. He has provided workshops on a variety of topics, including fund-raising and the organization of library support groups, has published numerous articles, and is the editor of both editions of *Running a Small Library*, published by Neal-Schuman and the American Library Association. Moorman has a master's degree in library science from the University of North Carolina at Chapel Hill and a PhD in library and information science from the University of Illinois at Urbana–Champaign.

Janet L. Crowther is Assistant Director of the Williamsburg Regional Library in Virginia. She co-authored the book *Partnering with Purpose: A Guide to Strategic Partnerships* in 2004.

Cy Dillon, a college library director for the past twenty-nine years, is currently Director of Library and College Computing at Hampden-Sydney College in Virginia. He writes a column on open access publishing for *College and Undergraduate Libraries*.

Karen C. Knox is Director of the Orion Township Public Library in Lake Orion, Michigan. She published the book *Implementing Technology Solutions in Libraries: Techniques, Tools, and Tips from the Trenches* in 2011.

Rodney Lippard is currently Director of the Learning Resource Center Information Commons at Rowan-Cabarrus Community College in Salisbury, North Carolina. Since earning his MLIS from the University of North Carolina (UNC) at Greensboro in 1995, Lippard has held librarian positions in North Carolina at Johnson C. Smith University in Charlotte, Catawba College in Salisbury, and UNC Chapel Hill and most recently was Library Director at Barton College in Wilson.

Elizabeth Terry Long is a librarian at the State Law Library, a division of the Supreme Court of Virginia. She received her BA from Stetson University and MSLS from the Catholic University of America.

Jessica McMurray has been a children's librarian in youth services and a young adult librarian in adult services for the Williamsburg Regional Library in Virginia. She is now a librarian/library teacher for a private school in Maryland, working with pre-K–8 students. She received her MLIS degree from Florida State University.

Laura Morales is IT and Technical Services Director at the Williamsburg Regional Library in Virginia. She received her BA from the College of William & Mary and her MLIS from Florida State University.

Patty Purish O'Neill, PhD, has worked in the field of higher education for more than twenty years, and since 1996, she has served in a variety of leadership roles in the development office at the College of William & Mary. She earned her bachelor's degree at the University of Central Florida and a master's degree from Florida State University.

Barbara Riebe is Collection Development Librarian at the Williamsburg Regional Library in Virginia.

Frederick A. Schlipf has been a professor at the University of Illinois Graduate School of Library and Information Science in Urbana–Champaign since 1970. He currently teaches courses on library buildings. Fred was director of the public library of the City of Urbana for thirty-two years, and he has consulted on about 150 library construction projects. He has a PhD from the University of Chicago.

Barry Trott is Special Projects Director at the Williamsburg Regional Library in Virginia. He is the editor of *Reference and User Services Quarterly*, past president of the Reference and User Services Association, and winner of both the Allie Beth Martin and Margaret E. Monroe Awards.

Linda Williams is the retired Coordinator of Library Media Services for Anne Arundel County Public Schools in Annapolis, Maryland. She received her BS from Radford University and her MLS from the University of Maryland.

Alicia Willson-Metzger is Collection Management Librarian at Christopher Newport University, a liberal-arts institution in Newport News, Virginia.

Index

CPSIA information can be obtained at www.ICGtesting.com
Printed in the USA
LVOW09s1932190515

439122LV00007B/45/P